More Havoc

BY THE SAME AUTHOR

Early Havoc
Marathon '33 (play)
I, Said the Fly (play)

HARPER & ROW, PUBLISHERS

NEW YORK

Cambridge
Hagerstown
Philadelphia
San Francisco

London
Mexico City
São Paulo
Sydney

1817

MORE
HAVOC

by JUNE
HAVOC

MORE HAVOC. Copyright © 1980 by June Havoc. All rights reserved. Printed in the United States of America. No part of this book may be used or reproduced in any manner whatsoever without written permission except in the case of brief quotations embodied in critical articles and reviews. For information address Harper & Row, Publishers, Inc., 10 East 53rd Street, New York, N.Y. 10022. Published simultaneously in Canada by Fitzhenry & Whiteside Limited, Toronto.

FIRST EDITION

Designer: Trish Parcell

Library of Congress Cataloging in Publication Data

Havoc, June.
    More Havoc.

    Autobiography.
    1. Havoc, June.   2.   Actors—United States—
Biography.   I. Title.
PN2287.H33A35   1980   791'.092'4 [B] 79–2732
ISBN 0–06–011811–3

80 81 82 83 84 10 9 8 7 6 5 4 3 2 1

For Tana Sibilio

Photographs follow pages 54 and 214.

More Havoc

1952–1954

I was a couple of years into the marriage that was to endure twenty-five years of my adult life. I had enjoyed a full decade of acceptance onstage. On film. Television, radio. I was within touching distance to the wonder. The letter came from one of the small cities of England, strung on what remained of a variety circuit. Gypsy Rose Lee was playing every remaining stop on every fast-disappearing route.

"Oh, God," she wrote, "even if Mother was a stranger . . ." The letter rambled. ". . . Must finish my bookings here . . . impossible to keep her out of our lives now . . ."

We were more than a couple of years into a mature relationship that, as children, neither of us could ever have thought possible. Friends, companions, sisters. We had lived together for four years. Traveled halfway around the world together. We would now find our way through this dark corridor together. Until my sister could return, I would be alone to care for Mother.

Mother. For years, we had communicated with Mother only through lawyers. That part was also over now. From this time on, any picture in my memory bank would stand as but a graying negative to the third-dimensional reel to follow.

Mother was fifty-six. No gray had appeared in the fine amber hair. Clear skin free of makeup revealed the tiniest of lines. She looked astonishingly as she always had. Since this operation, and for the first time in many years, Mother and I were together as often as three or four times a week, but I still received the familiar pleading letters. I replied by sending the requested television set, clock radio, electric blanket, two pairs of new glasses, and medical items. Even so, those letters still came regularly. I wrote to Gypsy, sending the evidence; no one person could ever use the quantity of medical needs itemized on those bills. They numbered enough to supply a small hospital. Gypsy replied that Mother, true to her style, had arranged for a kickback. "Of course," I thought, "irresistible." Watching Mother at the old familiar games began. She was up and about with remarkable strength in no time.

"I want to see your show, dear. I'll come to the matinee." Mother was back inside the skin of my life and I was trying to apply the experience of the years between to keep balance. Mother had come up losers, but that word wasn't in her vocabulary. We were to pretend this one out. Pretend.

We were in my dressing room at the Music Box Theatre following a matinee, regarding one another through the looking glass over my makeup shelf. Mother was aglow.

"Isn't this nice, dear? Here we are. . . . Oh, yes, I enjoyed the show. My baby. I couldn't take my eyes off of you, dear. Like old times. Your name up in lights . . . of course, it's only a straight play. I don't like so much talk. Talk, talk, talk. It tires me so. Now, your sister's shows are chock-full of action." She lowered her voice. "I suppose, now that—well, in your condition— how long do you think before it shows? You don't look too well, dear. Actually, June," she laughed, "pregnant is nothing! You know how they tore me to ribbons when I had your sister. Twelve and a half pounds!" Mother loved the old story. "Not a doctor for miles, only half the roof on the house during a blizzard— but I made it."

I didn't make it. I was told that I was fortunate to have had one child, and to settle for one only. When it was all over, Mother came to the hospital. She explained that I lacked the "steel" that ran through the women of our family.

"You'll be onstage again overnight, of course, but none of the rest of us ever lost a baby. We all had steel in those days. For instance, you couldn't last five minutes with this." She opened her skirt. I stared. "It's a container. I can't empty it alone. Look— here, and here . . . well, they say I ought to have a trained nurse all the time. But you needn't pay those foolish prices, because I have a friend who knows all about this, and she won't overcharge us because she is a friend. Look, look at this . . . June? June!"

I had quietly passed out. When I came to, the room was filled with people. "No steel," Mother was telling them. "Why, I've never fainted in my life."

A long time ago I started keeping a journal. In going back from here to there year by year, day by day, the landscape of life appears to have been designed for roller-coasters. The highs so high, the lows so low. I was in the middle of one of the lovely highs when the unbelievable became reality. The pretend time ended.

Mother was dying.

The first part of Mother's illness had lasted almost a year. The part where she had looked the same. Behaved the same. Almost. Deterioration almost imperceptible, until suddenly the inevitable was everywhere.

There were no more matinees now, no more trips or visits. The amber hair no longer glistened. Body skin was loose. The violet of her eyes deepened into purple. Mother's younger sister, Aunt Mina, had looked like this, I remembered. In a room like this. Airless. Dark except for one too-bright light over the bed. The family had all been present. Mother's mother, Anna, whom we all called Big Lady; Anna's mother, Doddie; Mother's older sister, Belle; and Mother's two daughters, Louise and June. These women were the whole family. Someone lifted me onto the bed. Aunt Mina smiled crookedly. "Too small. She's too thin." I felt ashamed to be small and thin. I hung my head.

"It's the drugs talking." Big Lady had said that. A little while later the light had been turned off and I had been lifted down from the bed. "She put up a good fight."

I don't recall who said that, but it was what I was thinking now about Mother. They all took such pride in being "good fighters." They always fought as though their cause could never be lost. Mother had yet to come face to face with her own calendar.

In and out of hospitals. A rest home on the Hudson that lasted two days. Finally, a series of nurses at Mother's house. The list of failed efforts to contain this unquenchable spirit was growing.

Even after drugs had dulled perception, as well as the awful pain, Mother summoned the old steel.

"Who is paying for that woman out there, June? Gypsy! I

don't need to pay anyone for living in my house, eating my food, and drinking my beer. Taking advantage because I'm down—well, I'm not that down!"

The last nurse to go was a real trouper. Mother took a particular dislike to her because she had an advantage. She elaborately turned to the off position on her hearing aid just when things got going. Tall, angular, remote. I was almost sure she would last. Almost took the bet. But Gypsy had the odds. My sister had returned from her music-hall tour in England months before. It was she who had found this paragon. We relaxed. Too soon. One night, while tucking Mother into the rented hospital bed, the tall, angular one missed a cue.

"Closer, please," Mother's small voice implored. Her smile still had the old, hypnotic lure.

"Never happened to me before," went that report. "I leaned over her just far enough to hear? And POW! She slams the side of my face with this metal water pitcher she has hidden under the sheet."

That one cost a boodle, because of the dental work. The paragon lost a half mile of bridgework.

Winter deepened. More drugs, then more. In Mother's lucid moments, she always asked one or the other of us to find something for her. We stumbled over a dozen radios, eight television sets, and boxes of electric blankets. Several shopping bags filled with watches, rings, underwear, toys. It was a scene from my childhood. The same rainy feeling. I didn't want to see—to know. Kleptomania wasn't a glib subject then. We weren't all amateur analysts. We were bewildered. Why steal? She didn't need—need? She had a home . . . car . . . annuities. We were frightened. Why? She was always so angry. Angry? She had everything she asked us for. Well, almost. We hadn't responded to her pounding requests—appeals—demands to be together. Not for a long, long time. Years.

"Some people can never have enough attention. Enough love." It was easy for that doctor to say. I had run away from the melodrama at twelve. My sister remained until the combined hurdy-gurdies weakened the lining of her life. Putting Mother on the other side of a lawyer had been the ultimate necessity. Life insurance. Gypsy and I had never known the pleasure of each other's company until that triangle of distance had been formed. Never been sisters, even friends. It had taken half our lives to realize one another. To understand and enjoy how similar and still how different we were from one another. The differences never again eroded the affection. Respect. The laughter. While husbands, lovers, and life styles separated us occasionally, we never were too far apart.

We had this vision. We were going to live together at the lengthy end and enjoy the fruits, so to say, of growing old in a luxury-riddled fashion. Yes. After the purple smoke of all the hazards of the long long-distance run, the peculiar assortment of men buried or left to sunbake along the way, the gullies of tears, the moving walls of fury. We two, dressed majestically in yellowing ermine and dusty diamonds, would be a "must-see" at all first nights. Moving slowly down whatever aisle, with shining if slightly blurred eyes, we would nod to left and right. The well-earned surge of affectionate recognition would warm our old, no longer active flanks, and—well, it was a very comforting sort of game we played.

But that game was called, too. Later. First it was Mother.

Mother was dying.

1 ༝ᴇ༝ᴇ༝

I saw the ad when I was at Western Union. I planned to send for the fare, but I saw the ad; it wasn't anyone's newspaper, so I tore it out. The scrap was covered with magical words, so I didn't send the telegram. Instead I ran, I ran all the way.

> SHOWGIRLS WANTED:
> Big New Show
> Apply 41st Bdwy.

I was too scrawny for a real showgirl, but maybe . . . I wasn't seventeen yet, I needed to fill out and round up, and . . . but maybe . . . "SHOWGIRLS WANTED" . . .

The mob had formed all the way to Forty-third Street. I heard a voice giving directions over some kind of public address system. I pushed on until I was so wedged into the crowd of women I could no longer move.

"Oh, God," I thought, "at the eleventh hour, rescue! A real audition for a real Broadway show." I tried hard to hear what the voice was saying. No matter, I was ready to sing, dance, show them, anyone, that I belonged in one of these theatres—any one of them—but I didn't belong where that telegram would send me. If I could get back on the stage, I'd never have to do that again. Today I saw that ad—today when I was about to send that telegram . . .

Today had to be my lucky day. I scrutinized the field of flowers. Long-stemmed American beauties. Pristine lilies. Shy, tiny forget-me-nots. My competition were perfect specimens all; but which of us would win the day? I gritted my teeth in determination. This very blossom was going to be selected at any moment. Why me? Easy! I was the most dangerous piece of fluff on the premises, that's why! No living, breathing human tissue could possibly fail to be drawn in my direction on this day.

Trembling in the icy sunlight, I smiled. I thought I smiled. Then a miracle happened—they all stopped! Right there in the middle of Forty-first Street, only a few steps from Broadway itself. Stopped long enough to hear that voice loud and clear: "Step up, ladies. All of you—"

I didn't want to be with "all of you." Would someone look at me? Just me?

"Toward the theatre, ladies."

Theatre. We were going to a real theatre.

The army of feminine pulchritude was inching forward in such tight formation that my choice was limited to either moving with them or inviting them to move over me. So we moved together in our colorful mass toward cascading tiers of fire escapes adorning what would seem to the uninitiated an unremarkable gray building. Once within that shabby door, like Alice through the looking-glass, you were surrounded with magic. . . . Behold! A palace of vintage beauty. Red velvet, golden tassels, gilt, and alabaster. A thousand cushioned seats under the faceted gaze of huge crystal chandeliers. Plush carpeting to empty the sound of footfalls. All that and more was inside, from Forty-first to Forty-second Street, right through the entire block.

The handsome front entrance was a whole street away. This was the rear of the theatre. This was the outside of the rear: STAGE DOOR. This was the place, all right. The very back of the front. The rear. The tide of us were swirling past the door toward the iron stairs. I caught a few electronic words on the way up: "If you will please make room for the others . . . that's right, ladies, all the way up . . ."

Soon we were indeed all the way up. The fire escapes were loaded. Some of us must have heard whoever was doing the directing, for we began waving to the street below. The few spectators on the street waved back, then slowly disappeared. Presently there was no one to wave to. We waited awhile, still smiling with our secret hope of someone, somewhere watching. Selecting. Perhaps at this very second picking out this one of us, or that one . . .

I checked the ad again. "Showgirls Wanted," time and place were here and now. I looked up, then down. There were three tiers above me and two below. Even the stairs between were lined solidly. Females and semi-females. All ages, sizes, shapes. Showgirls? Actresses out of work? Who were we? I wondered how many had real jobs. Homes. Families. The last four years of my own life had been a rigorous exercise in survival. Whoever we were, we were being taught to use substitute food, substitute sleep and shelter, even substitute pride. The only human ingredient more than plentiful was hope. Hope abounded in my year of 1934. So, even when the voice no longer scratched its way through that speaker, when the world below seemed to have forgotten about us completely, we smiled. Hope was real.

"Oh, look! Cameras!" The girl squeezing against my back was breathless.

"Whadya whispering for? There ain't nobody here but us chickens. That's a joke, kid!" The big growl came from a small, square female pressed into my right rib cage.

"What cameras?" I asked anyone. "Where?" I scanned the street below. Perhaps the audition came next.

"Right over there, see?" Three or four of my close friends pointed downward. I squinted my eyes. No camera passed my view, though there was another signal of some kind, because an orderly dispersal was beginning, similar to a Miss America Parade—granted the fire stairs were a bit more awesome to navigate than a nice, flat boardwalk.

"At last," I thought, "on our way to the theatre."

The tall lady at my side chuckled. "Can't find the camera, huh? Yeah, you'll make a helluva actress."

We moved on as though picking our way through a minefield. Someone must be somewhere watching. Someone who had the power to change everything. One pointed finger, a single word, "You." The finger beckons, and POW! Just like in the movies, the whole world sprawls at your feet. Who among us would be the lucky ones this time? I glanced about. Dare I dismiss the hairy lady over there? Is it possible that, having done so, I may be stunned, while viewing some future evening of Oscar awards, to see the Golden Tribute to Talent pass into those pudgy fingers tufted with reddish-blond fuzz? The seemingly hopeless was always a possibility. It had to be, I thought, or we wouldn't be here, hoping, on this cold day. A bouquet. A Duke's Mixture.

Reaching solid ground gratefully, I looked back and up at the now abandoned tiers of ironwork. The sun lay flat at the very end of the street, lighting the old building with an amber caress. Grubby windows gleamed in response like gold cloth in a spotlight. Up there in that glowing pink aura, what had I looked like? Was I in any way different from the others? Different enough to be noticed? I stared at the posterior of the regal old theatre.

"A star," I whispered. "Even your rear looks like a star in that lighting."

For that brief time, had I glittered like that, too?

Stand still now. Wait for an invitation to enter the theatre now. I closed my eyes, waiting. . . . It would be like returning home. All the familiar sounds, scents—home.

Secret prescription for the aura and perfume of a real theatre of that time: Take a smidgen of whatever you cherish most in your secret heart. Distill that with the deep longing of any unquenchable wish, a wish beyond your wildest hope, but leave enough hope for seasoning. Let it simmer most of your life; breathe it in small doses until you just don't need it anymore.

Well, it's a hard act to follow. Beware what you substitute, if substitute you must.

My reverie was splintered by a long, low scream. I recognized the tall, striking lady now standing in the middle of the darkening street. The hairy woman pulled at her hand.

"Don't," she pleaded, "please don't!"

The tall lady screamed again. "Showgirls? You want to see showgirls?"

"I'm not with you," the hairy woman said, but she pulled at the other's hand again. They were joined by a small girl of lumpy proportions.

"Let her go," the small girl said, "let her scream, and let's hear it for all the rest of us!" She took the tall lady's other hand. "Now," she smiled, "let's have it, huh?" They looked a second into each other's faces, then screamed together.

"I'm not with you," the hairy woman repeated as she walked

away. It was then I realized there was no audition. No theatre. Nothing.

My echo to their helpless fury carried me toward them. We screamed it out together. We might as well have been at the bottom of the Grand Canyon. After a deep breath and a brief silence, the tall lady called out, "Who wants to audition showgirls?"

Silence.

"Anyone know what in hell we were doing on that fire escape?"

More silence. The lumpy girl smiled.

"You have a lovely voice. Such projection! You never been used free for some promotion? Watch the ads, honey—you could be featured!" The girl walked away.

"Come out, come out, wherever you are!" the tall one sang toward the empty storefronts. "Look at me, I dance!" She lifted her skirt, exhibiting a few yards of flabby thigh.

"Tough," I said to myself, "like the alligator girl in any sideshow. Tough, inferior hide."

I moved away, too, pondering on the lady's mismanagement of her dubious resources. The sound of her yelling diminished with every step I took. Even though I walked toward the brilliance of the dusking sun, her image remained in my mind's eye, itching like a loosened eyelash. There she was: her outer package tall, orderly, almost dignified. But under the wrapping that blotched skin loosely covered the unsuspected whistles and pipes of a discordant, disorderly system. Survival again, but toward what end? Did she too worry about who she was? I'm not going to be like that, I'm not—am I?

The sun flattened in the distance. "There," I thought, "is the ultimate in the realization of one's potential. How old was the sun when she learned her exact Fahrenheit? How old when she discovered how to use it? And the moon, all that pulling power—when did she learn who she was in the crowded night sky?"

Wasting gas again, I told myself, standing at the curb with your motor idling. The process of image elimination had been going on most of my almost seventeen years. The word "time" still meant "o'clock." I had yet to confront that other word, "urgency." Perhaps with such a full tank I hadn't begun to worry about how far I had to go.

2

I went back to Western Union. Clutching the pencil connected to a small chain, I composed my surrender.

"Shoot the fare in care . . . that's good, it rhymes," I said to myself, "but shoot the fare where?" I looked up to see if anyone could identify our location. A few people were busy with the protected pencils, but the clicking machinery behind the counter was unattended.

"Hey!" The voice was as galvanized as a fire door.

"Hey, anybody? Where are you?" Flushed and angry, the girl of the voice banged a reddened fist on the counter.

"Yeah, yeah!" she yelled. "You got a job, so why aren't you on it?"

Her frizzy hair bobbled like electric live wires as she darted under the counter, facing our startled group, arrested in mid-action—our pencils frozen resembled small weapons. She stared belligerently a second, then let the tears loose. They didn't flow or course down her cheeks, as the poets say—they spurted from her eyes in the same jetlike stream produced by a water gun.

"Don't anybody ask me whatsa matter, see, because it's nobody's business and nobody gives a damn, and I don't like strangers anywhere, but most of all not in this flea-infested, animated sewer of a city! Just shut up, all of you, and mind your own business, see!"

There were no sobs or gulps, just the spectacular waterworks. We were an attentive, fascinated audience.

"Whadya staring at?" she bellowed. "Write! Go on, send home for money. Tell the folks back home you're getting out of here because you're sick of getting screwed, yeah—screwed—yeah, with nothing even to show for it, not even clap or—or crabs! Hell, you're not even knocked up, no! You're just screwed!"

The tirade built to a wail which attracted a few interested spectators from outside. They leaned against the storefront, peering in at us. Finally the wiry-haired girl dribbled onto the worn carpet bit by bit, at last gasping in painful sobs. Released, we gathered around her sympathetically. One man offered a ragged hand-kerchief. The girl looked up at us.

"You know where I just been?" she demanded. "I been three stories up on a goddam fire escape, that's where." She stumbled to her feet. "Hundreds of us, all packed ass to ass because some son-of-a-bitch lying ad said 'Showgirls Wanted.' Me? I'm a showgirl if I could. Only it wasn't nothing but another screw. Just get a couple hundred wishful thinkers hanging on the rails, smiling away, so they can show how many women are outa work in this cesspool town—I'm gonna be in the papers! Hooray! As a 'unemployed pretty'! I'll take it home to show the folks, 'cause that's where I'm going—and everybody here, they can screw theirselves, not me." She blew her nose positively. "Thanks, mister. That's the only thing anybody ever gave me for nothing since I left Kansas City." Sighing noisily, she pocketed the handkerchief. "So," turning to me, "who's sending you money to get where, huh?"

I looked at the half-finished message I held. She whirled on the small group.

"Okay, jokes, I mean folks, the flood's over. Thanks for witnessing." She picked at her dress, then whispered, "Wanta give it just one more flap? C'mon, I saw you up there—couldn't find the camera? Hell!" She pushed us both toward the door. "Nobody here, either, to take that S.O.S. of yours, see? That's a sign. Try once more. Okay? Come on."

I went. Of course I went. We moved swiftly, too breathless to communicate. The familiar little fountain of hope kept pushing up somewhere inside me. Wouldn't it be too strange and wonderful to be saved, as it were, at the very moment of defeat?

"Shoot the fare, etc." forgotten, I bumped along through the crowds, following my new friend in need. She turned into a side street, stopping at what seemed a long, high brick wall.

"You okay?" she asked, peering into a compact mirror. "You wanna fix anything? Jeez, you shoulda left that paper bag at W.U. You look like you're smuggling out somebody's remains or something. . . . C'mon."

We went through a narrow passage in the prisonlike wall. In the dimness ahead was a sign that sent my heart leaping: "STAGE DOOR," it said.

"Hide the bag here, we'll get it later, okay?" She reached toward me; I drew back.

"Oh, no," I whispered, "I'll need it—my things—toe shoes, and . . ." Her eyes opened wide.

"Your what?" she hooted. "Never mind, just hold it down, or—or back, or—ah, c'mon."

We crossed through the stage door into another corridor. This one was suddenly a subway scene. More girls. Women. Females. The sea of femininity flowed into a smaller stage entrance.

More stairs. They went up and they went down. On the upgoing stairs were dozens of legs, feet, all shapes and sizes. On the downgoing stairs were unmatching shoulders, heads, and arms. A huge fire door pushed forward, causing the sea to ripple and roll. There were no men in sight, but an unmistakably male voice was heard above the babble.

"That's it, girls! The rest of you gotta hold it in the alley. Okay, now, easy! Ready for bunch number eight. No pushing . . . c'mon. Now, let's tippytoe like ladygirls . . . c'mon, now, quit pushing, you bums!"

A clatter of females disappeared into the iron-jawed door without making a dent in the crowd. I struggled to stay upright. My friend seemed right in her element.

"You okay, kid? This your first cattle call, huh? Well, rule one is stay on your feet. You let 'em knock you over, you miss the holidays and your birthday—life just goes on without you, see? Here, let's look at you." She pushed my hair out of my eyes.

"Thank you. What—what kind of show is this? Is it—?"

She adjusted her bra. "It's a musical-type sort of thing—say, you undernourished or just young?"

My spirits rose. "Oh, that's good. I can sing and I dance, and I . . ."

She gave a yank. The bra slipped down her sleeve.

"Yeah, me too. Only I don't want to work up too much hope for this job, because I got an inverted nipple."

She put the bra in her purse and began tugging at her girdle. An attempted advance from the rear of the crowd almost downed us both. She turned and bellowed: "ALLLL-L-RIGHT, Madame Doo Farge, get those needles outa my armpits! Uh-uh, you claw at me, baby, you're gonna draw back a nub!"

My friend stepped out of a soiled girdle, which she rolled

neatly into her pocket. Just in time, too, because the male voice now announced: "Okay, next bunch—easy on the wrestling, girls! . . . Here's your big chance, so light up those teeth . . . move it, ladies—center stage!"

We had made it onto the stage itself. A galaxy of giant showgirls preened. Someone noodled on a piano. A huge Arabian Nights type of oriental urn was the only inanimate object in sight. From out front a man, invisible to us, was walking back and forth surveying the girls. Heads followed him with smiles and coy gestures. I squeezed boldly between two Amazons. The back-and-forth voice in the darkness out front was hairy with authority.

"Velvet? You gained a coupla pounds, honey? Never mind, they're all in the right places. Hullo, Dada Baby—you're looking nice and juicy—*ssllllurrpp!* Ah, ha! Cushions! You added to your upholstery, too, huh?" The girls giggled and nudged one another.

"And you . . . heeeeey! What's your name, honey?"

A giant blonde oozed vapidly downstage. She spoke in a lisping squeak. "Mabelle. Mabelle Glory. I just arrived in this man's town from Akron, Ohio, and I'm here to . . ."

The producer interrupted. "AAAAHHHHH! A singer, eh?" The ladies giggled. His voice dropped into the depth of sincerity.

"Now hear this—the painful truth. Galli-Curci herself couldn't get on this stage in this show. Nossir! This is for a very special few. Only some are true artistes of pictorial perfection. It's a rare talent. A special gift."

There was a moment of heavy silence. All posed in attitudes of great respect. The producer's voice lifted somewhat.

"You—you there in the middle."

The Junoesque beauty next to me spoke to the top of my head. "He means you. Go on, honey."

I was aglow. I knew I was. "Me? You mean me, uh—mister?" I tried that ooze movement downstage, hoping to land somewhere within the orbit of his gaze.

"Yeah, you. Will you kindly tell me what the hell you think you're doing here? Get outa that line, will ya? Go on, get! Hey, you with the frizzy head—in! Okay. So now, ladies, you see that phantasmagoria urn? Almost as gorgeous as you. This is a Grecian tableau—you are princesses—on the Nile—Ancient Greece. . . ."

My friend threw a glance of mixed emotions at me as she moved into my place. On the sidelines I dissolved with envy.

Of course I tried to be glad for her and the other girls, but it wasn't easy.

The voice went on. "I want to see you move like royalty. You are Queens of the Nile. Just like Cleopatra. Now, move real regally upstage . . . that's right . . . okay. So you're all just like some legend outa the past . . . ah, say, that's lovely. Whatta picture. So, okay—now, drop 'em. Let's see what we got—drop 'em—all the way . . . we're all artistes here."

Skirts and dresses dropped from the girls surrounding the urn. Bare bottoms began to shine forth. The producer's voice didn't alter one note.

"Okay, let's add this up, see where we are . . . uh huh . . . hey, Joe? That one fourth from stage left. It's outa line, too low. Sorry, honey, take it out. That pear-shaped butt there—put it center. Ah, yeah . . . very nice. Over there, third stage right. Honey? Is it always red like that or are you blushing? Okay, okay— a little makeup can fix that. Holy God! I never saw a furry one before in my life. Get it outa there before it bites somebody! . . . So! Fine! You're all gorgeous. You can back into my room anytime. Go on over and sign in. Joe? Name 'em, will ya?"

There was general reaction. My friend pulled up her skirt. She was starry-eyed.

"Whooooeeeee! Oh! Did I look nervous? Well, I was! Oh, I'm so sorry for you, kid, but I could have told you. He only likes high-pocket girls, you see—'cause he? He's almost five feet tall himself. It builds him up. But he's not unusual. Producers! As far as they're concerned, a woman's social position is strictly horizontal. C'mon, I'll buy you a cup of coffee. Whatsa matter, that guy scare you?" I made a casual gesture—I think. Her voice lowered.

"Oh, am I ever relieved! Understand, I get by fine just only bare ass, but that damn inverted nipple screws me good if they want total naked. It's because it's so noticeable it detracts from whatever else, see? Of course, a weird thing like that—with any break at all—can make you a star. Look at Myrna Loy—she's got one blue eye and one brown eye, you know that?" She slapped me on the back playfully.

"Honey, you wanta be a actress? Think hard. You got anything commercial? I mean, besides only singing or dancing, or . . . you know—something you can really sell. Something they might take notice of?"

3 ༘༘༘

Alone once more, and on the way back to Western Union once more, I wondered, What if I had been one of the chosen? The confusion was that all my early life had been a continuous lesson on the value of skill, craft; my school, the demanding stage of vaudeville: the actual experience of wing-watching such standards of the period as Jack Benny, Belle Baker, Willie West and McGinty, George Burns and Gracie Allen—oh, on and on. Sure, they were the grownups then. I was a kid star observing from the wings. But, when I did my act, I did it on the same boards, with the same audience. There was no copout on value then, so how in hell could I now equate competing with only my mute behind? How could it get me back to where I felt I belonged?

Considering my alternatives, I sent two identical wires. Whichever answered first could claim me. Only dance marathon stars could wire collect for fare, could send out laundry without paying in advance. Naturally, stardom was earned. By definition, "star" in dance marathon terms was a combination of "horse," a contestant who had the endurance to stay on the floor until the near end, and "clown," a contestant with enough additional stamina to entertain the crowds continuously during the endurance show.

I was a star.

Had been a star since age thirteen, when in my first marathon I had managed to stay on my feet for fifteen hundred hours—unimpressive, but I was established. By this time, I had several thousand hours to my credit, during which I had sung and danced, as well as "marathoned," with no additional favors other than fare and laundry. The twenty-four-hour-a-day audiences wandered in and out of the dance arena continually and without notice. Add the fevered militance of the other contestants, and any sneaky favors such as extra sleep or an occasional five-spot were quite impossible.

But then my lifelong admiration of the trapeze artists, the

acrobats, the genuine dancers and tumblers was based on their passionate pride. They were not fakers. They were skilled craftsmen. It followed, I now suspect, that the same "no fake possible" element in the marathon was a source of pride to me, too. Survival, as well. Survival with a certain kind of honor. I had learned to walk on three-inch calluses, to keep them from cracking with regular applications of olive oil. I knew how to sleep upright, hands in pockets, chin pointed straight ahead. To keep my mouth shut, never fight, listen to no one but the management, and endure.

I was a star. A sort of athlete.

After each of the marathons in which I participated, I took my savings and my hope to New York. Making the rounds of the casting directors, I never got past an outer office. So, once again, I sent my wires. Grimly. This made the sixth? seventh time? I was beginning to lose count. There were a lot of punchy marathoners who had lost count. I was determined to get out. Get out soon.

What is it "they" take notice of? I wondered. My sister was in New York, and she certainly had been "taken notice of." As the spieler on the sidewalk of the theatre she was playing bellowed: "Like a banana, watch her peel! Watch Gypsy Rose Lee take it off, right down to the fruit!"

These days, Mother insisted loyally that Billy Minsky's Forty-second Street Burlesque was equal to the best of Broadway. She ignored the fact that there weren't any spielers outside the Lyceum, where actors were billed under their real stage names.

How many times had the acts playing on a vaudeville bill with us been led by Mother, all refusing to stay at the same hotels, or even eat at the same restaurants with burlesque people? A certain snobbery was prevalent. Mother chose to forget.

"Why, burlesque is the womb that has borne great big stars— I can name you eight or nine easily, and the *Ziegfeld Follies* at the Winter Garden is no different in any way from *Ada Onion from Bermuda* at Minsky's!"

Rayon or silk, they were both shiny, weren't they? My own theories were so fragile I never dared expose them. Besides, I was in no position to voice opinions. Though temporarily, I was a marathon dancer—with no spieler at all. Mother had made a happy segue, now it was up to me to do the same. "How?" was the major question. The place I yearned toward was the legitimate Broadway, just a few blocks away, but a moon trip if you wanted to deal in realities. As usual, the most immediate major reality was my very empty belly. Hardly a viable topic for my mother and sister, who were convinced that I marathoned for fun; but then they had managed to sidestep hunger. After all, it was I who had abandoned them. In all fairness, my hunger was my own concern. Why expect them to recognize the value of twelve meals every twenty-four hours just for staying on your feet? A value which I consider, even now, a pretty fair deal. But it was the external me that worried them most.

"I can't understand how you expect to be noticed, June." Mother shook her head sadly. "Doing the rounds looking like that, dear. You are as plain as a piece of homemade soap."

Mother's concern with physical beauty was new. When I was killing the audiences on the Orpheum Circuit at six, seven, and eight years of age, I was downright funny to look at; but back then she told me, "Beauties are those supers in the last row, honey; the talent is down center in the spotlight."

So I hadn't grown up feeling cheated that my nose was too big—"that Norwegian beak," Mother called it fondly. My legs too long—"great for high kicks," Mother said. "Dainty June wouldn't be worth fifteen hundred a week if she was just a pretty kid!"

So I felt special—until 1934, when "beautiful" became Mother's byword. So "pretty" was an important word for the first time. I was panicky about emerging from the endurance mass to walk the solo plank, with an overlarge nose, elongated legs, and an impossible secret dream.

"Your sister is the most beautiful girl on Broadway," Mother beamed. It was true. Everybody agreed on that. Perhaps it was because I had been totally happy with what "Dainty June" had been that I had no understanding of beauty for itself. My actress idols would never have scored with "Ada Onion" anymore than they would have won the approval of that little man with the cigar who said, "Hey, you! You there in the middle!"

So, somewhere inside my life machine, there was a mechanism that kept me from regret when I failed at the beauty parts. And the record proves I failed consistently. But, like the rat or the sparrow, I didn't stop to sort out the "why." I concentrated on survival. If we didn't possess the weapon of beauty, we created the next best armament, fortitude.

Besides, I was spoiled. Hadn't I enjoyed the laughter and applause before? I looked almost the same, only longer. Cold appraisal of one's personal equipment is a private and painful business for any teenager. I was no exception. Not only my nose and skinny arms—my hair was unmanageable, and there was a crooked tooth smack in front.

Get the wrinkles out of the belly, sure, but get to work on those externals, too, What does a plain piece of homemade soap do about the packaging of the product except to justify it?

4

The sun felt good. It lit the Western Union window like an arc. I snuggled into myself and smiled. I was empty enough to be experiencing the same floating sensation as on one of those previous excursions to Broadway two or three marathons ago.

Mother's voice had rippled joyously on the phone.

"Come and see the beautiful big apartment your sister and I have found, a real home at last. . . ."

Visions of a full pantry, a sneak trip into an icebox bursting with goodies, had filled my mind. I invested another nickel on the subway.

The apartment was a ten-room doozie, right on Riverside Drive.

"Someday, dear," Mother mused, "we'll have enough furniture so we can have guests."

Proudly she had given me the tour. In time, we reached the kitchen. I leaned against the door, faint with the familiar smells of German food. All around was the portrait of Mother's singular homemaking. The unforgettable still-life was intact: A small table covered with newspapers; the bare bulb hanging above, casting a glow on neatly placed mugs, familiar from their previous life at Thompson's One-Armed Cafeteria; a coffeepot sporting brown stains from many overboilings. The Carnation evaporated milk can—the ice pick had neatly made two identical pouring holes, now thickly clogged with yellowing excess.

"Don't look at the walls, dear, or the ceiling. I'm going to have to borrow a ladder." Mother's tone was grim. I looked. There were many lumps large and small mixed with wide streaks in a miss-and-match pattern on the walls. The ceiling design was even more elaborate.

"I can't stand the smell of food because of him. Imagine, June—" She sat at the small table opposite me. I breathed in the sweet scent of stuffed cabbage as I suggestively fingered the stains on the coffeepot.

"Your sister's shady friends are not all to my liking, June." She moved nearer. "If you're going to be a cop, *be* a cop. Don't be sneaky. Pussyfooting around—"

I ventured, "Is that wonderful odor what I think it is?" She slammed her fist on the table. I grabbed the evaporated milk just in time.

"Yes, by God, it is, and he is skulking in the vice squad, mind you—won't even be called a cop, oh no!"

I swallowed. "You mean it's stuffed cabbage? Your wonderful stuffed cabbage, Mother?" I could taste the sweet-sour gravy. I looked around for a plate.

"He'd better never show his wop face in this house again. Your sister isn't going to throw away all I've done for her on some two-faced dago imitation cop!"

I found a plate. Edging toward the huge pot on the stove, I murmured, "Mother?" She stood up so suddenly the little table danced.

"Let him show his shifty eyes here once more!" Little blue veins were beginning to protrude at her temples.

"The stuffed cabbage," I said quite firmly. It was my empty voice speaking.

"The cabbage!" she shouted, rushing at the stove. I stood back so I wouldn't be in the way, but I held my dish in front of me. Mother grabbed the pot and swung it over my head. I ducked.

"He got me so mad I missed him once—twice—every damn time!" She was swinging the pot wildly about.

My stomach called out, "Mother, the cabbage!"

She was arrested mid-swing. "The cabbage," she yelled,

"never even once hit him, dammit to hell! There is the cabbage—wasted on the walls, the ceiling. Wasted! That damn, dumb cop!" She wilted onto the chair in tears. "Someday you children will be grateful to me. Life's lessons will prove that men—men are no damn good!"

I yearned toward the walls, the ceiling, but that visit had ended, and I was just as hungry as when it began.

Just as hungry as right now, I thought, hugging myself in the sunlight streaming through the Western Union window. I closed my eyes and gave up to the floating sensation. Rest period—use it—let every fiber go . . let go . . . rest. . . .

I knew the bus fare would come from the promoter of the dance marathon. I was among the needed. In fact, the negative points in a lineup of pretties were positive blue chips on a marathon dance floor. Hollow-eyed and skinny? Weak-looking and wispy? Great assets if you had the staying power to put it all to use. Because the usual "horse" looked just that. Some horses—trade name for pros—got through fifty or sixty contests, stacking up around a hundred and fifty or sixty thousand hours before the shell began to peel away, exposing impaired speech and mobility. A glassing of the mind. Punchy? What a good, descriptive word that is. Well, on the glorious journey toward that term, the horses basked in fame and fortune. Not in tangible forms, of course. I never knew one who had ever been inside a bank, except perhaps to clean it. But they thought they were in the Olympics, and that was more than enough.

Comparing what the politicians call "underprivileged countries," there was about ninety-nine percent illiteracy dancing away in any of the contests in which I participated. I was right in style. I couldn't spell and "decimals" was a dirty word to me, too. Four shows a day on the circuits had limited my formal education.

Among the connective tissues that grafted the endurance show to my childhood was the arrival at any new dance marathon location. It was not unlike coming to opening day at a vaudeville theatre. There were always familiar acts on the bill, people you knew, the orchestra warming up, a similar ritual of preparation. Only difference was the arena air. It was redolent of onions, hot dogs, and popcorn. The vendors' cry, "Get yer three-point beer, ice cold." It would be a long time before a lunch counter at the movie houses would be such a big concession—and the Winter Garden or the Empire never would smell like that. But here was an audience, an orchestra, a sort of, kind of show business . . . a substitute with twelve meals every twenty-four hours.

With all the semi-likeness to what I had known before, I wonder how it was that I never found a single soul with whom I swapped dreams—no pal, no buddy, no personal exchange. That's why I'm not positive how many others managed to surface. Sure, there were Frankie Laine and Red Skelton, but we were never even on the same floor, so I never met them. Not there, not then.

Getting out of marathoning wasn't easy. Staying out was harder. But out and away for good must be my next move. This one just had to be the last circle for me. When the fare came, I'd do my usual thrifty job: stash it away in my bra and hitch a ride to the location. No interest rate, but next-to-the-heart savings.

I was almost seventeen years old, and I had to find a route back to the kind of theatre that had instilled this fierce pride in my gut in the first place.

5

Just as Mr. P. T. Barnum knew the net worth of a two-foot-tall honest-to-God man, or Florenz Ziegfeld what shade of blue light was enough to clothe a bevy of beauties, so the marathon promoters knew where to pitch a tent, promote a Grange hall, and/or enlist the good right arm of the local American Legion.

Jamie Smythe didn't fit into the scenery, perhaps, but he was organically pure to the brethren. He was a big-time promoter, but unlike the more obvious-to-the-trade, Jamie was well mannered and gentle spoken. No diamonds or manicures, no checks or stripes. A real gent of the soft-sell school. Even "the boys" treated him with affectionate respect. He was almost delicate in stature, and his shadings went from semi-Latin to mid-Italian. He wasn't afraid to spout poetry, but he didn't know how to dance at all, he had never learned; and I loved him with a burning that made my eyes sting.

From the beginning I knew the dizziness would pass. Even though it was my first trip to the peak, I knew. How? . . . Blood. My veins bubbled in equal doses of positive-negative family impulse. Had I been born into some other tribe, perhaps the opposite sex would have held more mystique; men would have been meaningful to an entire life, actually important—for the long run, I mean. But in my family tradition has always been the fast-start-and-sudden-stop-to-drop-off syndrome.

It didn't limit appreciation of the opposite sex, only the duration of the appreciation. Companion to this condition was an under-the-skin knowledge of one's own time clock. The greatest gift of all was absence of judgment. So love was enjoyed in all its painful glory while it lasted, because it was never considered to be life's main attraction in the first place.

Mine was a family trait: to want everything that being alive suggested; so, if only one's quality gauge didn't break down, and one's motor kept running, nothing was impossible. Not in my family. I mean, of course, the females of my family.

Doddie was my mother's mother's mother. An early bride, mother, and widow, she had no power to control her own daughter's headlong rush at life. That daughter, Anna, married at fourteen, by seventeen had produced a brood of four: one boy, three girls. Later, weary of stage-managing a cliché, Anna composed a more liberating sonata. The opening strains conducted her fourteen-year-old middle daughter, Rose, to a convent, "to learn manners and obedience from the sisters." The boy selfishly drowned, the two other sisters strayed, and my grandma Anna, the tall one known to us as Big Lady, was free for the final movement, the freedom movement.

Grandpa Charlie was bewildered for a little while, but then the understanding lady next door brought in the milk and laid the table. He was one of very few lucky losers.

The fourteen-year-old, temporarily imprisoned in the convent, was my mother, Rose Evangeline Thompson. Mother's intimacy with religion, which vividly colored my childhood, stems from that incarceration. She was convinced that, when people ignored His rules, God was the victim of His own terrible tantrums. That's why thunder-and-lightning storms are so prevalent. All the time it's God up there, letting us know He saw everything, knows everything—and if you are guilty, He might just let loose, in His uncontrolled rage, and hit you with a piece of lightning.

Mother's inside track seemed to protect her from any fear of His personally directed wrath. She didn't need church, she said, because she didn't need to go through channels. The closest she ever came to a Bible was in the convent, when she cut out the saints and Family into a paper-doll collection. She related that the nuns said nothing, did nothing, but took away the scissors and the book.

"They knew," Mother said, "they knew I needed the paper dolls but I didn't need the book."

Both sides of that family were religious. Grandpa Charlie Thompson was not only a highly respected member of the Northwestern Railroad, which ensured free family travel, but he was also a 32nd Degree Mason. His wife, Grandmother Anna, believed in the Bible, but declared, "God wouldn't like the way men have turned everything around to make things easier"; while Doddie had a view of her own.

"I gave God back to the Indians seventy years ago," she'd say. "Yup, God is running out of the money, girls. The fear of Him has fizzled to a punk tip, because men are much more afraid of each other now. Why, any spoofball with a tight-packed gimmick that really rocks mankind as a self-propeller could grab this day and ride it right into eternity. Some clever spoofer could easy outrun God as a bona fide faith. You watch. If God fumbles this chance, right now? Just watch, some other order of hope is going to grab off heaven sure as hell!" She always chuckled at her own jokes. Mother thought Doddie was asking for it.

A thread of adolescent marriages runs through the family tapestry. Early marriage was escape to early independence. Sink or swim, it was all yours. If you perished of failure or were killed by your success, you had the satisfaction of knowing you ran your own show. On that premise, my family were closely united, without all that stifling togetherness.

In the working stage of Big Lady's marriage to Grandpa Thompson, they lived in a little house and had little children, just like people. Belle, the firstborn; my mother, Rose, the second; and Mina, the youngest, were the sticky center of a buzzing beehive: all beautiful—not just in the way that youth alone is beautiful, not brunettes or blondes, and certainly not redheads—the features uneven, totally unalike, but with an eerie inner fire that was peculiar to this one litter. Oh, yes, they were wonderful-looking women, with a built-in magnet that might have drawn the force of the universe.

They all ate and drank of life in operatic gesture, enduring occasional heartburn to the clash of cymbals. So it followed for me that what I felt rushing through my veins was equal to the procession of *Aïda*. Who would bother to consider the amount of time it took that great crowd to arrive, flood the premises, and then recede to darkness? This was now. The rushing was dominating my metabolism, and Jamie had happened.

Jamie. He was an education to envy. What I learned from Jamie helped prepare me for anything and everything that was to come.

Jamie. I was meant to meet Jamie.

So it was that Fate, or some other patsy, had to take the fall for the fateful early spring afternoon, a year or so before I sat hugging myself in the sun of that Western Union window. That was the spring I had sat waiting in the smelly, dark office of Jamie's confederate promoter, Dinky Valoon. I was waiting for a coupon good for one meal and a ride to the site of the ever new dance marathon operation. Dinky didn't know the bus fare he had sent me was stashed in my bra. If he had known, I don't think he would have appreciated it. Anyway, I sat in the corner, trying not to inhale the stale air, when the hackles rose at the back of my neck. I couldn't hear all of the exchange, but I had a fine northeast view of the gent Dinky seemed to be in conversation with. My hackles told me this was no ordinary meeting: automatically I blended into the wall.

Dinky wore a pasty grimace as he stared into the spitting end of a large gun. He seemed so fascinated he was speechless, which didn't matter because his new friend did the talking.

"Partners," that oil slick was saying, "fifty-fifty, see? One of us will be in the cashier's office, a couple of us keeping an eye in the arena—and me? I'll be with you. Partners, see?"

Apparently, Dinky had no eye for it, because he quietly slid down and out of sight, like jello off a plate. The visitor put his gun on the desk and leaned over the unconscious Dinky. Only Scorpios do what I did then. That's right, I moved stealthily to the desk and grabbed the gun—and I didn't even like Dinky. Some words must have gurgled in my throat, because the brute turned and rose to his King Kong dimensions. I held the gun in both hands, so he wouldn't see I had no idea of where the clicker clicked from. I guess I fainted standing up, because nothing seemed to happen for the longest time.

Then there was laughter. It came from behind me. I didn't look around. I got credit for that later. "The boys" thought it was cute—I never told anyone I was too paralyzed to turn. Then King Kong was laughing, too, displaying what seemed to be as many rows of huge white teeth as the ivories on the grand organ in the pit of the Roxy Theatre.

That's how I met Jamie. He was the main laugher. It wasn't until King Kong's purple lips fell over the ivories and the sudden silence was pointed away from me that I knew another outsider was in the room. Jamie was gently rolling Dink into a sitting position. No one else moved. He looked my way.

"You can't tell me," he smiled, "that such a huge weapon belongs to such a little girl."

Kong's chest heaved. "It's not hers, it's mine."

Dink's eyes glazed open, still staring into the same muzzle, but now it was I who fingered the trigger. His eyes traveled upward, meeting mine before they went dead. It wasn't until I realized that I was the only one in the room holding a cannon that I began to come to.

Jamie's voice was velvety. "Does that gun belong to this gentleman here?"

I forced my tongue away from the roof of my mouth. "I was . . . I was just holding it for him," I said.

6

In any dance marathon, walkathon—whatever those promoters chose to call it—the number of original contestants thinned to less than half during the first five hundred hours. The trick was to force your mind into accepting the routine your body was experiencing, and to keep feeding your furnace. Strangely, an easier task for the mind than for the body. The human machine, unaware of being overused, gained weight. Some were frightened, others just alarmed.

Me? I was delighted. I was tired of being skinny, so "filling out," as Mother would say, was thrilling for me. By the "2,000 Hours" sign, I actually began to look female. However, there was a penalty, because by then we would be into crowd pleasers such as derbies (run-in-a-circle-until-someone-falls), sprints (a handicap race-until-someone-falls), and other treats. It was wiser to resist the mounds of greasy eggs and stew-style grub, because it was possible to gain fifty pounds in a thousand hours. That stuff sure stuck to your ribs, as Mother would say, but it also stuck elsewhere, right in that place that is hardest to get off the ground.

I remembered the desperate struggle my sister waged with her weight. "Baby fat," Mother called it. Hardly a man alive could fail to concede it was fun to be beautiful—sure, but to tip the scales at a consistent twenty-five- to thirty-pound overage? Louise didn't care to hear Mother's "She is large for her age," anymore than I enjoyed the "Yes, her eyes are too big now, but she will grow into them."

During one of my sister's early heavy periods, it was fated for me to be confined in a hotel room on Chicago's North Shore. The act was on a forced lay-off because I was the angry victim of a breakdown. The hotel doctor who was in charge suggested quiet, and that's what I got. With the exception of his visits, and the hotel maid, I saw absolutely no one for two weeks.

I did a lot of thinking. I couldn't believe hard work was the cause of a breakdown; it had to be something else. As I lay staring out the window at all the so-called normal people on the street below—going to, then coming from work, shopping, or just plain loitering—I tried to sort out my ten years of existence. Something was going wrong. I was the one in bed, too thin, too nervous to work. Shame and disgrace. It had to be on me, and I had to find the cure.

I pondered—hard. What was I doing wrong? My fourteen-year-old sister was attempting a solution to her problem: she was going to stop eating. I was always full of pickles, hot pie à la mode, popcorn, and all the other things I doted on. My dollar-a-day was secure, along with the freedom to go where I pleased. There was only one rule: Don't miss a show! Get in the theatre half an hour before the first act, all in one piece, or else. Hard-and-fast rules are a cinch. It's those half shades like "If you really want to" or "What do you think?" suggestive-style dictums that bring out the self-indulgence in me. I never missed a performance. Considering the four-a-day with five on Saturday and Sunday, which was the fashion in vaudeville by the time I was ten, staying thin and nervous was easy. It helped, too, that of the nine numbers comprising the act, I appeared in seven, making lightning changes: singing sweet (Mother's term for straight), low and high; dancing—tap, tap on toe, adagio; comedy complete with slides and falls. All in all, the act tired me considerably. As long as audience response was exciting, it was a breeze; but the vast theatres were beginning to suffer from radio competition and talking pictures; so working that hard for smaller and smaller audiences became depressing, hopeless—therefore exhausting.

I looked around that empty hotel room in Chicago and stopped believing that vaudeville would live. That any of the way of life we had enjoyed since I was "Baby June, the Pocketsized Pavlova," had a glimmer of survival.

But Mother believed.

"There is no substitute for flesh," she said. "Anything mechanical hurts the eyes or the ears." Mother was loyal to her dream, which was born when I stood up at age two on the points of my toes. Right then she decided there had to be someone who would want to buy such a phenomenon. If so, she had the longed-for passport to freedom.

She was right. The market bought "Baby June," whose film career began at two, even though no dialogue was possible. I refused to speak until I was three, and then only because a role came along I couldn't refuse.

My first remembered meeting with my sister occurred a couple of years after Mother's plan was working well enough to bill me as "The Hollywood Baby." There was no "The Darling of Vaudeville (Reg. U.S. Pat. Off.)," yet; that came later. But there was triumph enough to send for Louise. Not for a brief visit, but for always. The "good part" was under way. It would last just long enough to change the beat of my heart forever.

Huddled in a cluttered dressing room of a vaudeville theatre somewhere in that theatrical limbo are a few little boys; myself, approximately five seasons young; my mother—who, contrary to a popular cliché, was not a calliope but a music box—small and vulnerable. She wore no makeup, nail polish; her hair curled about her blue-eyed, innocent countenance naturally. No high heels or silk stockings. Way ahead of her time, Mother was, in truth, natural and as delicately weighted as a stiletto.

Standing apart from "the boys" was the brunette, ruddy-cheeked big sister. She wore a "store coat," an honest-to-God hat, and—to top off the incongruity—real gloves. She had arrived complete with a whole set of clothes in a brand-new suitcase, along with an assortment of educational toys. She had actually attended school. Had been living in a genuine home, eating three squares daily at a family table. She had been reluctantly released from the protective embrace of Mother's first discarded husband, Daddy Jack. Said release marked *finis* to any attempt on said husband's part to assist in the rearing of his first two children. Us.

After Mother's umpteenth departure from his bed and board, he had discovered how easy it was to live without all the high winds, the turbulence; eventually nesting in a marital tranquility of kinder climate. Mother never forgave him for that. He cherished his second family and feared for his first. But Mother's new independence was to guarantee his nonexistence. From this time on he would be the lead in a horror story Mother enjoyed telling. Nothing more. No flesh, no bones—just a running character in a thriller about what marriage can be if you don't look out. So, from that time on, Louise was all Mother's very own, like me.

We stood apart, regarding each other soberly. My sister finally extended one long-fingered glove. We shook hands. Her eyes examined the ash-shade roots of my peroxide hair, while I concentrated on the geranium-red button which secured her coat. It was just over her heart, I thought, red. Heart red, only it didn't beat—it hung there at my eye level. I looked up to remark on this fascinating discovery, but my sister's eyes were uncomfortably on our mother.

"Please, will you show me my room?" Laughter swept the strangeness away.

"My room," mimicked Bubsy.

"Pleeze," exaggerated Sonny. Mother picked up her cue.

"Now, now, boys." She smiled warmly toward the stranger. "We're all one big family here, Louise. We would be lonely in a room by ourselves, wouldn't we? Of course we would, so all ladies share one room and little gentlemen the other, see?"

Louise turned to look at "the little gentlemen." In her steady gaze, the back-alley façade of these mongrels slowly developed before my unbelieving eyes. I saw them myself for the first time. I wondered if the others felt as unfinished, as grotesque as did I.

In the weeks that followed, Louise did seem to bring out the best in all of us, although there was much more gold to be mined. The boys became more conscious of their language; Mother stopped steaming open other people's mail, and I even began to wonder about those ducks painted on my dress. Not that Louise actually did or said anything to create this new atmosphere of self-evaluation. On the contrary, she remained aloof. Cool. Even dissociated. It was a long time before she was "worked into the act."

Many gnawings might have been detoured from the sensitive inner skin of this child, if the voice Mother wished to hear had sung out, or the dancing she yearned to watch had erupted. But Louise, like a chilled canary, didn't sing; didn't dance a single step. Didn't care to try. She didn't do anything Mother could consider useful. We never did appear onstage together. Not then, not ever.

Mother said she "made a beautiful picture" in the opening and the finale of the act. That was enough for the present. But Mother never gave up hope. She knew there was a spot waiting on some stage center for my sister. It was going to take a little time, but there was enough time to balance Mother's dream. Besides, there was more than "working into the act" for Louise. It was going to be just as big a job to find a line of communication between us offstage as with an audience onstage. Louise stood away from both tasks for a long time.

We were walking to the hotel from the vaudeville house we were playing in Buffalo, New York, after the fourth performance on that Saturday night. By the time we had stopped at the Chinese restaurant for a bowl of yak a mein, it must have been two in the morning. A warm drizzle had just begun, so that the street lights were many-faceted diamonds, and the black tar of Buffalo's main drag glistened. We straggled along, the little boys in the act following my mother and sister, who held my hand. Mother was telling us something she wanted us to remember.

"Now, a border town," she explained, "is always a place where people who are on one side are trying to get on the other side. Many of them aren't wanted on the other side."

"Why?" asked one of the little boys.

"Because," Mother went on, "they are undesirables. I mean, they don't obey laws, they—" she took the opportunity to stare at Bubsy pointedly—"they have been caught stealing and telling lies, and forgetting to wash—and, well, they just aren't wanted on either side. But the side that has them, naturally, has to keep them whether they want them or not."

Bubsy stopped dead in his tracks. I almost bumped into him. A dreadful comprehension spread across his angelic features.

"You mean," he said, "like, say, Buffalo or the place on the other side is your parents, and it just can't get rid of you anyways—and it's stuck with you?"

Mother smiled, patting his cherubic face. "Now, that's right, that's exactly it. And so, with all these undesirables and parents who have just given up, what do we have?"

Bubsy cried ecstatically, "A reform school!"

Sonny jabbed him with a bony elbow. "Naw, ya stupid bastard, ya got two bordertowns!"

Mother deftly grasped Sonny's topknot; leaning down to his seven-year-old height, she spoke right into his face: "Now, that's an undesirable speaking, you see. Little boys who spit in the street, use gutter language are not little gentlemen, and I won't have it. Now . . ." She released him with such force he almost fell. Mother drew herself up.

"Apologize," she demanded majestically, "first to us ladies, and then to the little gentlemen."

I hated these training sessions. I hung my head and tried to avoid Sonny's embarrassed face. Still remote, my sister watched us all with clinical interest. Bubsy, Chinky, and Merv stood miserably on the sidewalk, looking anywhere except at Sonny, who eventually pushed a word or two out into the silvery air.

"Louder," Mother commanded.

"I apologize," Sonny mumbled, "to the ladies."

At five my blush always began at my feet and worked upward at an alarmingly quick rate until my face bristled with blood.

"And," Mother prompted.

"And I apologize," Sonny's voice choked over the final words, "to the little gentlemen."

"The little gentlemen" snickered. Mother had found these mismatched urchins in an assortment of tenements and back alleys in much the same fashion an old-fashioned dog catcher scooped up strays. She dressed them in "knickerbockers" and cleaned them up, never understanding why there wasn't an immediate shine from within, as well as from the polished exterior.

The crisis over, we resumed our straggling procession hotelward. Passing an arched doorway, we were startled by a loosely sprawled figure. It convulsed once or twice before Mother, regaining her composure, herded us into the center of the street. Lurching into a crouching position, the figure rose to its feet and bellowed deafeningly.

"Keep walking, just keep walking! Stay close, Sonny, Bubsy." Her grip tightened on my hand. There was a crash of glass as the man dashed an empty gallon wine bottle onto the curb. His bellowings, while thick and jumbled, became more coherent.

"Mine, mine!" he howled. "Thieving, sneaking son-of-a-bitch!" He staggered into the shimmering light. The rain-wet black street, reflecting light, held him and his flat, spreading shadow grotesquely in that instant—for all time for me—a portrait, larger than life and twice as gaudy bright. Organic to the night, anywhere, anytime. My mouth hung open with the beauty of it. This was better than *The Phantom of the Opera*. Mother tugged my hand as she directed us to the opposite side of the street. Unexpectedly, a second figure appeared, lurching and staggering toward the first.

"Ya goddam liar."

"Liar."

"You're a sniveling, stinking liar!" The two voices intermingled. The second man yanked the first until they spun around disjointedly. They confronted one another—bleary, violent.

"Yeah, yeah!" Bubsy yelled. "Hit him!" He broke away and crouched on the fringe of the circle of light.

"Hit him!" he yelled. The two enormous figures swayed, glaring into each other's bloated faces.

"Son-of-a-bitch!" the first man bleated, his grubby hand clawing into the face of his opponent, who raised his fist, arc-like, from behind, upward—then brought it down like a pile driver onto his tormentor's skull. There was a cold clattering, very like ice cubes being emptied into a pail. The second gladiator buckled, sinking slowly. Sonny and Merv joined Bubsy.

"Get up, ya stupid bastard," Sonny yelled, "get up and hit him! Get up and fight! Yella belly! Yella!"

Mother hesitated only a moment. "Get up!" she yelled. "Let him have it! Soak him!"

Heavyweights spark a special kind of fury. These warriors connected with such impact that my teeth chattered at each blow. The thin piping voice I heard was my own.

"Kill him," it spiraled, "kill him!" It didn't matter, of course, who killed whom.

An unfamiliar voice topped my squeal. It was my new sister. "Shame, shame! Uncouth! Vulgar!" My jaw dropped. I thought a Grimms' fairytale queen would sound like that. We must all have stared at her.

Then she joined the family. "Just a couple of bums! Dirty, filthy bums!" she hollered. "Go on, skin him alive!"

We were banshees dancing and howling on a deserted street with the soft rain on the wet pavement reflecting the street light. It was a tyrannosaurus and brontosaurus fight, clumsy and ludicrous.

The tyrannosaurus was gaining momentum. Suddenly he let go with an unbelievable impetus. The brontosaurus, as though shot from a cannon, careened across that shimmering street, penetrated the black fringe, and disappeared into the surrounding dark night, all in one deafening second. Tails of our screams overlapped the clipped action, followed by the vacuum of silence. A watching, listening second only. Presently there came an agonizing scream, then total silence. Not total: the rain had begun and the drops made a tiptoe sound.

The apparent winner swayed under the street lamp. In a second, or an hour, whatever it was, the other man staggered onto the edge of the circle of light. He whimpered. We peered into the darkness, knowing he would re-enter the arena, knowing we would see him—knowing everything, it seems now. Moving toward us, he stepped uncertainly, almost gingerly, as though his feet might penetrate the substance of the street and carry him downward. The light disclosed what we must have known. His head was split open from between his eyes, upward through his shaggy hair, the blood gushing, streaming. His hands hung palms outward, apologetically. Tiny whimpers bubbled through the blood. His friend moved toward him sobbing, softly at first; but as Mother herded us away, the sobs grew and grew. I looked back, I couldn't help it. Those huge men clutched one another, hugged one another, their stinking rags glistening in the spattering red blood, there in the center of the arena. Mother hurried us up the street.

"Look straight ahead, children. Don't look back. Don't stop. Louise? Take June's hand. Now, everybody hold tight. Stay together, that's a real bunch of troupers." When we had safely reached the steps of the hotel, we gathered closely around her.

"Before you go to sleep tonight," she looked at each of us affectionately, she touched Bubsy's face, her hand trembled, "I want you to say a little prayer for those poor men. Drinking and fighting and swearing in the middle of the street in the middle of the night. Not just in border towns, but anywhere. And in front of women and little children, too. No shame. No shame at all. You remember that. Selfish, selfish men. Not that prayers can help them—you can't finish what God didn't begin, and God made a mess of so many men that I sometimes wonder . . . ah, well, sleep tight, darlings."

We went inside, up in the elevator, to our beds. Mother tucked us in, kissed us goodnight, and turned out the lights. I sighed, closed my eyes in the safe, warm stillness of the shabby hotel room. Were they still out there in the middle of the street, holding one another and sobbing in the blood? I wondered. Did no one come? Mother had once said that we were our brother's keeper. Did that mean them, too? How could we have helped keep them? Were they alone out there in the arena? Had it really happened? Were they real? Would I remember it tomorrow?

Eventually a truce was called and Louise no longer struggled with any of the traditional vaudeville tools. She read a lot, and in those few years, with the assorted help of stagehands and acts on the bill, my sister rang up grades upon grades, and even came up winners in some civilian school competition somewhere along the road. As for the overweight—well, she wore a lovely cape most of the time.

Mother said, what with four-a-day and all, I was too "high-strung" to learn how to read. She said book learning wasn't as important as the lessons life teaches you if you just keep your pores open.

7

I had emerged from that long-ago two-week solo in the Chicago hotel room more recovered from my breakdown than I realized. I had pondered my way to discoveries, solutions, convinced there was no law decreeing my own death along with vaudeville, that I had the right to die on my own terms. The real hurdle was my status as a sub-adolescent. Being ten was hell, because I was convinced I was stuck in a muddy track going nowhere.

The following two years became one of those nightmares of silent screaming and stationary running. I reached middle age by twelve. The quality of life, like the quality of audience, resembled a slow-motion nose dive.

Fortune's decline had also created disorder within the ranks of the boys in the act. The turnover was so fast now that we were rehearsing in the wings. Mother's promise to pay these sullen recruits "as soon as vaudeville gets on its feet" didn't inspire loyalty. To her dismay, these adventurers turned mean. They "skipped the act" right and left, until only a few faithful misfits, who had no place to go anyway, remained.

Before this exodus was total, I took out a contract on one boy I liked well enough. Bobby had failed Mother by demanding at least part of whatever salary we were getting on the current shabby tour. He was eighteen—small for his age—in fact, we were of identical height then, and I would be thirteen in a week. He played saxophone, clarinet, sang, did imitations, and danced. Very impressive, but the act itself, by the time Bobby had joined us, was awful; my gangly frame so embarrassing to me in my "Dainty June" kid getups that I had developed a stammer and dropped almost every prop I handled. Bobby understood my frustration. We vowed escape and partnership.

Although we were almost totally separate during the long teardown, my sister vividly expressed her own resentment of life in general. She was more and more withdrawn. Haughty. Around this time, overweight became fat. The boys called her "The

Duchess." She looked right through them. There wasn't a boy in the act she would favor with a word. She, most of all of us, had outgrown the act, even though she had eventually appeared in three spots. She never did try singing or dancing. She spoke the introduction verse and stood regally by, "making a beautiful picture." Dignity and disdain suited her tall, dark presence more and more. Besides, it won Mother's approval.

"Stay away from the boys, be like your sister. She knows what they are, why don't you?"

How could I tell Mother I admired those mongrels because they had the guts to at least try the world. It was stimulating to hear anyone planning the future, any future. Recognizing that there was indeed a future at all.

"I'm not learning anything here," one boy said.

I realized with a dreadful stab that I hadn't learned anything for years. All during the bad time, which had gone on now as long as the preceding good time, I had learned only that I didn't want to sneak out of hotels in the early dawn. The thrill was gone from walking out of a store fearing the touch of a hand on my shoulder, because my sleeves were loaded with things I had swiped. I had learned that I didn't like myself. Because I didn't like myself, my mother and sister didn't like me, either. What was left of the audience didn't like any of us. I was secretive, solitary, bewildered.

"Malcontent," Mother accused, "after all I've gone through for you. Ungrateful, selfish—oh, God," she wept, "you were put on earth to make my life a misery."

My sister always held Mother now, as though Mother were the younger of the two.

"June, it's bad enough everything's so rotten. Why must you be a . . . a . . ." Mother looked up from her handkerchief. "A Bolshevik!" she screamed. "Undermining the army, changing the rules!"

I screamed back, "Yes! Yes I am!"

Her mouth opened, then closed. The blows were unexpected and, considering her small stature, real haymakers. I careened against a chair as I fell face down on the threadbare carpet. My mouth was filled with something sticky. I spit into my hands. The sight of so much blood surprised me. I turned, holding out my hands toward Mother as I tried to rise, a scream trying to bubble through the stuff.

"Look at yourself." Mother wasn't weeping now. "You're going to look just fine on that stage, just fine. See what you make me do!"

The part that tore me up the most were the bad performances. Exploding with frustration, I was a dangerous weapon. At night, when Mother and Louise were asleep, I took the bedding from my cot and sought asylum in the same place that had comforted me ever since I could remember. Lying within the deep cold walls of the bathtub, I could recall all sorts of directions from Mother, but no conversation. How could she know how I felt? She knew me no better than I knew myself.

There was a scratching at the door. I unlocked and opened it a crack. My sister pushed in. She held a finger to her mouth.

"Shhh," she said, "Mother's asleep. She is exhausted, June. These fights are getting worse and she can't stand it." I relocked the door.

"What fights?" I said. "She just slugs me. It's always one slug and out. That's no fight."

She sighed. "Shhh, I know how you feel. About the act, I mean."

I looked at her. "You do?" This was the first confidence we had ever shared. "But you don't have to do the act—you never have."

She nodded. "That's right. All that sweating, practicing every minute. I've watched you enjoying your broken toes and scratches. Dancing so hard you black out in the wings. No, you do the act because you enjoy all that. I never have and what happens? You don't enjoy the act anymore than I do now. Do you? So, we sit here in the same bathroom with the same problem." I didn't dare the words so I waited. She got up and listened at the door.

"Why do you think I'm so fat?" She yanked her nightgown up, slapping her bare thighs viciously. "Look at that!" she hissed fiercely. "Fat, fat, fat!" I stood up in the tub.

"Please don't," I cried, "you aren't meant to be that fat! You can get rid of it!" Her face crumpled. "I didn't mean it like that," I babbled. "Oh, please—I only meant it's not permanent like—well, like my nose, for instance. Look—look how awful it is. And—and, Louise, look—look at how long and skinny my arms are. Those things can never be fixed, but you can be any shape you want. You can." I was in tears now, too; speaking earnestly, leaning out of the tub toward my sister in the first intimate exchange we had ever known.

"Shhh," she sniffled, "keep your voice down, June. This would make Mother so unhappy." I unreeled a few yards of toilet tissue, tore it in two and offered her half. We blew.

"It's all right for you," she said, "you're never alone. Those boys, those common alley fighters—you're always with them." I looked down. Why was I ashamed?

"I like them," I said, "I've always liked them."

She sniffed. "Shooting craps, climbing trees with them. June, not one of them has even finished school."

I stared. "Well, I've never even started. So? Besides," I said guardedly, "one finished high school at seventeen, isn't that good?" She was at the sink mirror looking deeply into her own eyes.

"That's the one you are always kissing. You like that, too, don't you?"

I wasn't ashamed now. There was another sensation, and I had never shared the acknowledgment of it before.

"Yes, I do," I admitted softly, "and holding hands, and sitting close, and . . . and . . ." I leaned over so I could see in the mirror, too; but she didn't look at my reflection, only into her own.

Finally she said, "Mother thinks all of that is . . . is dirty. . . ." She turned and looked at me now. "Do you?"

I shook my head. "Mother says everything she doesn't like is dirty, and I stopped believing what she says a long time ago."

My sister almost gasped, "Why?"

I went back to the beginning. "Well, she told me that if you kiss a boy you have a baby, there's no way out. . . ."

Louise looked uncomfortable. "I don't believe that anymore. I'm too old."

I agreed. "Me too, but I was nine when I first heard it from her. I knew then it wasn't true because I'd been kissing since I was eight."

She looked at me now until I squirmed. "That's disgusting," she said.

"You kissed Stanley. I saw you."

She frowned, then turned pink. "I am almost grown up, June—and I didn't start when I was eight just because I liked it. Besides, Stanley sneaked away, didn't he? So Mother is right and I hate him. I wish I had never seen him!" She was angry now. "Anyway, June, it's all going to be easier for you because you can't see how disgusting it is. You won't be alone like Mother, but you have to decide what you want and stick to it no matter what." There was a moment of heavy silence.

"Louise? If Mother is right, and that's all men want, then—whatever it is—perhaps that's all they ought to get." I smiled tentatively.

"You don't understand," she answered, "you can't just give them what they want. Not for just nothing. Because that's all there is. All you have, see?"

I digested that, then: "So, what did our father give Mother? She must have felt different than she says about him—after all, she married him."

Louise shrugged. "She got out of that convent in the middle of the night, didn't she? Big Lady and Grandpa would never have let her get married at fifteen, so what she got, I guess, was out."

I considered this. Yes, that was Mother's escape. "But, there's us," I said.

"Well," my sister mused, "maybe she felt that anything was better than a convent." We were very still for a little while.

"But she wanted you," I offered. "Remember when she told us that?"

Louise nodded. "I remember. But I was first, before she knew anything about life and—and all that. Then, four years later—I mean, by the time she knew she had to have you, it was too late. Poor Mother—" My sister's voice broke.

"It's not fair," I whispered. "She punched her belly, and, and—"

My sister picked up the tale. "And sat in boiling water, and—"

"But I wouldn't budge . . . and that's not fair!" I cried, "I'm not going to have babies unless I really want them!"

Louise looked at me. "Well, you better stop kissing boys until you make up your mind!"

"I'm not kissing boys," I said. "I'm kissing Bobby!"

"Everyone knows," she retorted, "kissing gets to be a habit."

I was getting angry. "Kissing isn't a habit, it's being—oh, being people. A habit is—is smoking, and I gave that up when I was ten. Besides, Mother may think it's all dirty and ugly, but if the rest of the routine is as nice as kissing someone you really like, it's got to be great, and I just don't believe her."

Louise looked thoughtful.

"What about you?" I said. "What do you want to be?"

She almost smiled. "Me? I'm going to marry a king or somebody. In any case, I'll be rich, really rich." It was an announcement.

"I want to learn to be an actress." I almost didn't get it out.

"Poor baby," she said. "Keep kissing Bobby and you'll be a hoofer. Just like him—only you'll have to call the team Mutt and Jeff, because he isn't going to grow one more inch. You are only thirteen and sprouting like a weed."

8 ꭹꭹꭹ

She was right. Within a year after eloping with Bobby, I was a hoofer, too, and he came almost to my shoulder. But that union served the purpose. My coven would cheer the early freedom, and clean break. Most of all, the natural demise of what they would have recognized as a marriage of convenience.

During the fated alliance, Bobby struggled to maintain what were termed "masculine prerogatives." Perhaps if I had not learned so fast and grown so fast the whole experience would have been more satisfying to him.

We were staggering through a crowded hotel lobby. The usually inexorable hammerlock my groom had on my neck was, for a split second, broken because he stumbled. Displaying a style that should have made my mentor proud, I pounced on the opportunity, threw him over my shoulder, and was astride him in a flash. His arms and legs pinioned by my own, I smiled into his astonished face. It was a feat he had demonstrated—in reverse position, of course—many times.

"Say 'uncle,'" I prompted.

Apparently, "uncle" was a word reserved for females, because the fight that ensued on the flowered carpet of that dingy hotel was the high point of my puissance and the low spot of my consanguinity with that member of the opposite sex. Bobby's love didn't end, it just burned on a different part of the stove.

It was during these labor pains that we were starved into dance marathons. Since we were too young to be on exhibit as a married team, the first outside wedge was driven by the promoter, who said we had to be brother and sister or the audience wouldn't like it. He meant the authorities, who never did show up to inquire what anyone was. From there on my efforts were bent on getting back out of the marathons while Bobby, who felt dramatic kinship to the underworld heroics surrounding us, was striving for recognition within.

Bobby found his heroes among the Dinky Valoons and the rest of the hoods who graced the shadows. I was in search of that childhood cameo of the legit star taking a flyer in vaudeville. The one who smelled so fresh, and sounded so nice, so classy.

Separate quests, separate routes. I was alone and nowhere, very busy combining two full-scale operations, grubstaking in marathons and combing New York for a toehold on the invisible ladder.

He was learning to carry a gun so it didn't protrude.

I gave up on Bobby. Watching him defect from the big hope—giving up—arguing that the big time for him was the postage-stamp floor of a speakeasy . . .

"I'm somebody here." Sure.

I began to value time. To understand how, if you used it with thrift, it was like money in the bank. So I was grateful for what I had managed to absorb during the hand-to-hand contest of our wedded bliss. There were other enlightenments as well. I had learned to run at a breaking wave in a high surf, not from it; to tap-dance; and to drive a car "like a man." That was the platinum tribute. His methods of teaching were similar to field combat, so I also learned how to duck and feint.

Meanwhile, like Alice, I grew and grew, just as my sister had predicted. By my fifteenth birthday I was looking over Bobby's head. By that day in Dinky's office, when Jamie asked if that gun was mine, I was almost seventeen, and I had given up looking at Bobby at all.

9

Jamie had arrived to search for a soft location in pal Dinky Valoon's vicinity. That's how I happened to be Jamie's official chauffeur at five simoleons a day, plus box lunch.

Jamie didn't know the territory. He could have saved the box lunch and the fin by traveling with a road map, but I got the job. It was interim work while waiting for my fifth contest. I'd leave the digs where marathon stars roosted free between shows, pick up Dinky's hearselike car, pick up Jamie, and we were off for the day.

It was easy on the feet, for a change. Jamie read the map and called the shots. He was all business—for a while. Then we found the location. It was the skating rink in one of those amusement parks on the rocky shores of a beach in Maine. Nothing else for miles around. A perfect spot for a murder.

On a chilly New England early spring day, that marathon began just like the others I had known. Within the usual five hundred hours, we were down to the regular small assortment of amateur flotsam and a larger group of jetsam horses.

Unused to actual romance, I was overwhelmed with Jamie's style. He was, by legal trade, a cartoonist and writer, so I received entire booklets with hilarious illustrations warmly relating whatever had transpired between us up to that point. They made me laugh right out loud sometimes, as I stood rocking from foot to foot.

"What's so funny?" the floor judge asked, as he flicked at my ankles with a thin wooden ruler. "Keep movin'—lemme see."

But I never let anyone see. The booklets were funny, but also very, very personal. It was a rare talent Jamie had for communication.

The law said we had to have fresh air every twenty-four hours or so. This put us on the dawn-lit street as a long straggle of semiconscious rag dolls. We wore whatever was at hand, and if a partner was asleep, we tied his hands with a soft cloth, draped him over our shoulders, and shuffled along with the partner hanging on piggyback. The procession moved slowly, which made conversation possible. That's why Jamie took the hour for wooing.

He couldn't help me lug my partner, it was against the rules; so sometimes his prose and lovely poetry must have infiltrated the battered ears of the exhausted comic I carried.

Unused to such elegance, I was mesmerized. Jamie's dark, brooding intensity was thrilling, the flashes of bright humor delightful. Most of all, his attitude: he regarded me as a woman, and that's how I made the transformation.

Oblivious of the crude reaction of the rest of the gang, I must have glowed in anticipation of these sunrise strolls as Jamie and I trailed the diminishing army. Then later, walking the circle alone, perusing my daily booklet, I would still be smiling. In my growing intoxication, the floor judge's "Keep moving" was less tedious.

Eventually there were stolen seconds of aloneness. This was possible because each contestant was permitted a few minutes out of a twenty-four-hour span in the hospital. A curtain was drawn, and Jamie waited. It was worth losing my turn at getting my feet oiled to be alone with this perfervid hero. He brought me wildflowers, which by now lavishly carpeted the fragrant hills surrounding our amusement park, little dainties completely alien to our menu, and words. Words. Words.

Jamie took it for granted I understood the words, and in many ways I did. If they failed to penetrate my unawakened mind, the effect they had on my psyche was profound.

At a little over twelve hundred hours, intelligence spread that, because the community was small, the show would wind up less than the usual three thousand hours. Therefore, sprints, grinds and derbies would begin soon, eliminating the flotsam and digging into the jetsam.

My booklet at around fifteen hundred hours graphically informed me not only what happened if a lady ran in these races, but what could happen if she didn't. It was thought provoking. At fifteen hundred and twenty-four hours, I believed I had had enough time to know my heart.

"Jamie," I whispered. The odor in the little airless hospital was by now hard to describe, unless you had more than a few thousand hours to your own credit. "The little cartoon of me wearing a crown and sitting on the big package with the ribbon?"

He nodded. "That's the first prize, Jeannie."

I rotated a swollen ankle. "I don't think I can ever get to first." It was hard to admit that I was weary of the screaming audiences and the lung-bursting races.

"Dear Jeannie." His eyes were deep and clear. I loved what I read in them. "I hoped to hear that. The package in the cartoon is filled with pretty things to make you smile. To make you look as sweet and fresh as you are. I mean to give you everything you want—everything." He leaned nearer. "At the very bottom of that package marked 'handle with care' is my heart. Let me give you my love, Jeannie—let me take care of you."

I gulped. The starch holding my spine upright melted. I collapsed in his arms. "I can't," I mumbled through a veil of tears, "I can't marry you, because—"

"I know," he whispered, "I know about Bobby. I have a plan."

I looked. "A plan? And—and you're not angry?"

He held me close. "I'm not anything but so in love I think the world is mine—it's all here in my arms." Everything sounded vaguely like song cues. I was dizzied and deeply content.

"You say you are an actress. Do you believe that you can convince everyone inside, as well as that whole audience, that you aren't well enough to complete the first sprint?" I looked into his adoring eyes. I saw no guile. Not even a flicker of impish humor. It took a moment to sink in.

"You mean, take a dive?"

He sighed. "Not exactly, Jeannie. It would be really acting, not easy at all. No one on this floor could know." My mind raced through quick pictures of the possible drama.

"But my partner," I murmured, "leaving him solo now seems so . . ." I trailed off.

Jamie was laughing softly. "He never goes into big hours. I've taken care of him for twenty-two shows, Jeannie. Those flat feet can't sprint."

I pictured the marathon clown: sagging posture, mouth agape, the comic shuffle. No, they never tried for the prizes. All they asked was laughter and expenses. They were stars.

"You've made so many friends, Jeannie, it will be a big, noisy goodbye. Thrilling." I looked down at my calloused feet uncomfortably.

"Isn't that what the horses call punking out?" Jamie had been kissing the palm of my hand. He looked at me now from between my fingers.

"The horses," he scoffed. "Surely you don't think of yourself as a marathon dancer."

I tried pulling my hand away, but he held firmly. "Maybe. I mean, I do when I am out there trying to last, even though I know it's all part of something I have to get through to—to . . ." I closed my eyes. The tip of Jamie's tongue was delicately caressing the soft areas between my fingers. It was a sensation I had not experienced. The glow began, slowly igniting my exhausted senses; it spread warmly all through my body until I became breathless.

"Oh, let me love you . . ." Jamie's voice seemed far away. ". . . My little girl, my own . . ." He lifted me to his lap; we were suspended in space momentarily like dancers. His hands found my small breasts; they were as cool and gentle as rainwater.

"A baby," he was smiling, "only a baby girl." He sort of burrowed his head between the little hard beginnings, which were now covered with goose bumps, closing his warm mouth over a straining, throbbing nipple. I gasped.

"Shhh," he whispered, "you won't be afraid, you are going to let me love you, let me take care of you . . . you are my little girl." He bent his head once again and the chills raced through me—I felt like a flag in a storm. It was too glorious to be me.

The air was split with the sudden clanging of a bell. Jamie rearranged my blouse, set me on my deadened feet, and pointed me toward the floor.

"Don't tell," he whispered, "not about the plan, or—" he laughed softly—"or anything."

I made it across the floor to my cot, where I lay bathed in a warm, undulating haze.

"This is what it is," I thought dreamily, "this is the poetry, the music and songs. This is what it feels like being a woman—not a girl, but a woman. . . ."

Wearing my new-found maturity like a magic cloak, I accomplished a near-perfect fall during sprint one. In fact, all would have been perfect but for "the improvements."

10

Oh, that interim before sprint one! Lulled into a semi-catatonic state, shrouded in a pink bubble. Well, it may have been pure coincidence, but that was when Aimee of team number 28 decided to improve me. Whipping up a batch of Lux flakes with peroxide and a soupçon of ammonia water, she explained: "Highlights in your hair—that's what you need, kid—and your whole face falls off at the sides, too. I'll just fix your eyebrows while we wait for the Lux to cook."

Almost covering me with a towel, she then worked the creamy lather into my shoulder-length hair. Checking the huge time clock at the side of the arena, she said, "Lessee, now, we got forty-five mintues on the floor before rest period—it took ten to get the gook on your head. O.K.! So in another ten minutes you go ask the floor judge for toilet excuse, see? But instead you wash all the Lux out fast and just wait'll you see those highlights!" Aimee then proceeded to improve my eyebrows. She was tall enough to walk alongside me, tweezing as we moved.

"Keep moving," the floor judge growled.

"Yeah, yeah," Aimee muttered, "I'd like to tweeze your hairs you know where, you big baboon."

Eyebrows removed and the ten minutes up, I asked the judge for excuse.

"Got two offa the floor already, no go."

I looked up at him. The sudsy cloud had begun to de-bubble. "But, I'm being timed, and I just have to—to go."

He turned his wall-like back to us.

Aimee chirped, "It's emergency!"

He stared coldly at my new needle-thin eyebrows, the mound of now rapidly melting frosting piled on my head.

"She don't look no different than always to me," he said, as he lumbered away.

"I'm going blind," I whimpered miserably. "Look, the stuff's going into my eyes."

Aimee was suddenly all business. "Gimme what's left in that bowl," she ordered. "O.K., girls, I got something I'd like to say here." Her voice was loud and commanding enough to gather a fair-sized group. "Just get around us, willya?" She spoke now in a conspiratorial whisper.

"C'mon, cover us and keep talking. Go on, dummies, just talk, willya? Here, Jeannie, pull up your skirt."

I hesitated.

"Pull up your skirt and pull down your pants."

I looked at the circle of faces surrounding us. There was interest and even encouragement, but no surprise. I pulled up my skirt but could go no further. Aimee lost her temper. She yanked at my middle.

"Goddammit," she whispered furiously, "you're gonna ruin my effect. That big flapjack's gonna keep you on this floor till the bell rings, so hold still, willya?" She was sliding the remains of the suds down my belly and onto my pubic hair.

"Go on," she ordered, "work it in. That's right. Good, there's just enough to fill your pants. This'll fix his wagon." She smiled in triumph as the empty bowl was displayed.

"Ooooohh, it stings," I chattered.

"Shut up, willya? You wanta be a emergency, so we won't screw up the timing, don'tcha?"

I nodded.

"Well, then, you gotta look like one to convince the big slob. You go over now, let him see how red your eyes are getting, then show him how something mysterious keeps runnin' down your legs. He'll give you a excuse. Anybody wanta match me on a bet?" She got a few takers as I moved toward the judge.

I babbled a renewed request, but that stalwart barely flicked an eye.

"And look," I had saved the clincher for the end of my plea, "something mysterious is running down my legs." He cast a jaundiced eye over the foaming trickles coursing slowly toward my socks.

"That don't look mysterious to me," he basso profundoed, "I seen that lotsa times on lotsa people." He moved center in order to be distinctly understood. "Problem here is I don't see it on enough of the present company. I'm talking now about the use of soap. S.O.A.P." Having made his point, he threw a final tip in my direction: "Just keep movin', kid, that way you won't puddle up."

That's how I happened to look like I was trying to be Jean

Harlow. The highlights turned into silver on silver.

"See, your hair is the kind that takes fast." Aimee wasn't displeased. "Now me, I woulda turned red, maybe. Interesting, huh?"

But Jamie scowled. He didn't appreciate what he could see of the improvements at all.

Anyway, when I took the fall it helped my credibility to be red-eyed, and the big purple splotches on my legs seemed to impress the audience, because they yelled encouragement like mad, even though some asked later why my hair had turned white overnight. Those audiences believed marathon dancing could do anything to you.

I had my prescribed sleepout in rest quarters: one hour, then coffee and a walk around. Then two hours and a walk around, then three of the same before the dreamless, uninterrupted long sleep. You could leave after that, but ex-contestants had to stay in the building for the long sleepout, because early on in the marathon business promotors didn't know so much about endurance and its results. Well, the record says that there were a few incidents of a contestant falling out of a marathon after getting way up in hours. He was allowed to go directly into the long sleep, and he just slumbered right into eternity. A thing like that could stop a successful show dead in its tracks, so naturally it had to be avoided.

According to the plan, after I woke up from the long sleep, I was supposed to pack and stand by for the bell; then, when the gang left rest quarters for the dance floor, go to the rear exit, where Jamie would be waiting with the getaway car. It was a pale blue Packard and it gleamed in the moonlight. It had everything but six white horses.

After sharing sleeping as well as waking hours with the equivalent of a family carnival, the cool, pale lobby I entered seemed an oasis. The tiny hotel was typical of resort towns, but to me at that moment it was a palace.

Jamie let the bellboy take me across the wide veranda through the antique-cluttered reception room, pausing at a carved rosewood desk to sign the register. There were an assortment of bowls and vases containing delicious-smelling wildflowers peculiar to the area. I leaned into one bouquet and inhaled deeply.

"Take your pick, Miss Reed." The clerk was smiling. "Felt

pretty awful last night when you dropped out. Sure put up a good fight, though. Here—" handing me a tall vaseful of trailing blossoms. "You get all rested up now, won't you?" He turned to the bellboy. "Luggage?"

The boy took my key. "It's all upstairs, sir. This way, Miss Reed."

Smiling my thanks, I followed up the winding stairs, through a dusty pink corridor carpeted in yellow roses.

"What luggage?" I thought. The brown paper bag, being carried so properly by the young man now opening my door, was all the luggage I had owned since I began marathoning. Could I still be dreaming? The door opened, revealing sunny windows bedecked with ruffled white curtains. More flowers everywhere. And quiet.

The door clicked softly shut. I stood motionless, holding my breath. What now? The blissful silence was broken only by occasional birdsong from the green treetops outside my window.

Would the serene beauty of everything here help me find the grace to enter this mysterious part of life? Was the tingling throughout my body going to melt away the apprehension of my mind? Or was it fear? Was I afraid of Jamie, or was I fearful of discovering the colors artificial, the beauty superimposed on a truth that would fill me with what Mother called disgust? What was the truth about men and women? Was it the same for everyone?

I knew the childish fumblings, the wild releases of my relationship with Bobby were basic and crude; that I had enjoyed tenderness and a sense of sharing pleasure for the first time in the moments alone with Jamie. That was surely true.

At the far end of the room a wide door was ajar. Dared I push it open? Would I be suddenly confronted with a moment for which I felt ill prepared? How could I have prepared? How could he find me anything but gauche, insipid, inchoate? I felt heavy with ignorance, then paralyzed with sudden stage fright. My eyes traveled about the room. Everywhere were beribboned boxes, all shapes, all sizes. Just like in the cartoon booklets. I took a deep breath and walked resolutely toward the partly open door. Hadn't Jamie called me his little girl? Smiled at discovering the immaturity of my body, saying "a baby"? Well then, I wouldn't pretend. I'd admit my ignorance. Insecurity about the script wasn't new to me. I remembered this same bone-numbing stage fright from some years earlier, as I stood trembling in the wings of a forgotten theatre, trying out a new number I wasn't sure the audience would love as I did.

Just before my cue, a grizzled face thrust itself between me and that circle of light onstage. "Just remember, honey—'To thine own self be true.' It works every time. Go on, say it."

I swallowed the dry lump in my throat.

"What does it mean?" I croaked.

"Mean? Well, it's clear, isn't it? If you're true to yourself, to what you believe, see? You won't ever screw up on somebody else. Say it!"

I said it then, I said it now as I opened the door wide.

More artistic than any fountain in Rome, more thrilling than the falls of Niagara, the gleaming white bathroom was a masterpiece. Was it all mine? Could I submerge the tense muscles and soak the knotted nerves loose all alone? A huge basket of fruit sat midship of the old tub. Ornate bottles lined the shelf above. I had never used scent in a bath. Now, placing the fruit on a stool within easy reach, I half emptied a particularly fascinating bottle. I let the steaming water cascade, inhaling the sweet pungency as I dropped my clothes to the floor. Spotting another door, my hand went convulsively to cover the recent bleaching of my pubic hair when Aimee had emptied that bowl of Lux into my pants.

I crossed to the other door. It was locked. Oh, glorious privacy. The bubbles were almost overflowing as I turned off the water and sank slowly, gratefully into the panacea. How long the fragrant steam enveloped the universe, how far away in relaxation I wandered is not remembered, but eventually I became aware of a low, rhythmic purring. It was me. I reached for the fruit.

Perfumed water, peaches, bananas mingled in a heady feast. I thought of the immaculate double bed in the next room, actual sheets and pillow slips. Such luxury was drunk-making. To stretch my half-dried frame until I filled the entire coolness, then with no siren waiting to screech me back to the noisy, smelly arena, to stay semi-asleep until I simply didn't care. I stood up, letting the bubbles run down my body. It wasn't until I opened my eyes enough to look for the towel that I saw Jamie.

My memory projected a series of large closeups. Faces I would always remember because of a curious mingling of innocence and red-eyed fanaticism. We were playing somewhere in the South.

It was routine to attend a Holy Roller–style camp meeting.

Jamie's face fit those closeups. I stood frozen, dripping opalescent bubbles, unsure of what the next frame would reveal. Finally he breathed a single word: "Impossible."

His eyes were riveted to the result of Aimee's efforts to make me an emergency. The heat of shame enveloped me like a fever. Tears dimmed my vision of Jamie's measured move forward. Covering the damned spot with trembling hands, I tried to sob out words of apology, explanation.

"Oh, no," the voice was hushed, "don't cover it, don't hide it from me."

He stood close now. I hung my head abjectly. "The Lux . . . " I murmured wetly.

"Oh, so impossibly beautiful, the only perfect little girl in the world . . ." His voice continued, but I began to hear music, far away at first; it sort of underscored his words. It grew in volume as Jamie lifted me from the tub and carried me toward my mystical room. Jamie's awed, ecstatic tones—with music under—continued as I slowly began to realize that he had not made the connection between the "improvements" he so deplored and the phenomenon of his delight. He was gently abandoned in his rapturous explorations.

The music I heard was an exordium. Little by little, fear and guilt vanished. In their place, a growing desire to be worthy of this valorous knight. "Let me love you" had far exceeded my most tangled illusions, and Mother was wrong. This must be part of the best part of being a woman. Regrets of any kind were unthinkable. Except for one, I thought. Nothing must in any way cloud Jamie's pink sky. It was my responsibility and I felt it deeply.

"Oh, please," I spoke to whichever gods might be in charge of such a situation, "please don't let the roots grow out too fast."

11 ᵜᵜᵜ

The weather that summer was benevolent, resulting in a most spectacular display of ragweed. Within a week, the pastel view from my window had turned to muted gold. It was a very positive season for weeds. And me. Sitting at the little desk, the ruffled curtains swaying gently with the soft breeze, I tried sincerely to concentrate on the problem Jamie had given me. Desks should never look out onto beguiling terrain. Perhaps a blank wall could force the mind inward. I inhaled the intoxicating mixture of sea, ragweed, and goldenrod.

"You're not thinking of numbers, are you?" Jamie's voice was thick, his eyes and nose swollen and red.

"No," I admitted, "I'm thinking of the hills and fields and flowers everywhere, and—"

He sneezed. "Flowers! That is a view of poison. Filthy weeds that won't let you breathe!"

I waited for the wheezing to die down. "Jamie? Why is it your legs are all covered with sores from the poison ivy, and you can't breathe because of the flowers—I mean the weeds— while none of these things bother me at all?" I looked earnestly in his direction, avoiding direct eye contact. He was shy of being seen in leg bandages, and it was true that his face was puffed and splotchy almost beyond recognition.

"Just get the answer right this time on your arithmetic and we'll get to me later."

I looked down at the sprawling numbers on the lined paper. "I'll never, ever learn the multiplication table, let alone problems." There was a hint of a wail in my voice. "If I hadn't told you I've never been to school, would you have suspected?"

Jamie started to put away the lesson. "Maybe not, but you'd know, wouldn't you? And, if you don't learn even the elementaries, you're going to be embarrassed and ashamed all your life. People will think of you as inferior, even stupid."

Hot tears clouded my vision. "How would anybody know? How could they tell?"

Jamie sighed. "A million ways. Let's say as a housewife you must take charge of expenses and things . . . if you were a salesgirl, you'd have to use a cash register. Even a waitress has to make change, and—"

The tears spilled. "Housewife? Waitress? You know very well I'm an actress. Nobody can tell how great I am at arithmetic or geography by my acting, can they?"

He patted my head. "Now, now, Jeannie," his tone was sympathetic, consoling, "your biggest lesson is going to be accepting what you really are."

Something burst inside me. "What am I?" It was almost a shout.

"You are adorable," he said, "you are my sweet darling, and you mustn't worry your pretty little head." He would have taken me in his arms, but I had turned into a statue. Holding me at arm's length, he smiled down into my cloudy face: "Sugar and spice and everything nice."

I pushed down the rising fury within me. "I'm not," I said dangerously, "everything nice—a pretty little head—and I may not be the one who knows everything, but my legs aren't all poisoned, and I'm not wheezing and swollen up and runny-nosed—and just maybe whatever inferior equipment I'm made of just might be good enough to outlast the expensive kind!"

But I let him hold me. I even leaned on him.

"My baby, oh, Jeannie, Jeannie, my poor baby."

I pushed away. "Listen, now," I said evenly, "I'm not your poor baby. I'm nobody's baby. I'm growing up, and I don't feel like a poor anything. You mustn't worry about me. I'll learn to spell sometime, honest I will. But that's not first on the list of what I've got to learn. You said yourself I wasn't just a marathon dancer. Well, I have to prove that first of all—and it's midsummer, almost, so it's a good time right now." I was breathless.

"A good time for what?" he asked.

"For me," I answered earnestly, "to go to New York and try again."

Jamie sniffed. "To New York?" he said quietly. "What about me?"

I moved closer. "You'll get over this hay fever, Jamie, and I'll write and tell you what happens to me."

His watery eyes were blank. "You mean you can just go away like that?"

I waited for a sneezing spell to stop. "God bless you," I said. "Casting for the new shows is just starting. And in a day or so you'll be off to find a new spot anyway."

"That's different," he said.

"How?" I asked. I really wanted to know.

"I'll send for you as soon as I get the setup." He was being reasonable.

"To marathon?" I asked.

"Of course not," he snapped. "To be with me."

I thought for a moment. "I can't afford that much time between jobs or marathons, Jamie. I'll just have enough to pay this bill and for the time in New York as it is."

He wavered to his feet. "You aren't marathoning anymore, that's number one. Two, you aren't getting up on any stage to be ogled. And, finally, I pay my own bills." His vehemence brought on another wheezing attack.

"Me too," I agreed heartily. "I don't believe in skipping hotels, either."

I had found it endearing that Jamie wanted to educate me. He neither drank, nor used profanity, and he felt strongly about tobacco. He believed that no real lady ever smoked. The ban on swimming, because he said men would "ogle," had made me very unhappy, but it was warming to be cherished. I had reluctantly forgone the salty embrace of those inviting waves.

Watching him gasping and choking, the weakened victim of an invisible dust wafting through the fragrant air, I wondered why such suffering failed to arouse compassion in my usually tender heart. It was almost embarrassing to be witness. Worse, to be bursting with energy and in perfect control of my perfectly functioning parts. Pretending not to be aware of his obvious discomfort was impossible.

I looked out the window, speaking amiably. "Are the fields in Michigan full of hay fever, too?" I asked.

"What do you know about Michigan?" His tone was suspicious.

"Well, we played all through there when I was in vaudeville," I said, "but I don't remember fields, of course, or hills like these. Mostly theatres, hotels, and certain restaurants. I remember—"

He interrupted. "Why don't you remember Ohio, or Montana, or—or—why pick Michigan?" He fixed a watery eye on me.

"Well, it's your state, isn't it? That's where you live . . . home . . . isn't it?"

The splotchy coloring on his face deepened. "It's nobody's business," it was almost a growl. "I have no home, do you understand? Nobody knows anything about me. It's all talk, talk, talk from a bunch of mongoloid idiots, and it disgusts me that you spend your time listening to them." He was choking in fury.

"Please, please, Jamie—there's no reason to be so angry.

The early years in the biz.

Christmas card vaudeville-style, Orpheum-Keith Circuit.

Toward the end of "Dainty June and Company," Louise second from left.

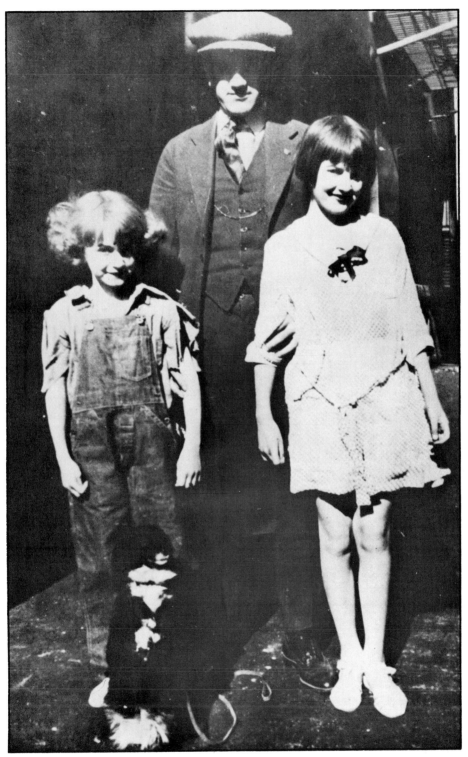

Who is wearing pants? June, Gordon and Louise the doll girl.

Grandpa Charlie Thompson.

Daddy Jack and mother.

Louise at fourteen, weight, 165 pounds.

Rose Louise, Auntie Belle and the usual homeless victim.

Mother at Rego Park.

Louise, Bobby, June.

Jean and Bobby Reed.

"The Act," Jean and Bobby Reed.

Please now, come and sit down. Come on, now." I felt I was consoling a child. "There, now—perhaps I ought to call a doctor? Maybe some kind of medicine would help—"

He staggered to his feet. "No!" he almost shouted. "Nobody comes in here—nobody! I'm all right. I'll be all right." I watched him sit heavily at the desk.

"I don't know what to do for you," I said helplessly.

"Just don't pal around with those morons on the dance floor. Don't talk to them. That's one thing you can do."

I put my arms around him. "But some of them have been with you ever since your first show. They're really fond of you, Jamie."

He relaxed enough to let me cradle him. "They told you about—about Michigan, didn't they? How long ago did they tell you?"

I was almost rocking him. "Just before I left the floor. Shhh, now—it doesn't matter, Jamie. Please don't be upset."

His breathing was thick again. "I didn't lie to you, Jeannie. We just never talked about me. And it couldn't change how I feel about you. Nothing could change that."

I murmured, "I know, I know. It doesn't change anything for me, either. After all, Jamie, in a way I'm married, too, you know." I smiled into his face. "It's just that, with Bobby and me, it doesn't count."

He lifted me onto his lap. "Well," he said, almost paternally, "with me it does. It counts a lot after all the years we—well, I've been married since before you were born, Jeannie." I thought he was going to cry.

"I know," I whispered.

"Jeannie, ah, Jeannie, I'm sorry." His voice was so low I could hardly hear.

"Sshh," I answered, "I'm sorry, too. I mean, I wish I knew why you are so unhappy, and angry. I'm sorry." For the first time since I had known Jamie I felt a pang of sympathy. Jamie in his big candy box of an automobile; Jamie—impeccable style and elegant clothes; Jamie—feverish and humble, clinging to a nondescript teenage girl in a small-town resort hotel room. Poor Jamie. Old enough to know all about being happy. What had he done wrong? Why was he here at the mercy of a stranger who hadn't had enough rehearsal to know how to exit gracefully?

"That's why you won't stay with me, isn't it, Jeannie? Because I'm married? Because there's no future for you?"

I sighed in relief. "Oh, no—no—oh, Jamie, I don't feel that way at all—oh, no!" I laughed. "I don't want to marry you. Not you or anybody else. I just want to get organized. You know, find out how to be what I'd like to be, and—and get started."

He was breathing better, I thought. "You mean, you don't care—you don't love me?"

I hugged him—hard. "I do," I cried, "I love you, love you, love you! It's just that I have to go now." I looked into his face for understanding, but he remained perplexed. "Look," I explained, "you have to go find a new location, right?" He nodded. "Well, then, you'll have to check in sometime, won't you? With your wife, I mean, so—"

He stood up, almost dumping me on the floor. "Don't ever talk to me about my wife," he commanded, "my wife, or Michigan, or my home, or anything at all that is part of my private life. If you really love me, you won't ever question me."

It was my turn to be perplexed. I began in a placating tone. "I don't understand what one has to do with the other."

He began to sputter.

"All right," I continued quickly, "you don't understand how important it is for me to make my own life. To hold a receipt in my hand for a hotel bill I paid. Me. Myself. I paid. I'll trade you what I don't understand for what you don't understand. That's fair, Jamie, isn't it?"

He turned away. "I can't believe it's my little girl. You let me love you. You even seemed to love me back, and all the time you knew that you could never expect more. That you could never expect to be more than just—this." He regarded me balefully. "It's hard for me to believe you hold yourself so cheap."

I wondered why I didn't feel it. The cheapness. Surely it would be painful.

"I don't feel cheap," I said, "do you?"

He closed his eyes and shook his head. "Of course I don't." He was being patient. "The difference between a good girl and a bad girl is how she feels about what she does." He cupped my chin in his hand, looking tenderly into my eyes. "But a man is different."

My head was swimming. "I do feel ashamed that you think

I hold myself cheap," I swallowed the tremble that tried to enter my voice, "but I don't see that I should feel different about us than you do. Or because you have to go on now from here. The fact is I do, too." I gathered up a few things as I moved about the room. "I—I'm sorry about the arithmetic, I mean . . . I wish I could have been wonderful at the problems."

Jamie blocked the door. "I won't let you go," he said sternly, "for your own good. I'll find a place for you so you won't be afraid—"

I stared. "I'm not afraid. And you're not listening," I accused.

"Shopgirl's dreams," he spat. "Movies and thrills and trashy adventures. You won't end up in the gutter because I won't let you!" He paced as he spoke, and I guess there was a lot more, but I went into the bathroom, through Jamie's room, and out his door to the hall. I could hear his voice halfway down the stairs. I guess it never occurred to him that I would just keep on going.

I bet he was surprised.

12

But no more so than I. I was surprising myself more and more. It was hard to believe it, but my legs carried me down to the beautiful carved reception desk, where I paid my bill, then out and on until there I was, dozing in the window of Western Union: untraceable, in limbo, just barely containing the missing of Jamie.

Somehow I managed to put the entire maze of the past on a mental sidetrack. At least that was true of the first week or so, which was quite full enough to deaden the turmoil within. The days were spent going from call to call. Rehearsal rooms, theatres, hallways, even lobbies of buildings, where the same agent who now carried his office in his pocket once ruled a floor-through dynasty a few flights above.

My arrival budget had permitted a street hot dog dripping with sauerkraut for breakfast. Later, rounds of prospects were interrupted by a lunch or teatime treat consisting of a huge pretzel, salty and hot from the peddler's charcoal. At day's end I lingered over an Orange Julius and jelly doughnut dinner. This schedule provided just enough time to plan the next day's attack before the sidewalks filled with chattering theatregoers released for intermission of the current Broadway shows.

By season's end I had seen the last half of most of them, not once, but I had returned to my favorites many times. I occasionally managed to sit down in one of the plush seats with time to breathe in the glitter and dazzling beauty of the theatre itself. It never occurred to me then that these treasures were doomed.

The season of Jamie, when I desperately needed to believe in my choices, was a banquet. I returned six times to stand at the back of the Booth Theatre, listening to the gentle music of what vaudevillians termed "legit" speech. There was evidence enough to banish all my doubts with one performance alone. In a play called *The Distaff Side*, Sybil Thorndyke was making her first appearance in America—oh glorious being. But the same play included Estelle Winwood, Viola Roache, Mildred Natwick and Viola Keats.

At the Broadhurst I watched through a slit in the velvet curtain at the back of an upper box; mesmerized, I heard Eva Le Gallienne and Ethel Barrymore in *L'Aiglon*.

The Martin Beck was home for Katharine Cornell as Juliet, with Edith Evans as the nurse. There were men onstage, of course, but my attention was for the realization of a secret dream. Single-minded, I watched the perfection of actresses only. There were no playwrights or directors for me then. Just the magical creatures of my very own sex, proving up there in the light that they could hold the whole world's attention all by themselves. Brian Aherne, Basil Rathbone, Orson Welles—wonderful!—but easy to take for granted. They were men.

Every evening was spent like this. As long as hot dog and pretzel money held out, and I was successful finding an unoccupied bench in the bus terminal for a few hours' sleep, I could look forward to the thrills of the evenings. Going from theatre to theatre, mingling with the first-act intermission crowds, it was easy to saunter into the lobby as though I had a ticket, too. Of course, I missed all the first acts, and much of the plot, but I was there for the nods. I loved the curtain calls. Then I waited in hiding until the last of the audience departed so I might have a moment all to myself in the awesome emptiness.

No wonder New York sojourns were stretched until the hot dog was seldom, the pretzel a memory. Only when the gnawing at the pit of my stomach threatened to chew would I send my wires.

The few confidences I had ventured regarding my sole interest had met with either derision or sympathy from my peers, so I didn't seek out other young people who gathered for gossip and information. I held an NVA union card made out to "Dainty June," it's true, but National Variety Artists? That union was something to hide. I could have claimed a few of the three hundred thousand free meals for indigent actors on the presentation of that card, but it would have been advertising the awful truth of failure, and I wasn't ready for that. There were over a hundred shows on and off the boards during this period, employing thousands of actors, however briefly. I just had to stay alive so I would one day be in the right place at the right time.

That part I had down pat, but the inner conflagration burned barely within control. Some of the second acts I had devoured in the past few seasons had dramatized the nobility of women who thrust aside all personal dreams and desires to stand lovingly in the shadow of the men they obviously could get no other way. Nobility didn't appeal to me. But neither did denial. . . .

My reverie was interrupted by the sound of a bell. I leaped to my feet automatically, heart pounding—did I make it to the floor in time?

"You're Reed, arencha?" The disinterested voice brought me into focus immediately. "Don't spend it all in one place."

It was response number one. Bus fare to a faraway hamlet even the wireless operator had never heard of. Promising myself fervently that this would be the very last grubstake—the end, the turning point—I decided actually to ride the bus for once, forgoing the dubious pleasures of hitching. I'd save every cent from then on. To celebrate, I would spend the night with my family, if invited.

I was certain Mother would be no help in a matter of the heart, but it was possible, if I didn't divulge too much, that my by now highly sophisticated sister would be keeper of some of the answers. Still single and traveling fast, she had obviously learned to cope without resorting to nobility.

13

I dropped a nickel in the pay phone. A muffled voice answered. The "Yes?" was far away.

"Who is this?" I asked.

"Tell me who that is and I'll tell you who this is," the voice quavered.

"Mother!" I accused firmly. "That's you!" I was sure it was.

"No, it's not," she answered, "and you haven't said who this is."

"Well, after all—" I was annoyed—"how many people call you up and refer to you as 'Mother'?" I could hear the intake of breath.

"You'd be surprised," she said.

"Wait, wait a minute—don't hang up—it's me, Mother." I knew she was still there. "Mother?" I said softly. "This is June."

She chuckled. "Oh, dear! June! How you frightened me! We can't be too careful. You see, dear, now that your sister is such a star, we are hounded by every jerk in town." She was eating something crackly, but I understood what she was saying.

"I have to leave early in the morning, Mother, and I wondered—"

She interrupted, "Have you any money, dear?"

The lie was compulsive: "I just bought my ticket, so I—no."

I could hear her chewing thoughtfully. "Well, come along anyway. And, oh yes! We have moved again, dear. Wait till you see the beautiful new home your sister bought us in the country, dear—Long Island, no less. And we have a car, too."

The home was attached. It stood sentinel fronting a block-long development of identical buildings called Rego Park. The style was neo-Antwerp. Mother's eye peered at me from a tiny aperture in the center of the front door, disguised within Roman numerals.

"Wait, dear, these locks baffle me so! I never can work them right—there!"

After a moment's struggle with the huge door itself, I entered a long darkened room devoid of furniture. The blinds were drawn, the floor bare.

"Want some popcorn, dear? I was just watching my evening movie, and I like to have everything just as though I'd taken the trouble to go to a real theatre." Mother wore soft felt slippers and a cotton wraparound; she was relaxed and smiling. "Your sister is upstairs, dear. You don't mind if I go back to my movie? Don't want to miss the story." She waved toward a staircase as she disappeared into the darkness, toward the clicking sound such as made by a film projector. "Plenty of popcorn, dear—come back and make comfy at the movies."

I stared up the stairs. "It's after midnight, Mother," I said.

"Well, I can't go to bed anyway, dear. I have to stay up until the furniture gets here."

I stopped. "Furniture? When is the delivery?"

Her voice came from a long way in the dark.

"Between three and five A.M., dear." A door closed, the clicking sound of the projector was muffled.

At the top of the stairs was a short hallway. The first door I passed was ajar, revealing a room that could belong to no one but Mother. A large, permanently unmade bed, piled high with nondescript pillows, would be the "comfy nest" she doted on. Two side tables littered with empty Vick's jars and a bureau with three legs.

"I like plain things," Mother told us repeatedly. "I'm old-fashioned."

There was a soft moan coming from a door further down the hall. An odor of sickness soured the air as I approached. Unprepared for the sight of my sister lying face down on the tile floor of the bathroom, I cried out: "Mother, come quick!" I knelt at the prostrate form.

"Shhh! Be quiet, June, don't bother her—aahhh—" my sister moaned as she turned her face toward me. Makeup had blackened both eyes, running into the smudged lipstick.

"But you are hurt. I should get a doctor." On the verge of panic, I tried lifting her.

"Let go of me, June—let go!" She pushed away with such force that I landed on the floor beside her. "I'm not hurt, dopey, I'm fine. Really." Her eyes didn't open, but there was a tiny smile.

"Oooops." She took her position over the toilet bowl and

let go. I scrambled to my knees. The retching was scratchingly dry. My throat began to ache in sympathy. Then I realized there was a certain rhythm to her sounds and movements. Eventually, between heaves and retches, I made out some words.

"Glow uurgh glow worm uuhh glow worm uhh glow little uuhhh uhh," etc.

She was singing. Just as she had in the act. It was called "talking a song." Presently she crawled over to the tub, rinsed her face and sighed.

"Helps," she said weakly. "I try to keep my mind on the lyrics. I can't get past the first eight bars, though." She made herself as tall as possible, leaning regally against the bathtub. Emitting a gentle burp, she inquired, "What the hell are you doing here? This is a private lesson."

I stared. "Lesson?"

"You heard me. A lesson in social amenities. I happen to be moving in a very special set of people and I've got a lot to learn."

I plunged in. "Me, too. Oh, I don't mean about social things— uh—I mean, about—about love and—and, uh—"

"Sex?" she asked. "Well, June, you've come to the wrong fount. With me it's one thing at a time. I'm such a great big sex star nobody ever dares to make a pass at me, so I'm going to have to rape somebody to lose my virginity. But first I've got to keep at this." She produced a bottle of brandy, closed her eyes and swallowed as much as she could hold down.

"That's a social amenity?" I asked.

"Uh huh. I've got to learn to drink like a lady." She gulped another mouthful.

"Louise—" I began.

"I'm not Louise. Never. I'll never be Louise again. Didn't Mother tell you? My stage name is who I am from now on. Gypsy Rose Lee. That's who I am for good." She put her hand on mine. "You call me that—Gypsy, I mean. We'll all get used to it."

I thought a moment. "But wasn't that name just temporary? Besides, you're not a gypsy."

She was bubbling up again. "And you weren't Dainty, either. You're just lucky Dainty June died with vaudeville— ooooops—'scuse—" She moved away.

Later, when she had relaxed once more on the cool tile floor, I tried again.

"I'm someone else, too," I confided. "Every day I'm more someone else, and I don't know if I'm as sure as you are about who it is. You used to say you were going to marry a king—"

She interrupted. "Yes," she smiled, "but it looks like I'm going to be so famous and so rich I may not have to marry any of them."

I blurted, "What does it feel like to be in love?"

She looked at me with near compassion. "You have to smarten up, June. You've wasted so much time already. Almost seventeen years old and playing dance marathon games." The scorn in her voice wasn't veiled. "You are unbright, June. You always said you'd be an actress."

I stood up. "I try. I go to every call I hear of . . . and I stand in chorus lines and . . ."

"Chorus lines?" she echoed. "Looking like that! Your nice long hair has disappeared, your knees are bumpy, and your eyebrows bald! You . . . well, you'll never make a chorus line."

She was right. I never did.

My voice wobbled. "A friend tried to improve my appearance, and—"

She was crisp. "That was no friend, June."

I began to cry. "On top of the Lux I got a permanent. Then, when it all dried, I put the comb in the waves and my whole head of hair came away with the comb, but that's not all that's gone strange—there's more. Oh, Louise—"

She stopped me. "Who?" she asked pointedly.

"I—I'm sorry," I stammered, "Gypsy, I mean." The name tasted unfamiliar. "Gypsy, if you had a friend who was in love—" I paused for courage.

"I do have a friend in love. Go on, June."

I sniffed. "You do? And is the man—older?" I asked.

"They are all older, June. And they are all married. Now listen to me." She settled more comfortably. "If you want to go through the whole marriage thing over and over, you'll come up losers, just like you did with Bobby. Or you'll be on some guy's payroll as his working nonentity. You'll never have a damn thing that belongs to you—"

I interrupted. "Children," I said. "I'd have children and a home, and—"

She snorted. "The only way to have a home is the way I have this one. Otherwise you're a sort of an unpaid gardener-cook type and nothing belongs to you. Ask Mother. It's all his."

I began, "The children—"

She shook her head. "Uh uh. You are just specially privileged to have 'his' children in 'his' home and that's it. I don't want that, do you?"

I bit on my retort. "What about love?"

There was a silence. She took a long swig from the brandy bottle. "If some man really loves you, June, he won't stop because you won't marry him, because you want to be more than a 'pretty little ornament' in his life."

I looked up in surprise at this new softness being displayed.

"Is that what you got called?" I asked. "A pretty little ornament?" She nodded. We began to giggle. "Don't worry your pretty little head?" I added, and we laughed some more.

My sister drew a deep breath finally. "The difference is that I wasn't having an affair with him, June." The laughter was gone. "You always liked all that," she continued, "and it's a sure way to wind up nothing, nothing at all. Not even a ring from Bobby. I don't think it's so funny to buy your own ten-cent-store wedding ring."

I stood up defiantly. "I got away, didn't I? And I'm free, aren't I?"

She sighed. "So what are you? You haven't any idea, have you? Listen, pin down whatever it is—no matter how hopeless it seems to be—and make a solid vow to it. Then, like me, don't let hell or high water get in your way. Believe me, June, nobody— I mean nobody—is going to be a roadblock for Gypsy Rose Lee. Hell, you haven't even got a name yet."

She would have helped me more that night, but we were arrested mid-confidence by the chiming of the doorbell. At first I thought it was a far-off church, because it chimed the first few notes of "Ave Maria."

"Gypsy! Gypsy, they're here. The truck is here with the furniture!" Mother's voice was jubilant. "Right on the dot . . . it's four A.M., dear."

"Oh, God, look at my face!" Gypsy said. "Quick, go help Mother and I'll clean up. Go on, June." She pushed me out the door. I ran down the stairs. Mother was at the front door peering through the peekhole.

"Helloooo! Just a minute, dear," she called. "I never can

work all these locks. June, hold this, will you, dear?" She handed me the bowl of popcorn. "There we are."

The huge door opened, revealing a group that might have been posing between chores on the Georgia chain gang. Before Mother could restore order to the panic this vision had thrown her into, a gruff voice inquired, "Mind if we check around?" Or some similar request, to which no response could have been expected because they spread through the house like the bubonic plague.

Mother found her voice as one furniture mover lumbered toward the stairs. "Wait, dear." She crossed to him quickly. "A lady is upstairs getting dressed."

His purplish lips parted to display a full set of cracked dominoes. "Sorry, Ma. I gotta check," he rumbled, "or no furniture."

"I understand, honey," she said, "but you follow me, all right?" They disappeared upstairs. The open front door framed the rear end of a truck. Dark and threatening, it seemed to lean against the house. I held the window shade aside trying to see the name of whatever store would be delivering at this hour, but there was no lettering on the truck at all. The invasion set Mother's dogs—Bootsie, Boola, and Glam—into piercing shrieks of outrage. They danced about the legs of the searchers in snapping hysteria.

I tried to place the familiar prowling gait, the beefy countenances and guttural voices of these men. Then it came to me. I felt I knew them because they were so perfectly cast. I went to the window again. Yes, there it was. A long, dark limousine idling at the corner.

"Whoever sits inside," I said to myself, "owns the store." These apparitions were all identical to the Dinky Valoons & Co. I had come to recognize on sight.

"Just like in the movies." Mother was wide-eyed. "Ooh, so exciting." She looked around. "But don't let the poor dear sit out there waiting. Here, I'll call him in."

There were two negative grunts as the boys executed a neat adagio lift, putting her down gently near the stairs; then someone must have let us all know we were to stand pat. That's how it came about that we formed the exact staging for the tenor's big entrance in *The Student Prince.* Only the gent now entering was no tenor. He wasn't very tall, and he wasn't hefty, but the empty room filled with his presence. He was well groomed and nicely dressed, and the memorable thing about him, I suppose, was the mustache. It was pointy. It was waxed.

The spell was broken as my sister tripped lightly down the stairs.

"I'm sorry I took so long," she called. We turned, just as the chorus did in *Blossom Time* for the entrance of Fritzi. Or Kitzi. Or was it Mitzi? She moved—hastily, I thought—toward the double door at the end of the room.

"The dining room is in here," she sang out as she disappeared. There was much clanging as the iron doors of the truck were pried apart. Mother stood smiling at the waxed mustache.

"Well, son," she said, "I am the mother of Gypsy Rose Lee."

And Waxy Gordon said, "Pleased to meet you."

Mother turned to me. "And this is my baby. She used to be somebody, too."

The furniture consisted of elaborately carved oak. The kind of pieces tagged "Mission style." There were at least thirty chairs and one very, very long table. The set spilled out of the dining room. Extra chairs lined the walls. Waxy spoke toward my sister, who stood in the arch. No trace of the smudged face I had left a few moments ago. She was ready for the scrutiny of a Technicolor closeup.

"Hey, Gyp," he said, "no excuse here for standing room only, huh?"

She smiled, "Thanks, Mr. Gordon."

"Anytime, kid, anytime. Why, we—" Mother took his arm. She walked him toward my sister.

"You have no idea how hard it is for a widow alone with two children—"

Gypsy stepped between them. "Would you like some coffee? I mean, all of you—or maybe a drink?"

Mother protested, "Now, Loui—Gypsy, you know we never have liquor in the house."

Waxy must have signaled, because the boys had clanged the iron truck doors shut and evaporated. "No sale," he said, "but a raincheck?"

My sister held out her hand and they shook. "The suite is lovely," she said.

He murmured a polite "Don't mention it," the truck roared; as he turned in the open door he was caught in a gray cloud of exhaust. "Wear them in health," he choked.

We closed our eyes against the acrid smoke. When we had recovered, he was gone. Mother sneezed, then sighed.

"Class. Class," she repeated firmly. "No pretense, just honestly himself." She started toward the dining room. "In this world of stinkers, just give me a straightforward, true-blue gangster every time."

Gypsy and I followed to stand gazing admiringly at the endlessly long table flanked on all sides by straightforward-looking chairs. My sister chuckled. "Just think, he sat at the head, there, and all of the rest sat around him, and on the wall was this giant-sized map with pictures of the precincts and all the detectives and police. It was in color, too. Very lifelike." We stood for a second's silence.

"Girls," Mother was solemn, "at this table history has been made." I looked down at the popcorn I still held and remembered my appetite.

"Let's celebrate by having a big meal on the table," I suggested.

"I'm too choked up to eat," Mother said. "Turn on my movie, Loui—Gypsy, dear, and I'll just unwind in the breakfast alcove." Gypsy moved toward the French-windowed nook.

"You have to learn to run this projector yourself, Mother," she admonished. "I won't always be handy to stop it when people come. Look, now this is how you turn the thing on and off—"

Mother whimpered, "Oh dear, you know I can't work mechanical things. Besides, you'll always be here with me." She threw a meaningful glance toward me. "Not like some ungrateful children."

The film clicked away. I stood uncertainly in the flickering light.

"Stay here," my sister whispered. "She really loves you best, you know. It's just hard for her to say so." She yawned. "I've got to get some sleep. If you are gone when I get up, don't forget what I said, and good luck." She moved into the darkness.

"Sit down, June," Mother whispered, just as though we were indeed at the movies. "Tell me why you look like that—no hair, no eyebrows—why?" I cleared my throat. "Shhh, dear—tell me all about it later. We are just getting to the funny part."

I looked at the screen. A girl was just dropping what appeared to be the last of her clothing to the floor. She stretched, gyrating her rather scarred abdomen suggestively; then the camera moved with her toward a bathtub. First she sat on the edge, opening her legs wide, displaying a formidable wilderness; then quite daintily she climbed into the empty tub. The male star in this opus now entered. You could tell it wasn't another girl, even though the camera was shooting him only from the waist down; that had to be, because it was important to hold the lady star in the picture, also. After all, it really was her scene. Catching sight of him, she reached for a large bar of soap; then, as he urinated over her shoulders, she used the soap. I put the bowl of popcorn on Mother's lap. She was laughing softly as I went up the stairs.

Did she really love me the best? I wondered. The last two rooms were empty, but in the corner of one was a rolled-up carpet. If she did love me, why had I never felt it? I patted my sweater into a pillow shape and put it under my head. What did love feel like? Not only family love, but the overpowering emotion I was suppressing at that moment? What does it do to or for your life? Why would my sister tell me Mother loved me the best? What difference would it make, and how could she know? If Jamie really loved me, he would love me as I was—even forget the arithmetic lessons. But then, what about my investment of time? In truth, my sister was right. Jamie was a luxury I couldn't afford. There was logic in her theories. I envied her strength, her ability for appraisal. She would certainly attain whatever she set out for. Observe the determination to "drink like a lady." One had to be truly committed to a plan to go through all that. My weakness and indecision shamed me. I simply had to be more positive in spite of this ache in my heart, this sense of loss.

The plan was simple. I'd use the solitary time on the marathon floor. This final contest would be more than endurance. It would settle my route from here on in. I'd stay in that show until I knew who I was. The prisonlike discipline would help cool this fierce burning until it was under my command, and the pursuit of whatever life I chose would not be jeopardized by romantic excursions piloted by my heart, ignoring the collaboration of my mind. In the ceasefire isolation provided by the endless marathon circle, I could ruminate on recent events, their impact and possible destruction of the one road I knew well enough to take toward a way of life. Warm and familiar like my memories of the far-off "good times," my life should end where it began. In show business. No doubt about that part. How to convince the world? How to know what the so-called "normal" life would be like? I had been inside a real "home" perhaps half a dozen times in my life, so there was no pull there, only mild curiosity. The desperate homesickness that fringed every emotion I had was for that pinkish smell backstage, when the lights warmed those long colored borders, when the unpacked trunks and newly hung scenery exuded their mysterious scent. The other-world stillness when the house was sleeping . . .

I put my hand to the little "grouch bag" pinned to my bra. The bus fare was intact. The rolled-up carpet wasn't the best bed I had known, but good enough for a nap before the journey.

14

Standing in the entrance of an archway, I looked back into the brilliant Midwestern sun. There were no buildings as far as the eye could travel. Only telegraph poles, which seemed to be strung into eternity. The main thoroughfare lived about a mile away. Our tent was at this end of a connecting new road which would bring us our yelling, brawling audience. It was a freshly opened artery, spilling red earth into ditches, and it looked like a jagged scar on the face of otherwise innocent farmland.

Ten miles away sprawled a big, workable city. No airport then, no smog, just the sweet smell of recently wounded earth. Standing still, breathing in the sky-blue-pink air, was as good as soaking in perfumed water. I took my fill—then on to the business at hand.

I waited until the girls' rest quarters settled down, then dragged my scavenged furnishings to a dark corner, where I set up for comfort. Using an upright apple box as bureau, I arranged my few belongings, folded the sides of my travel case (a worn brown paper bag), which obligingly became a wastebasket, then covered the marathon-issue army cot with the ditto olive blanket.

Checking out slumber spoilers, I was happy to see Faye at the opposite end of the tent. Good. I liked her, but in her sleep she innocently made firecracker pops with her chewing gum. Eloise was well meaning but unaware of a powerful body odor. I guessed I was far enough away to miss that, too. Rosie talked in her sleep, which was harmful because it was interesting enough to keep you awake listening. We nodded greetings across the cots.

I had just finished putting away my gear when my eye caught a very familiar figure standing under the flap of the tent to the girls' rest quarters. It was Jamie. He looked wan. Pasty. The corners of his mouth twisted into a doleful smile. Even his blue serge suit was limp. He started across the littered floor, and as he came toward me tried bravely to disguise the limp that completed the pathos. How unlike the dapper sophisticate preserved in my own private gallery. I wasn't prepared for the alteration.

"I ran after you when I realized finally that you had gone—left me—paid your own bill and deserted. . . . I fell." His head dropped with the awful memory. Again I was afraid he was going to cry. I turned away, but he stopped me with a bandaged hand. "The wrist was turned," he said, "when I fell." Jamie swayed. "Sorry, I have to—may I please sit down?" He crumpled onto the cot. I glanced about but the rest quarters were now deserted.

"Jeannie? I can't sleep." His eyes were red rimmed. "Please stay with me a minute—you have hours before the first bell—that is, if you are determined to go through with this." I looked down into his face.

"I didn't know this was your show," I said.

"Only part of it," his voice strengthened. "Dinky is going to run this one while I scout a spot further west. I did tell you the truth. Dinky wants me to take Bums Malloy to help, but I want you as guide. You know the West, you told me you played every spot on the map, and the job pays better now, too, because it's a long-distance haul, and—"

I sat down next to him. "Bums can't even read a map," I said.

Jamie continued, ". . . and there won't be any expenses at all, because the syndicate picks up the bills." He could see my feet beginning to relax. "So, instead of wearing yourself out here, you can pocket even more than floor money while staying pretty for when you go back to New York to try again." I studied my hands. I didn't want him to see my confusion. "And best of all, Jeannie, you don't need to know arithmetic or spelling, or . . . or . . . well, you're a great guide and you drive almost as well as a man."

I searched his face. His eyes had cleared. "Truly now, this is a real job? I mean, from Dinky and . . . and the syndicate?"

He raised his bandaged hand easily. "I swear it, on my honor. And you stash twelve bucks a day in your bra. What do you say? . . . Jeannie, I really do need your help."

That's how I got to see Yosemite again, and the whole West, of course, as well.

Jamie had never been a father, although he could have been mine. Little by little I learned that his marriage had long since faded into an old family portrait, while his own image retained the indelible outlines of youthful vigor. Marital ties were sentimental, and he was gallant and respectful. I liked him all the more for that.

Meanwhile, my eyebrows and the other "improvements" were returning to normal. Jamie was gallant about that, too. He attempted to make me less guilty by insisting that he had been enjoying a sort of self-delusion. It didn't matter anyway, because as I became more and more my own natural coloring and so on he seemed more and more in love. As for me, I had no regrets about postponing decisions. Life was waiting for me up the road somewhere. For now, I blended into the furry pastels of a Technicolor dream.

The question, viewed from this end of the telescope, is: had I invested that early autumn differently, would the riches of a later autumn be more satisfying?

My contemporaries were going about the business of learning their craft and serving their apprenticeship, while I was loitering on the way to the forum. A small voice solemnly informed, "You will not be among those enjoying moments such as these again. This time is the only time of its kind for you."

I have always believed in oracles. And so, with eyes, mind, and every pore wide open, I followed. Over the Black Hills, through the badlands of South Dakota, through the wind caves and along the peaky rim of the Continental Divide, I followed the camp of Jamie. Through Grand Teton to Cody, where I wept among the dusty, sad-eyed buffalo heads leaning from every wall of the inn. All dedicated to Buffalo Bill himself. The Shoshone River yielded not a single trout for all of Jamie's expert casting. Not even the magical streams of Yellowstone favored his line.

But we drifted on, avoiding anything that was more than a village. At Flathead Lake Jamie caught cold, but no fish. At Bonners Ferry he recovered. He decided he was using the wrong bait. It wasn't until Jamie stood midstream of Priest River in the tip end of Idaho that it came to me. In spite of the sun, I shivered. We hadn't scouted a single location. It was most unlikely a dance marathon could find an audience along the route we had followed.

The glistening water danced over the rocks as Jamie cast his line further downstream. He was tanned and lean. Wrapped in many sweaters, I sat atop a huge boulder, concentrating hard on my secret Norwegian curse. I had thrown all my powers at Jamie's fish hook as usual. Pleased with my continuing success, I watched in a relaxed, dreamlike mood, confident there would be no display of the beautiful silvery things flailing about, gasping, fighting for their freedom, their lives. We had been enjoying picnic-style meals. Cooking over campfires. Sleeping in Jamie's capacious candy box of a car. Bathing in streams and lakes. Sometimes standing under a waterfall or in the dashing shallows of a rapids. We were glorious hoboes. It was only the last few nights that had been more than chilly.

The streams too cold for bathing during the days, we had begun more and more to stop over at roadside inns. I guess that was part of what started my considering apparatus.

"Do you think these little towns would like an endurance contest?" I asked.

Jamie grinned. "Not unless we could work in a medicine show."

A fringe of light began to grow around the fringes of my enchantment.

"Jamie," I asked, "does the syndicate know it's taking us on months of wandering like this?"

He was struggling with a can opener, sitting in the sun, wrapped in a blanket. I watched as he emptied the baked beans into a pan. Smoke from the campfire spiraled between us.

"Do they know what it's like to fish for Columbia River salmon?" he replied. "That's going to be something you'll never forget."

I nodded. "If your luck changes," I said.

"You've never tasted fish right from the stream, Jean. Just wait." What would he say if he knew that I had that good luck of his under my bad-luck spell?

The beans were great, but as the sun disappeared and the campfire dwindled, the presence of winter enveloped us.

We backpacked over miles of crunching pine needles, the forest aroma pungent enough to taste. Crawling over a fallen giant northern pine, Jamie suddenly stopped. Holding a finger to his lips, "Shh, don't move." We halted mid-step, listening. A smile of deep pleasure curled about his mouth. Then he lay prone on the length of the mossy trunk, reaching downward. Fascinated, I watched as he pulled a great glistening handful of wet green through the ferns. He held the bouquet over his head in triumph.

"I knew I heard water! Look! Fresh watercress. Taste it, Jean. You'll never forget!"

He was right. I've never forgotten. Never found a forest even vaguely similar. Tasted watercress that had any relationship to that. Saw a fallen tree of such majesty. Walked on a carpet of pine needles of that depth that exuded that aroma—never. It was an only time.

15

When do we find our total perception? Familiar landscapes thrill me more at each encounter. The lavender shadows that slowly veil the Grand Canyon; the magnetic lure of the desert; the stabbing reverence that humbles the soul at sight of a flock of geese overhead . . . but then, at seventeen, did I experience the intoxicating impact, the numbing awe?

Is it possible the plan could be to increase appreciation as the mortal shell slowly powders to dust, leaving only that one ever-increasing ability, to perceive glory, forever embracing the wonder of beauty? Forever and ever?

Jamie had acquired a tentlike awning. It flared romantically from the side of his car. When closed to the elements, the temperature inside was almost comfortable. I huddled near enough to the camp stove so that my warmed blanket gave off a musky odor. I was alone.

We had camped near the Grand Coulee on the Columbia River long enough to look like squatters. A line of washing extended from the tent to an obliging tree. Our box for garbage hung despondently from another tree, a fire line ringed the tent. We had learned how to live in the forest safely. At night, we heard bear, bobcat, and moose moving about us, but so far our only close acquaintances were snakes, which, lured by the warmth of the fire line, came to bask within touching distance. Far from being afraid of the creatures, I longed to know them better, to feed them. But that was taboo.

"Just like anybody else," Jamie explained, "give them a finger, they take a hand." So I admired them from a respectful distance.

This was my first solitude since we began our journey. Down river was another campsite, another man who stood midstream by the hour. This man and Jamie had discovered one another. One had a grand catch, the other none at all. One thing led to another, and that was the day of our only real fireworks. Jamie had presented me with the Royal Prince of Salmon. Laying its dawn-hued majesty at my feet like a trophy. He was overwrought because I tried to revive it with artificial respiration.

I dined alone on my can of beans that night. Revengefully wanting to prolong his worry and fear for my safety, I let him call my name as he prowled searching way after dark. It never occurred to him to look under the car.

"Murderer!" I had cried. "Why can't you pick on a fish your own size, a fish armed with a hook big enough for *you?*" Then I hid, carefully taking a can of beans with opener along with me.

The next day Jamie's fisherman friend had to go to Spokane on business. It was a good place to scout, so Jamie went with him, finally looking for a location. I was alone.

Strangely, this place was the State of Washington. State of Family Origin. Perhaps the mysterious vibrations sought me out. I am more and more inclined to believe that all that works to compel my destiny comes from within my veins.

This was the climate of all "their" beautiful beginnings and eventual failures. This was the seat of learning for the sisterhood, the garden with the luscious fruit that covered the seed of hate. For they had all arrived at that. All had finally mistrusted and, openly or secretly, hated men. Had they always? Searching my memory for a man who had lived within the coven even temporarily, who had been loved, trusted, or even tolerated over any period of time, I drew a blank.

Then I turned the X-ray inward. Try as I might, I recalled nothing negative toward the few men who had so far played prominent roles in my life. My father I remembered entirely as the thoughtless ignoramus pictured by my mother. One grandfather was considered a foolish sort of clown by all his women; the other, the Norwegian, as a harmless boor. The men who pursued Mother during my early childhood were lumped together with "All a man wants is to enter your room." Apparently what he sought in that retreat tagged him "no damned good."

I had indisputably loved one of those men, the man named Gordon. The one who taught us all to brush our teeth and to bathe regularly. The one who taught Mother how to make a lot of money on "Dainty June." Just as the "bad times" began to hurt, he had been removed. Someone said, "Removed, eh? Like a wart," and everyone laughed. Except me. I loved him. He hadn't stayed long enough to show Mother how to keep all that money we made during the "good times."

Mother and the family of women had kept on marrying as though marriage were a miracle drug, a cure-all. Or perhaps a lease: easy to sign—then, on a dark night, move out quietly. Tired of a person? A place? Abandon, eliminate. No trial, no inquest. In the artificial flavoring of self-right, there was never a sense of loss. They were starring in one cliffhanger after the other. Writing epics on the wind, but moving all the time, and moving fast.

Was it congenital?

There was a dread of being Mother. Or any of "them." And yet we were like them. Sometimes we knew. Then there were times we didn't. The worst times were when we scolded one another: "Don't—you sound like Mother!"—all the while choking with laughter. We couldn't stop laughing and it wasn't funny.

Not ever.

But that was decades later. This was a time when the campfire lay glowing before me, hissing its melody, while all the diverse people within me were in mortal combat for my life. There had been signals. This listening, watching self wasn't indelible. The color was already fading.

Bobby, then Jamie—and I was just seventeen.

"Admit failure now, and stop. 'Oh, God—stop.' Be the one to stop before distrust erodes the pleasure of love. Avoid contracts, because it is not your nature to honor an agreement that demands continuity. New leases, perhaps, but not new names. Don't be like them. Don't depend. You are all you will ever have for certain. You are and always will be on your own. Take care of you." I stood up suddenly, the blanket almost falling into the fire.

"That's it," I said to all the other selves. "I've been doing that all along so far." I told the fire ring, "I've never pretended." I turned to the car. "And I've paid my own way." It was somehow very funny. I laughed. There was Bobby, being a five-foot tough guy. Funny. And Jamie, across the table buttering a piece of bread for me. Funny. Funny. Not hateful. I never felt contempt. I never had any strong negative reactions. No. There was this slow diminishing of heat, that was all. A gentle disinterest. Disapproval, but mild, as though I understood how everything was temporary anyway.

That was what had been happening to me along with my height and breadth. I was growing!

The thought sobered me. I might live a long time. Like Doddie and Big Lady. My spirits sank, remembering their fierce aloneness. The crust upon crust of glassy contempt for life, which grew and grew over them until only tiny rays of light penetrated. Not enough to live by, if it was true that aging meant growing.

"The last eight bars," I said directly to the fire, "ought to be the best part of the song."

But what about that aloneness? Didn't that mean the eventual being alone from men? "They" had one another. Together unto death. Each returning to the others—always.

It suddenly dawned. If you could make a life on your own without losing the enjoyment, the pleasure of men . . .

"Of course, if they are all like Bobby and Jamie, marriage means dissolving into their shadow. So then men must remain outside the legalities. Men must never be family." The fire stared back. "You don't have to be alone," I heard myself say. "Strong— you are young and strong. Have a child. A girl. Now—right now. There won't be any other time for you. The rest is going to be toward making a life that will bear no resemblance to your nightmare."

Could I avoid accumulations of crust? A layer of distrust, a layer of suspicion, one of hatred, another of contempt—avoid joining the all-female choir of my family cackling their unified solo?

Yes. The answer had to be yes. Simply make a family of my own.

16 ꙮꙮꙮ

Dusk had faded to a chalky gray. I sat so near the fire my skin began to sizzle.

Something had happened to my heart. It was lighter. So light it had moved upward like a pink balloon until it swayed near my throat, almost stopping my breath.

Elation!

Crouched over a small fire in the enveloping wilderness, with a lowering sky threatening to close down on my head like the torture chambers in a thriller serial, I felt the juices of elation.

For months there had been no words from the real world. No radio. Just the voices of rivers, lakes, and birds. Or the wind rustling musically—sometimes bellowing or screeching. No newspapers. Instead I had been reading the changing of the seasons. Rain fell with a whisper, fragrant and soft; or it was driven, bucking against a blurred landscape. The shadings of Nature were so gradual I experienced little shock upon recognizing the first chill mists of autumn. And now the sky was about to send down rain in the form of minuscule crystals. Some of the wild animals had already retired for the winter. It was quieter than quiet. I sighed.

This trip to Spokane was the first effort Jamie had made to find a location since Minnesota—or was it North Dakota? Any short visit with a local newspaper office could have decided if the territory was viable. Next stop would be city hall. Then, of course, a friendly American Legion Post, because all the civic subsidiaries followed the leaders—the Kiwanis, Lions, the Jaycees, the Ladies' Guilds. With such sponsorship (for an affirmative pat in all publicity, to be sure), the rest of the populace would have followed. Jamie hadn't tried—until now.

And Jamie had a story about Spokane, too.

"Town is ruined for any decent operator," he scowled, "sleazy promoters—pretty good show, too. So they got up to a thousand or so hours, six couples, one solo left on the floor, when the backers packed out with the wad." Jamie sat holding a mug of coffee I had warmed for him.

"Did they get much?" I asked.

"Much?" Jamie's eyes narrowed. "Only a hundred thousand or so. The town suckers are ready to tar and feather."

I thought of the dancers. A thousand hours to nothing. Very few could send wires—"Shoot me the fare"—I shivered. Jamie's face reflected the fire.

"It's a real snow," I said, "the first real snow. We can't stay here even an hour."

His mouth was stubborn. "Plenty of wood and food and—"

I stood up.

"No, Jamie, we've squeezed every last ounce out of this summer. It's gone. That sky will be on our heads in a very little while." We looked up and around. Trees were green all winter here—it was something else they did instead of flashing all the warning colors. Something quiet but just as meaningful.

"I hate those cabins," Jamie muttered.

"Tacoma should be next," I announced. "It's a real city and it's only a cabin or so away." I started packing the few oddments comprising our campsite.

Tacoma wasn't interested, but the hotel was warm and friendly. I spent hours in the biggest bathtub ever invented, catching up on newspapers.

"Shouldn't Seattle be next?" Jamie examined the map carefully. I could see him bent over the small desk. We had the usual adjoining rooms. No "Mr. and Mrs.," ever. So I could pay my own bill. Whenever we arrived at a city where mail was expected, I received a formal check. It was from a corporation— the syndicate of promoters. I had turned the accumulated paper into a few big bills because the grouch bag I wore in my bra had begun to lump out peculiarly.

I crossed through my room to the stack of newspapers leaning against the huge tub.

"Look, Jamie, here is a Seattle *Times*—read alla 'bout it!" I sang, as I flattened the paper on his desk, covering the map. "Cheer your favorites—how long can they last?"

Jamie grunted, "Beat us to it, eh?"

There was a news story alongside the ad with a typical picture of one partner asleep as the other dragged.

"There's a show in Portland, too." I looked for the other paper.

"Never mind, baby," Jamie smiled, "we'll go on to a genuine metropolis, shall we? San Francisco! There's a place that can support two shows."

There was no mention of a marathon in the genuine metropolis. I looked all through the six pages of "Endurance Show News," carried weekly in *Billboard.* So we went show hopping on the way to the big city on the Bay.

In the Northwest the air has a tangible taste, especially when all of summer is gone and the true flavor of the climate comes into its own. Driving along the highway, we saw the pennants flying from miles away. It looked festive. The big building had been many things but was born for a roller-skating palace. A perfect spot. I could see Jamie's annoyance.

"Maybe a little less fishing?" I teased. He laughed. On either side of the wide entrance was a twenty-foot pole topped by a small platform. A big sign shouted:

POST #48 Never Gives Up!
WE STAY ON TOP AS LONG AS THEY LAST!

Sitting above were two men dressed as Legionnaires.

"Isn't that against the law or something?" I gasped.

"No law says they can't make fools of themselves," Jamie snorted.

"I mean the costumes. The American Legion costumes."

He looked at me. "Costumes! Those guys are real. Now, how did they promote that?" He couldn't wait to get out of the car to see the show—to meet the genius. "Find you later in the bleachers," he called.

Standing in the aisle I picked up a dope sheet. It gave the daily news and gossip of the arena on one page; the flip side had the betting odds. You were supposed to find your own sucker. The scratchy refrain on the record player being tortured by a demented p.a. system was "Love Me or Leave Me." I hummed along as I climbed up the bleachers. Although a model of perfection, something about the place seemed different. It looked, even smelled the same. Then it struck me. There wasn't a familiar face anywhere. Dancers, trainers, judges, or matrons. All were strangers. That was unusual. I eyed the setup inside and out; success was obvious. Big money here. The audience was arriving rapidly now. Boxes filling with the ever-faithful, youngish-to-middle-aged fans. More blankets and picnic baskets. Oh sure, they were here for the long haul. The band arrived, tuning up against that awful record. I remembered we had put off dinner expecting to just "look in" and drive on. I searched for Jamie—no sign.

One good thing about this kind of show business, the audience came and went without offense to the actors. People yelled to friends, or to the dancers; wept and screamed when a favorite dropped out; fought among themselves. Audience participation indeed.

"Getcha ice-cold three-point beer." I beckoned to the hawker. Wouldn't be the first popcorn-and-beer dinner for me.

The microphone adjusted, p.a. off, the band sailed into a huge fanfare, seguing into the same theme song of every endurance show I had ever known: the diminuendoed strains of "Sleep, Sleep, Sleep." A dapper little man stepped from the shadows of the band-shell and addressed both audiences.

"Good evening, fans of the Beaver State Walkathon, and all you friends out there in radioland. Here we are, folks, still going strong with ten brave couples battling it out there on the dance floor. We have one little solo girl, hoping against hope some other girl will fall by the wayside, leaving her a partner, and soon—soon, because she only has another three hours to solo before she faces disqualification—and the end of all her dreams of being a winner. Let's give poor, exhausted Mamie Raye a big hand."

The growing crowd clapped. There were a few shouts: "Stay in there, Mamie," etc. She straggled up to the shell. Arms dangling, dank hair, pasty face.

"Here's a request, Mamie, from all the gang at Firehouse Number Eight. They want you to sing for them, honey."

With a couple of false starts, Mamie quavered her rendition

of "Dancing with Tears in My Eyes." She was a star.

I studied the dapper little man. I knew that swagger. The grandiose manner. Something was different, added. The sound—that was it. The speech itself was affected, but the voice was the same. Hidden behind a fancy waxed mustache, garbed in striped trousers, vest, and cutaway, shod in patent-leather shoes with spats: it was Bobby.

I stifled a giggle. Bobby like a child acting out a fantasy. Within the hour he had played his clarinet, then saxophone; he sang, danced, and did comedy routines with the clowns. The audience loved him and it was very, very clear that he felt the same way about himself.

I bought another popcorn. This vendor had all the earmarks of a punchy ex-marathoner. I smiled. "How long do you think you'll be with it?"

He caught the borrowed carnival code and handed me back my dime. "You a dancer?"

I nodded.

"Some show we got, ain't it?"

I agreed.

"I done six thousand, seven hundred and five hours in eight shows."

I oooohed.

"Yup. I'm resting in between, now."

I uh-huh'd. He flat-footed down the steps, calling his wares. I turned my attention back to Bobby. The dancers had gone to rest quarters, the band taking five; he was poring over a dope sheet. I supposed he was happy. Hoped so, anyway. I decided to avoid any encounter, to slip out as soon as Jamie reappeared. A sudden chill struck me. Where was Jamie? I looked around the arena. O.K., take five, but where were the musicians? And the cashiers and countermen? They had been present only moments before.

My personal alarm went off. Hackles rose on the back of my neck. Music from the p.a. had been turned up. It was loud—too loud. Voices of the audience rose to be heard. The resultant clamor was indicative. I scrambled down the bleachers looking for anyone connected with the show, finally catching sight of my friend the popcorn butcher.

"Where's the beef?" I whispered.

He grinned. "Follow me." The din from the arena grew fainter as we ran down a long ramp, then along a wide corridor backed by a wall of huge steel doors.

"Dead end," I gasped.

"Ah, no—nope, come on." I could hardly hear the rasping p.a. system now. "In here," my friend directed. We went through a small door cut into the huge one, onto a loading dock.

The brawl was taking place quietly in the very best marathon tradition. Voices in the main ring were so low I couldn't catch the words, but the atmosphere bristled with fury. Verbal exchanges seemed to be between a slightly graying, florid man and Jamie, who stood with his back against a sort of dump; the florid man with his backup crew in a semicircle facing him. Each time a point was made against Jamie, these scrubs waved fists and growled like dogs. Snarling and baring fangs, they slowly backed the lone defendant further and further into the small mountain of garbage. The congregation was poised, waiting for the signal to attack. Attack quietly, of course—the idea of a private beef being enjoyed by those townies inside was an outrage. Nothing for free.

I edged closer, knowing there was no way to help. Jamie was on his own—there was no way to change the rules. As I moved among the crowd, there was the roar of a motor. A big blue car almost drove through us, skidding to a stop at the edge of the fray. Its headlights were blinding, but I saw Jamie struggling with the florid man, in his efforts to keep from being forced into the seat beside the driver. I was close enough now to recognize that it was Jamie's own car. The man at the wheel raced the motor, spreading gummy fumes that stuck in my eyes. We choked as we pushed to see. Jamie's voice spiraled overhead.

"Not until I find my girl! No! No! I've got to find—" The scuffle began in orderly fashion. There were even odds I might make it to the car; I would at least end that part of the dispute. But someone behind me lurched heavily against my back. I sprawled among the legs of the skirmishers. The odds held. Down was an advantage. I crawled toward the car, hitting out at legs and banging my fist down on feet that were in my way. I got close enough to see Bobby push his way between the two battlers.

"I know him," he stage-whispered loudly, "come on—I know this guy and you're wrong. I mean it. My word on it, boss." He raised his right hand, as in court. "It's not his style, even though he is a first-class son-of-a-bitch."

Someone lifted Bobby out of the way as the crowd moved in. The car roared, Jamie was thrust inside like a rag doll, there was a screech of brakes as it backed banging into the dump before it took off into the night. So much for odds.

I looked around, dazed. People were drifting back to the dock, but a small clump of rags was moving in the garbage. It was Bobby. I kicked the stuff away and dragged him out by his legs. One spat was gone, the other flapped against a bare foot, but there was no blood.

"Popcorn!" I called at a retreating figure. He turned to try to find the voice.

"In the dump—here—please help? Quick, go inside, ask for a doctor, bring him here—go!" He was just punchy enough to do it.

Everyone came out. Doctor, too. We took Bobby to his room without too much comment. Doctor gave him a sedative after satisfying himself that there were no broken bones. Then everyone was gone. I was stuck with the gladiator. What was the charge against Jamie? I knew he would be driven to the state line, and I knew he was too wise to return for me even if he was innocent. Of what? Bobby would never have defended him unless he was positive he was safely in the right.

Poor little warrior. The fancy mustache now fanned across his cheeks. He looked like the bearded lady after a foldup with a Stunkey. Whew! He smelled of more than garbage, too. Booze— lots of it. It followed that what I had considered affected speech was, in truth, drunken. I undressed him, washed away the filth, then tucked him into his bed.

I was composing a note to leave on his night table when he began to weep, softly at first, but soon in deep, racking sobs. Whatever the dream, he certainly wasn't coming in winners. I put a comforting hand on his shoulder. He thrashed heavily, thrusting his face into my neck. I rocked him gently. The sobs subsided into whimpers, but I knew I was there for the night; so I moved us both into more comfortable positions, then turned out the light. Chuckling quietly, I thought, "Looka me, madonna and child-man."

I guess I must have slept.

17 ❧❧❧

I hadn't really seen Bobby's habitat until the aching of my bones caused my eyes to open. The lighting was different. Instead of the lone naked bulb hanging overhead, there was a biblical shaft of sun pushing its weight against my heavy head. Looking straight up, I blinked hard. A skylight.

Bobby was still in my arms, mouth slightly open. Was he smiling? I tried stretching my frozen neck. His grip on my middle tightened. I relaxed.

It had been about round four with Bobby that the truth had dawned on me. Hazards of the marriage relationship include the danger of bad casting. In every break-in period, sexual rewrites are invariable. Your role as female partner could slide from lover to wife to sister to mother. Most deadly of all: to pal. Buddy. The introductory choreography of lovemaking produces one lead dancer backed by a chorus. Improvisation can freeze into set characters within a scenario, impossible to play for more than a brief run.

How do other people outwit the given circumstances? Is it ever simple to love and be loved while going about the business of making a life?

The sun streamed down from the skylight like a spotlight. The only difference was the warmth of these rays. I glanced down at Bobby.

"Long time no see," he said calmly. Neither of us moved. "Funny," he went on, "I don't feel like a port."

I sniffed and raised my eyebrows.

"Meaning," he said, "that was one helluva storm last night!"

I pushed him hard. "You!" My voice had the old ring. "I was the port—you got flattened! Just look at your pretty costume over there."

He was out of bed in a flash, fingering those ridiculous rags like gold. "The goddam dump! I remember! But I saved your superhero for you, didn't I? Where is he?" He looked around the room as though expecting to see Jamie.

"You saved nobody." I was emphatic.

"They gave him the bum's rush?" Bobby asked.

"Right across the state line, I'm sure," I said.

"So that's how I get the pleasure of your company, huh? I must have waded in for the rescue."

My tone matched his. "I was the wader—you were the wadee. It's not the first time I've dragged you out of the garbage and put you to bed."

Bobby grinned suddenly. "And it isn't the last time, is it?" He jumped on the bed, pinning me down in the old "say uncle" style. "Is it?"

I tried to look stern and failed. "Uncle!" I yelped. We fell back laughing like a couple of chimpanzees. When order was restored I explained what had really happened at the arena.

"What was the charge against Jamie?" I asked.

"You came back here with me." Bobby reached for me.

"Not the way you are thinking." I held both his hands firmly.

He smiled slowly. "It's stupid enough for Old Smoothie to show here. Because the territory is rich, and it's all owned—from border to border—by a sweet bunch of creeps who just might have sent him home in a cement kimono." The smile vanished. "They're my pals."

It was my turn to smile. "I could tell by the quality of the garbage you were fed."

Bobby rummaged through some things until he found a pair of glasses. "It had to be an accident," he said. "I'll get all new stuff. Even brand-new glasses. Presents. You'll see."

I sat back on the bed. "Bobby, what was the charge?"

He sighed, "Okay, remember the time you got sold off the floor by that bunch of snatch peddlers?" My breath stopped. He went on. "Nobody figs about some little old bimmy flickering out, you know that; but it was a kid who disappeared from Jamie's floor. She was certified canned goods. A true virgin."

I swallowed hard before I asked, "Jamie's floor?"

Bobby nodded. "I hate the old ghee, but I'll lay odds he wasn't in on that shake." There was a moment. "You were lucky, remember? But that kid? Nobody's ever heard of her again." Having polished the lens, he held the glasses up to his eyes. "Old prescription," he said. "My pals will get me all new. You'll see." His eyes, through those lenses, looked like those of a magnified house fly. "We were teamed as brother and sister, remember?"

Remember? I'll never stop remembering.

It was the second show for us. We thought we knew all about it . . . and them. The only reason the man was noticed at all, sitting so far up there on the very top of the bleachers, was because even from that distance everything about him was obscene. Pinkish wisps of hair on a strangely large, round head. He kept dabbing at his eyes, lifting the very dark glasses just above his forehead to do so. The eyes were red and swollen beyond puffiness. He was never alone; at least two or more solicitous attendants kept dancing up and down the aisles. It was always around four A.M. when he appeared. He didn't stay long, but he certainly made a big impression on us while he was present, so it was easy to remember him later.

I didn't stay in that show long—only about sixteen hundred hours. The offer I got that made me drop out was one I couldn't refuse. It was a contract to sing at a nightclub in a nearby city, and it was all right there in black and white. It was so perfect I left the floor like a winner, with everybody's approval and a big silver shower tossed at me by the happy customers. Bobby stayed in the contest with an unlucky pal gone solo.

I slept out the prescribed hours in quarters, then shifted to the rooming house as usual for the long sleep. The rest unfolded like a slow-motion nightmare.

The rustling seemed part of a dream I was hanging on to. Saturated with sleep, my senses clung to the comfort. It wasn't until I felt the unmistakable fatness of a muscled palm against my mouth that I sprang to. A blanket, weighted, it seemed, with rocks, pinioned my arms and legs; I was lifted like a sack of squirming kittens. I heard my window being laboriously raised. Someone—outside?—was cursing sotto voce, but we must have left by the door because it slammed, cutting off the sound of those other voices. We went up, not downstairs, then we must have gone roof hopping before we finally descended. I was being passed from arm to arm. Then I felt feet pushing down on me. It wasn't until a motor started right underneath me that I realized I was in the back seat of a moving car. On the floor. The feet were to keep me there.

I gave up and lay still. I wanted to scream at them: "There's been a mistake! I'm flat broke—you've got the wrong package— I'm not of any value!"

But my mouth was taped shut. Fainting or passing out—whichever—I did one of them.

I awakened in a cold sweat, afraid to open my eyes—but I licked my bleeding lips. At least the tape was gone. I ventured a squinty look. The face leaning over me was more than wrinkled—it was corrugated, the eyes worn and dim; smiling sweetly with a generous sprinkling of tenderness which couldn't be anything but real. Best of all, it was female. A blast of relieved tears burst from me like a police siren. She held me while I let out all my terror and all my relief. She even gave me a handkerchief when it subsided to sniffles.

Putting her finger to her lips, she went out one door, returning almost at once from another. Smiling and smacking her lips, she put a heavy tray on the table next to my bed. She fed me pasta, the like of which I have never seen before or after the event. I say fed, because I was apparently sewn into my blanket. Ravenous, I devoured the gorgeous stuff as she talked on and on. If it was Italian, it was a dialect I had never heard before.

Three days at least must have passed before she appeared apologetically holding the tape. I began to cry, she wept along in a friendly way, but the tape went on—after a very special meal which literally knocked me out. Coming to, I found myself once more in a car. This time I was sitting on the seat like a lady, but my knitted cap was pulled down almost to my chin.

"Bus ticket in your pocket—New York. Better not come back here."

I had a million questions, but only a gurgle came through the tape.

"There's a classy, rich old degenerate likes tender meat. He buys it off the floor, see? Plays greasy games with it till it's sick, then sells it along the down line."

I must have made my reaction understood.

"Yeah, sure—well, okay—now, you don't know who went out the door with you kicking in that bag, just like you don't know who came in the window a little too late, okay? Maybe you never will."

I was gurgling in tearful gratitude as I was hauled out of the car. I noticed the quiet because the only sounds were coming from me. I pushed against the blanket—it came apart easily this time. I stopped gurgling and lifted my cap. There was no one in sight. I was behind the bus terminal. Every instinct in my being said "Run." I was on the bus before I realized I still wore the tape over my mouth. I felt for the ticket, closing my eyes in relief as my clammy fingers found it in the bottom of my pocket. The bus sputtered out of the depot. I peered through the dirty window, looking for a face, any face that might be watching. There was no one. No one at all. I removed the tape, licking my dry, cracked mouth as I pushed down hard on hysteria. It was over.

Oh yes, I remembered. Bobby was talking.

I shook my mind free. "What?" I asked.

"I am telling you about down the hall. It's no Grand Hotel, but it's got a kitchen." He smiled happily. "Well?"

I was coming together slowly. "What?" I said stupidly.

"There's more room, foolish." He leaned over me. "You'd be more comfortable there. I love your cooking—and there's a laundry in the basement—we could be together like the good old days."

I looked at him.

"Last night—and being here remembering and talking together—well, all of that must mean something to you."

It would have been so easy to tell him exactly what it all did mean to me. "The good old days . . ." I just didn't have the heart. How could he understand when I was only partly aware myself? Just now beginning to comprehend the balance. Females endured much better than males. So it was no novelty that in the thousands of hours I had invested in the marathon circle I had learned to drag, carry, lug my male partner eighty percent more than he dragged, carried, lugged me. Squirrelly time, time spent out of your mind, was almost exclusively male, as were the sudden crashing falls to the floor. Evidence was overpowering because it was on display twenty-four hours a day. Facts, however, were denied. Polite silence on the subject was imperative. The evidence was inadmissible. There was the question of injury to a superior ego. A superior.

"No." I said the word tonelessly. It came with astonishing ease.

"NO?" he repeated, laughing. "What the hell else have you got to do?"

I didn't join in the laughter.

"You would never believe," I said.

18 ༜ༀༀ

My hungry roots reaching for soil, for sustenance, had at last found a base into which they might furrow and feed—hopefully grow—not dependent on homestead or hearth, on matriarch or patriarch. These roots had to be unafraid of the unfamiliar. Why not? So far, there was nothing that had not been unfamiliar. The next stranger I would carry would be part of me, and when she was born, I would have my own birth. A double celebration, combining forces with all the contradictions within me. To grow alongside my sprite. We would combine roots.

My route wasn't exactly planned. It was dictated by whatever dates were available wherever, salvaged by the few remaining agents. This time I wasn't dreaming along, looking at scenery and resting my bones. I worked. I played every ladies' luncheon, bazaar, county fair, or turkey shoot offered. As long as I broke even on expenses, hoarding my cashier's check for the big event, I could see the whole rainbow. Thus I hitched, walked, and bussed when demanded, all through Idaho, from Boise to Pocatello.

Salt Lake City was good for two whole weeks of solid bookings; so was Denver. In Kansas I had to make a straight line to Topeka, but struck gold for almost a month because it was Christmastime. Tap dancing was big in Kansas over the holidays.

Kansas City was a bonanza, almost as busy as St. Louis. The wad was safe in the grouch bag, and I was eating enough for two. My weight began to show in January. I had worked my way through Illinois and Indiana. I began really believing I'd be in New York for the big opening when I got the warning.

I was singing "Tie a Little String Around Your Finger." It was a nice date, a "middle-class country club," the agent had told me. There were a lot of children in the audience, and I was very busy shopping for tiny features to compare. To remember. I had always done the act in a tramp costume, so I didn't worry about any giveaways on my secret. The soft-shoe routine was for laughs, too. There couldn't have been such an awful lot of strain; no pratfalls or slides like I was used to doing. So the first stab was right out of the blue. I didn't gum up the lyrics or anything—I even got through the dance. At least, all the laughs were there. I took a couple of quick nods and called the hotel doctor fast. He didn't have a real office there, so he came to my room. I had gotten out of my makeup, but I didn't have time to dress. I wore my robe, a typical backstage makeup rag. I didn't stop to consider that I was not the usual expectant mother in this Midwestern doctor-patient meeting.

After a cursory examination, he asked, "How long have you been hemorrhaging?"

I sat up in the bed, pulling my robe around my bump. "Well, about an hour ago, I felt an awful sort of stabbing—"

He interrupted. "You alone here?"

I nodded.

"Well," he mused, "I could send someone over to stay with you. Keep you on your feet—you know."

I didn't know, and said so.

He didn't sit, he stood. "You don't need to tell what you did to start it, and I don't guess there'll be any complications, although no guarantee is possible." He pronounced it "gharintee."

"What I did?" I asked. "I did? To start what?" I was lost.

He moved toward the door. "You're trying to abort, aren't you?"

The word floated between us.

"Abort . . ." I repeated.

"You have a good chance, so don't worry."

I connected fully. "Damn you! Damn you!"

The color flooded his face. "Shh!" He crossed back to me swiftly. "I thought—well, you're alone, and I thought—I'm sorry." He looked around the room. "You want to keep this fetus?"

That did it.

"Fetus?" I yelled. "This is no fetus, you quack! This is my baby, and it's very much alive! Kicking and dancing, and—" I yanked my voice back to semi-normal. "All I want from you is to tell me how to keep it alive."

He was uncomfortable. "Well," he said, "no guarantee—but try slanting your bed on an angle, and don't get up for a week. Do nothing, really nothing, and—I'm—I'm sorry," he repeated. "Call me if you need help." I reached for my purse.

"No, please . . ." He had the door open. "Forget it—on the house." He was gone.

It was a useful week. I guess my last adventure in resting completely was at that other hotel in Chicago when I was ten. This time was different.

Mind and body greeted a week of feet up, motor off, with gratitude. Oh, how I slept and dozed and dreamed! It was a rosy rest—the two of us in a warm cuddle.

Clara, the hotel maid, got bellboy and desk clerk into the act. They put boxes under the foot of my bed so I was upended. She said her grandmother was a midwife, so she knew about such things. The White Tower at the corner was open twenty-four hours a day. Whoever was on the desk shared a root beer and bag of burgers (with the works) whenever hunger set in. I guess it was the most enchanted week of my whole life. I was in no fear of losing baby if I stood pat. Standing pat with baby kicking vigorously made it the best of times. There was only one tiny pinprick.

Included in Clara's hair-raising dramatizations of her grand-mother's heroic deeds were tales of death in childbirth. All sorts of dyings, and all leaving orphans alone and unloved. Grandma never did save a mother when the chips were down. Naturally I began examining my own choices. What would become of my little one if I didn't make it through the mysterious ordeal? Clara's stories of cruel institutions, cold prisons for waifs and foundlings, had me in thrall.

There was someone other than myself who was aware, indeed wary, of family characteristics. I wasn't alone. Baby wouldn't be alone. I could confide in my sister. My sister would understand.

19 ୬୬୬

On the bus a fellow passenger shooed me away from a seat which was directly over the wheels.

"Shouldn't be on a bus atall." The stubble on his chin was grayish. "Too far gone. Whaddya?" I wondered why I wasn't embarrassed. "Don't let the driver see ya—" my friend was sly now— "he ain't running a maternity excursion!"

Chuckling his way to the back, he lit up a pipe whose fumes permeated the atmosphere like an open gas jet. Gas. I remembered something Mother had said.

"No gas, no anything—" she used her mysterioso voice, "only half a roof overhead, a blinding snowstorm, the midwife hours late . . ." Tears filled the violet eyes. "I was only a child myself." That was the part I most enjoyed.

"How old? How old were you, really?" I chimed.

"Only a baby having a baby," she continued, "in a snowstorm." The voice always curved upward from this point: ". . . ripped to pieces . . ." Shrill, now, ". . . torn apart and no doctors for miles and miles in that Godforsaken state." She fixed those hypnotic eyes on my sister's rapt face. "Your father had to live in the forest. Oh, yes—the ever evergreen trees of the Evergreen State of Washington. He loved those trees far better than he loved you." Her gaze usually shifted to me at this point. It sent shivers up and down my spine. I knew the rest of the story.

"And you, my baby." Here it comes. "You were supposed to be Olaf. His namesake. So he didn't want to look at you at all."

I prompted, "You could put my head in a teacup."

Mother picked up her cue. "I knew I was carrying a girl. All that time he was saying 'Olaf this' and 'Olaf that.' Well, girls don't give up, no sir. I tried everything."

Oh, the pride I felt at being such a sticker. "You punched," I reminded.

"Fell down!" She always came in on that. "But girls don't give up!"

We always laughed hardest at Mother's tag line: "Fixed that man, really fixed him! Two girls in a row, and all he wanted was boys!"

Cuddling my bouncing bump, I thought about the miracle, the unexplained sorcery implied, each time Doddie, Big Lady, or Mother chortled happily over our inevitable bringing forth of baby girls. With the exception of Big Lady's one slip, the line had indeed consisted of a single gender: "the gentle sex."

That was Grandpa's term.

Mother's stories were good, well performed. One wasn't obligated to believe. Given the mandate for accuracy, the highlights of Mother's tales would have flickered to the power of a lone candle. A birthday-cake-style candle.

Gazing dreamily at the frozen countryside flowing past, I wondered what it would have been like belonging, actually being part of one particular place during my childhood—say, attending school in a town or village, living the years of early youth in an actual home, with two parents, birthdays, celebrations. Imagine Christmas somewhere else than backstage and hotel, without an extra matinee. Imagine no trains, no eerie "whoo-whoo" on overnight jumps, no hair-raising stories. Imagine a solid adherence to truth, requisite in an environment that was acceptable to that vast majority who considered themselves "normal." Even given a different set of relatives and a whole other start, could I have made the grade? Having done so, would I swap what I had known so far of life on this planet for whatever that other route offered?

Unlikely. I closed my eyes. Unless there was something out there, something I had missed, some kind of wonderful, free roller-coaster trip, complete with heart-in-the-mouth highs, as well as down-in-the-depths lows—no, I wouldn't trade a moment—a second. I felt smug.

My palate had recovered from the bitter taste of my early failures. Even Mother would be proud of me now. As I drifted off to sleep, I decided to check *Billboard*'s endurance section, then send a note to Jamie. Not about anything in particular, no details. Just a note saying I hoped he had found a location, etc. Just in case he wondered.

At the terminal in New York, I wedged myself into a phone booth. The operator's voice cut into my excitement. "That number is dis-con-nec-ted." Click.

I realized my mouth was hanging open.

"Close up, foolish, pull yourself together. . . . Oh, no! What if they are gone? Gone, and I'll never find them—no! don't panic!"

All my voices fought to be heard. Trembling, I suddenly realized I knew no one in all of New York City to call for a possible trace. More, I knew no one in all of New York City. I thought yearningly of the hotel I had just left. Of Clara, the desk clerk, and the bellboy. I sat on a long bench in the waiting room, fighting tears. The long bench. I looked down through blurred eyes. There it was, the worn, many-times-varnished wood was supporting me, just as it had done when I was alone. Many nights

I had slept there. Perhaps on this very bench. No grouch bag in my bra then. That's when "second-acting it" and living on hot dogs and pretzels was my idea of heaven. But I had no one to care for, then—I was alone. I squeezed the tears from my eyes and blew my nose.

"Well," I said to the world in general, "I'm not alone now."

Crisis over, I scanned the theatre section of a discarded newspaper. Of course, there she was.

If You Ain't Got It, Come and Get It, starring Gypsy Rose Lee. But the ad wasn't for Minsky's. I'd never heard the name, and it was way downtown.

At Fourteenth Street, the Irving Place Theatre enjoyed being the only burlesque house in the neighborhood. I took a seat among a few empty rows at the very back. Rear seats were not desirable, therefore I had my choice. The original VistaVision, stereo appetite craved, needed to be as close to the action as possible—or secluded. Far up in the balcony and alone, alone with the action.

The audience. Customer. John? Examine the man in the front row center. Fiftyish, balding, overweight? A regular. The balcony is filled with similar customers. Regulars. What kind of society creates this regular? This father, uncle, brother, husband, son, who has been the major support of the longest-running, biggest-money-making flesh shows and/or flesh sales from here back to the stone age or beyond? A floating society, surely, with such a time span. Nothing changes but the music. Even the jokes live on. Perhaps prices are affected with fluctuating economies, but this regular—he is dependable.

Let the little woman worry about the rent, or how to feed the kids, this regular can always find the price for pornography or pimp. Marching through the ages untouched, this backer—angel—of the arts related to prostitution never rides in a Black Maria or feels the lash, because he is home with his family when the bust occurs. However, for the action, he is either down front or secluded way up in the balcony, whichever fits the need.

"You're a fortuneteller?" The chorus girl was probably married to one of the stage crew. She wore an everyday coat over whatever went on before, or came next, on the bill.

"Fortuneteller? Yeaaah, that's me!" Suspenders stretching to the floor, the comic leered.

"Well," the girl said, "do you read palms, or cards, or—?"

The comic snapped his suspenders. "Nope, I have a glass ball."

She patted his head. "Oh, you poor man!"

A VOICE IN THE DARK: Peanuts, popcorn, rubber balloons . . .
ANOTHER VOICE: Help, someone—there's a woman here who has fainted!
FIRST VOICE: Peanuts, popcorn . . .
NEW VOICE: Fainted? Rub her wrists, rub her wrists. . . .
FIRST VOICE: Rubber balloons!

Segue into big fanfare. The show moved fast. It had to, or the audience took over.

Uptown at Minsky's, the production numbers not only featured undraped female frescoes, there were jungle scenes complete with chimpanzees and zebras, circus numbers with dancing elephants; even the famous spider web strung across the entire opening of the stage. That one needed everybody's wife and/or girlfriend, because there had to be lots of leg and arm waving, and all in unison, too. Yes, Minsky's went in for spectacle.

Similar to the big unit shows that now filled the forestages of what had been vaudeville theatres. Some of these were called "Ideas," created by an erstwhile dance team whose billing had been "Fanchon and Marco." Unwieldy sound equipment for the new craze of talking pictures consumed all the upstage space, so the "Ideas" had to fill whatever was left downstage. They did, too. Although a single vaudeville juggler, trapeze, iron jaw, family act had been more than sufficient to please the pre-talkie public, the new demand was for at least twenty people doing the same act. So these performers, dumb acts—meaning, without dialogue or song—sold Fanchon and Marco "the act." Owner-creators then taught their secrets to the chorus. As a bonus the dumb act was sometimes featured somewhere in the crowd for a fraction of a moment. It took a while for the family acts to realize this was a once-around-and-out. But legal. Thus, the vaudeville tradition of handing down, from parent to child, an original invention—an "act"—was ended. The invention, mass produced by the new owners, became more and more diluted, until it was lost in a sea of mediocrity. Within time, the whole idea of "Ideas," unit shows, or presentations was as dead as vaudeville itself.

Burlesque, however, gained strength as vaudeville and its imitators weakened. My sister told me it was a whole different audience.

"Have you ever heard of any other public who sit with a newspaper covering their lap?"

I was the perfect foil at the first hearing. "No," said I.

"Oh, yes indeed." She told me later it was fun just watching my face. "You see, the reason for that paper is simple—it's because they're masturbating. That's right, and I guess they'd rather not be seen by the other Johns. God! All the stuff they bring in with them—it's an education! Milk bottles and raw liver, and—you don't believe me? Check the alley. See what they sweep out of here at night."

I wasn't amused. "That's not an audience!"

It was the exact ammunition required.

"How would you know, June? Where have you been? What does your marathon audience bring in with them? Picnic baskets—so they can munch and crunch while getting their jollies watching a bunch of rejects degrading the human race in public."

The brandy was an ally now. It lived on the makeup shelf, in the purse, or under the arm. Permanently.

"Well, let me tell you, June." She wasn't excited—almost factual. "My audience is no scabbier, no sicker than yours, but my audience is more useful. Oh, yes—while they sit out there jerking, I'm the one using them. Because there's another audience coming to watch my audience watch me!"

There was a comic savagery in her manner, in the way she informed, remindful of a magician. The ultimate trick. Watch closely. Watch now, because the art is in misdirection. You see, your attention is directed away from what is really happening. Otherwise there would be no amazement, astonishment. The trick works—except on the subconscious. Under the surface of glowing skin and shining eyes, hidden somewhere within folds of silken tissue, a thread of acid flows like an underground river. In some simple beings, the river is created by improper care—feeding or watering. In others, more complex, it is conjectured the acid is born of loathing. For either, it is hemlock. Insidious, without even the melodramatic scent of burnt almonds as warning.

I watched the stage. My sister was sing-talking. It was the same arrangement I had sung in the old act—a "paste-up." Mother used the standard score given free by the publishers to any standard act, then she snipped out the parts she didn't like, pasting the result together. The number was the same, but as Gypsy was doing it now, it had a whole new meaning. After the performance, I found my way through the familiar dark alley.

Backstage was heady. The remembrance odor dizzied me. Same sweet smell. Different time, different place, different me. I held my coat in front, hiding my bump. I didn't want bad timing to spoil my surprise.

The doorman was far from the traditional gray ex-hoofer-with-wistful-face. This solid wall of brawn would qualify as top turnip for any stiff joint. Pushing a wooden toothpick under finger-nails sporting baked-in dirt, he wore one cigarette behind a cauli-flowered ear, another dangling from a busted lip.

"On the phone—everybody's across the stage," he lisped. "Whyncha wait in her room? Up there." He pointed with the frayed toothpick.

Climbing the circular stairs, I thought, "Whole new audience out front, whole new attitude back here."

The dressing room did it. I sat heavily on a backless kitchen chair gulping in the beloved clutter. Rhinestones and feathers, spirit gum and Sterno, perfume mixed in equal parts with death sweat. Never-stop cooking of coffee. This combination of intimate odors floated in an atmosphere warmed toastingly by circles of mismatched light bulbs framing the cracked mirrors. An array of brandy bottles littered the shelf, with lipstick-smudged coffee mugs. Various plates piled high with cigarette butts completed the picture.

My head fell onto my arms and I let go. Someday, I vowed, I'll have a mess like this for my very own. I was homesick.

Awhile later I was roused by the wail of a siren. Not the kind used to wake us in the marathon, no. This one was moving— it came closer. There was much activity on the stage below. I got up, wiped my face, and went onto the little landing above the spiral stairs.

It wasn't a fight—everyone seemed in control. Then I saw the men with one of those stretchers carried in an ambulance. They were crossing below me, and in spite of the blankets and the people and the noise, I could see who it was they were taking away.

"Gypsy!" I yelled. "Gypsy!"

She looked up.

"Get back—get back, you'll fall!" It wasn't her full voice, but it carried. I clattered down the stairs—they had already slid the stretcher into the waiting ambulance. Just before they closed the door, she looked at me fully. An expression of deep pity clouded her face.

"Oh, God, June—no!"

The door slammed and she was gone. I ran a few clumsy steps after her. The ambulance careened out of sight. I sort of fell onto the curb, where I just howled.

Someone was lifting me to my feet.

"She's okay, honest. She's gonna be fine." The voice was strong.

"I didn't get to tell her, I'm—I'm—" Someone had got my coat; they thrust my arms into the sleeves.

"Yeah, I know. And you're June. C'mon." We tumbled into a cab.

"But I'm—I'm—"

The voice turned gruff. "Calm down or we'll have two ambulance rides. Now, listen—do me a favor. I'll drop you at your mother's, see? You tell her Gyp's back in, but she's okay. Understand?"

I sniffed. "She's okay?" I asked.

"Yep," he said. "I'm getting out here. Cab's paid—and thanks for taking over, okay?" He disappeared.

"Thanks!" I yelled into nothingness.

20

Mother's new apartment was on West End Avenue. The façade looked like a road company set of the Forty-second Street library without the lions. I looked for a familiar name up and down the long list of tenants. My grateful friend hadn't told me which of Mother's many favorite names she was using now. There, "Thornton." That was one of Aunt Belle's married names. It was the only one I recognized, so I pushed the button. An electronically distorted voice wheezed some wavy words. I tried wheezing back, but communication was impossible, so I pushed a few buttons at random, until the buzzer sounded for the door. The corridor was all tiny mosaic tiles. Cecil B. De Mille–style sconces lit the way. As I rang Mother's bell, I thought I heard whispering and a small army of padded footsteps.

A muffled voice inquired, "Who do you want?"

I was sure I knew that voice. "Mother? It's me—it's June." I waited. More shuffling, whispering. I was being examined through a peephole.

"June?" The door opened on a chain. Only part of Mother's face was there. I could see an eye, but it looked wary.

"What do you want?" she said.

"Well, first, I'd like to come in, Mother. I've just been to the theatre—uh, they took Gypsy to the hospital. 'Again,' they said—Mother?" I wasn't sure she was listening. The eye was wide.

"Oh my God," she breathed, "what in hell has happened to you? June, you are pregnant!"

I smiled, nodding.

"I don't know anybody," she was very firm, "I don't know anybody who can help you." I put my hand against the door. "My poor baby," she said.

"But, Mother, I want it. I want to be pregnant."

She shook her head. "No one ever wants to be pregnant, June." The door opened. "Who is going to foot the bills?"

Inside was even more like a stage set. A half-complete second act from *The Shanghai Gesture.* Mother led me to the kitchen.

"I'll call your sister and then we'll see." She disappeared into a long, dark hall. More whispering. Shuffling. Feeling watched, I sat still. Perfectly still. Who else was here? If it was Big Lady or Aunt Belle, they wouldn't hide.

The kitchen was huge. Cupboards and cabinets covered the walls below, above, and alongside a huge old gas range and refrigerator. The sink was restaurant size. I stood looking about nonchalantly, I thought, then moved, pushing open a pair of ornate swinging doors. The dining room. Paneled in dark wood. A crystal chandelier blinked sleepily in the shaft of pale yellow light from the kitchen. What had happened to the dozens of chairs and the historic dining-room table?

I wasn't surprised at the bare floors. Mother said she never missed carpets—"Just something more to clean." I wondered where anyone could be watching from. Trying to penetrate the darkness of the adjacent room, I realized I had been holding my breath.

"That's silly," I told myself. Walking firmly into darkened space without seeing fully, I perceived more emptiness. Dim light filtered through bare windows. Light from above? A court, of course. Always dark, always empty. Why should I expect this room to be otherwise? If it were filled wall to wall, with whatever had been of whatever it was, what would it be? If, say, any of us could select at random—and of course, without charge—what would be our heart's desire? Would our choices differ? Oak, mahogany, plastic, tin?

Mother lived in empty spaces. Given a space of my own, would I do the same? "Yet" implied intention. "No furniture yet," Mother would say.

My ears still tingled with the echo of that departing siren; my sister's pity-filled face blurred my vision. I had to set things straight. Could I get to the hospital, talk to her? Waiting for her to come here, to come home, would be hard to endure. "She's all right" was reassuring but not informative. All right from what? Why an ambulance, unless something was far from all right? I heard myself sigh. Well, my own direction was established. Once my family realized I was not a victim, but a victor, they would rejoice with me.

So far I had had no opportunity to share my secret plans, bu there were no doubts in my mind as to how they would be received after all the chips were down. We were family.

"Well."

I jumped, then giggled nervously. Mother was beside me. "I didn't mean to scare you." She took my arm, guiding me back to the kitchen.

"No furniture yet," she said.

"Where are all those chairs and the big table and things?" I asked.

"Your sister and I managed to get out as many things as possible the night we left that awful neighborhood, but that big oak stuff—too heavy." We were in the kitchen again. She brightened. "Fixed that summons man good, though. Pulled up all the rose bushes."

We settled down. "What—why is Gypsy in the hospital?" I asked.

Mother frowned. "That's today's mystery, June. Spends most of her weekends there. I'm sure I don't know how to explain to people." Mother snorted. "My daughter says it's restful? Fiddle! And that ambulance—why not go in a taxi? But no, she has to show off. Tells me it's an investment. Well, it does get a line in a few gossip columns. . . ." Her face turned reflective. "I guess if it's good enough for Al Jolson . . . today it's stylish to be exhausted all the time."

I was relieved. "When will she come home?" I asked.

"Home?" Mother's voice was brittle. "Oh, she can't live at home anymore. Oh, no—lives in a penthouse downtown."

My heart sank.

"Oh, yes, got a maid waits on her hand and foot—I'm only allowed in when nobody else is there. You'll be the same." Mother's eyes narrowed. "Wait till you see the food comes out of that jungle bunny's kitchen. Everything on fire. 'Flambay' she calls it. Last time even the damn soup shot flames. No wonder she thinks she is sick all the time!"

Alarmed again, I said, "What do you mean, thinks?"

Mother unpinned a key from her blouse. "It's all in the mind," she said. The key didn't fit the padlock on the icebox. "All that nervousness, too. Why, she is scared of her own shadow." Another key, on another safety pin, from another fold in her blouse. This one finally worked. "You can't ignore your own mother, treat her like a stranger. . . ." She was about to succumb to the sadness. "God will punish you for being an unnatural child." Mother began peeling a huge grapefruit. "I'd offer you a wedge, but it's pure acid." She ate the fruit sadly. "I'm here," she sighed, "a prisoner in ten big, lonely rooms, while she's enjoying ambulance rides and all that publicity." She reached into a cabinet. "Look—who was so important on this night I had to be dragged out of a bingo game?" Fumbling through a scrapbook—"Here," she cried, "front page of the *Graphic*. Four columns, if you please, and who is stage center in the pictures?"

The caption read, "My Baby Is Innocent and Pure." There was more, but I got stuck on the way Mother really took over the action in those pictures. Real pro.

"That's when I was important to your sister. 'A Mother's Defense.'" Her face was flushed.

"What was this one about?" I knew I shouldn't have asked.

"What?" Mother crackled, "It was the big number-one story, that's all. We were arrested—Black Maria, the works, 'Indecent,' they said." Mother was scornful. "Well, your sister's reply hit every wire service known to man." Taking stage, she quoted, "'I wasn't naked,' Gypsy Rose Lee said modestly, 'I was completely covered by a blue spotlight.'"

It was a pretty good impression. But Mother hadn't hit the high spot yet.

"'Just ask my mother, who is always with me.' It was true, I was. And they did." She drooped. All the steam was gone. I closed the book and put it away.

"I'm the one who is sick." A sob caught in her throat. "I'm the one. It's my heart. My heart is sick with shame for my daughters." She blew her nose and stood up. "Fifteen dollars a week, but no board. You do your own cleaning up and there's a pay phone in the hall."

Fair enough. "I'll take it," I said.

"On Tuesday and Friday nights, I have very important meetings, so you must plan to stay in your room." We were halfway down the long corridor running parallel to the rooms I had already seen. "I'll put you in here," Mother continued in a businesslike tone, "because it's at the very end and near a bathroom." She opened a door. The room was empty. "There's a bed somewhere," she said, "and maybe a chest. Don't burn too much electric, June. Remember, this is a home, not a hotel."

Outside, a tall, imposing iron grillwork surrounded the window. It was decorative, but the length of the points suggested bayonets all in a row and at the ready.

"I know." Mother said, "that's why I say it's like a prison. In the afternoon light, those bars cast shadows on the walls of every room on this side." We stood together at the window. "Your sister wouldn't let me live on a ground floor without bars," she said, "because I would be at the mercy of every single prowling murderer—she had the service door barred shut, too. I always use the peephole and chain like she says. My God," Mother shivered, "she's so nervous she makes me nervous. And that's how she makes herself sick." She started toward the door.

"You told me she wasn't sick," I said. Mother turned. She was still hugging herself in a protective way.

"It's in the mind, June. Even the doctor says so. Half brandy and half black coffee—and chain-smoking every waking moment of every living day? Of course she's nervous! Any girl who pals around with famous hoods, and—and worse—"

I tried to think. "What's worse?" I asked.

Her face tightened again. "Moving her own mother all the way across town, that's what. I tell you, June, the day you both decided you didn't need your mother, you put the covers on your own graves." She went down the hall. "Wear slippers, June," she called back. "I can't stand the clatter of shoes on this floor."

The old guilt pricked at me. The new fear crept in. Would I be such a stranger to my child? How could I learn to speak the same language? Share the visions of my daughter? I yearned to be the perfect mother. I wasn't sure it was something anyone could learn.

Prickles in my feet notified me that it was time to sit. As I looked down, it occurred to me that I hadn't seen my knees in a while. I had to bend sideways or front, otherwise my bump hid them from view. It was funny to me, funny enough so that I laughed. I loved that bump so very much that I laughed because it came to a point these days, and was so big it obstructed my view of those loyal, hard-working knees.

"I wish I knew what you could possibly find to laugh at, June." Mother dragged a rolled-up single mattress into the room.

"My knees," I chuckled. "If I want to see them, I have to bend over this way." I exaggerated. "Or like this, see?" Mother's laughter curled into my own. Finally we had to drop onto the mattress.

"Oh dear," she pulled me into her arms, "it's so easy to forget all the fun we have." I rested against her. "Anyway," she murmured, "it will feel good to have a baby girl in my arms again—your sister swears she'll never, ever have a child—d'you know that?"

I was surprised. "Why not?" I asked.

"Well, dear," she said, "she has this little internal thing wrong, you see, and before this there was that other—well, nervous thing that was wrong, and so they hurt. Not bad. Nothing in the world to compare with the godawful hell of birth pains, but she says this is pain enough and she'd need a damned good reason to go through the agony of having a baby. That's what you are going to find out about." We sat quietly for a moment.

"Mother? What is the other pain, the one she has now?"

Mother stood up. She put on her impatient face.

"It's just nothing, June. And she brings it all on herself. It's nothing but an ulcer."

Unfamiliar.

"It's a pimple. Only it's inside," she said.

"Inside where?" I asked.

"Well, it's not inside her toenails, silly. Just somewhere deep, like that other thing that hurt so much. That one was inside the— oh, you remember, I used to warn you about those little men working inside your tummy putting away everything you ate?"

I remembered. "They have to sleep, too," I quoted. We laughed.

"Well, they do," Mother said, "and if you don't take care of them—"

I picked up the refrain, "They won't take care of you."

Mother nodded. "Well, June, if you ask me, dear, your sister has a couple of those poor little men trapped in there—they are stone cold dead, and she killed them herself. What she has to do now is find a way to eliminate the bodies without killing all of us in the doing."

I winced. "Oh boy," I breathed, "that was the highest kick in the chorus! Wow!"

Mother knelt quickly. "Can I feel?" She held out her hand, I put it palm down where the action was. Her eyes seemed to change color as a slow smile grew into a grin. We giggled softly.

"Strong," she whispered. "Good and strong! Oh, yes, June— that's a girl. A feeble kick means a boy." She straightened. "I'll find a chest of drawers somewhere." She looked around the room. "You'll be all right here. Remember, stay inside Tuesday and Friday nights." At the door she turned. "Enjoy her, June. You'll have a few years, anyway. She'll be out of there soon, then she'll let you hold her until she can crawl. You'll have to catch her when she starts to walk. Then, before you know it, she'll be running like hell—right out of sight!"

Mother sort of sighed before she turned away and disappeared in the darkness of the hall.

21 ✹✹✹

Mother had to be right about the importance of a firm bed. The parquet floor under my mattress filled that bill perfectly. Sleep was instant.

My energy was boundless. It was when I tired of walking the breadth of the Upper West Side that I discovered the park. I wish it had been sooner, because across the park were all these big, beautiful buildings. Anyone at all could go in; everyone was welcome, and it was all free. There were pictures from all over the world. Huge and small statues and precious things, and if you had a question, there were people all over to tell you the wildest stories about everything. It was the first time I ever realized how long ago was past.

Sometimes there was music, not like the pit band I knew, but tinkly sounds from the instruments like in some of those pictures. If you walked down Fifth Avenue, there was a zoo. Vendors sold hot dogs and popcorn. Further down was the library, where you could read all about it. Everything was free but the hot dogs and popcorn.

Mother's fanciful descriptions of what was hurting my sister stuck in my mind. Eventually I got over the worry of intruding. I knew I'd never get an invitation, so I called and asked if I could please sit bedside for a bit. "Well, June," my sister's voice was weak, "it's a tatty floor show, but come on. Only a few minutes, though."

The limited visit with my sister somewhat allayed my concern regarding what Mother referred to as her "nervous conditions." She held forth at a midtown hospital. The room was large, but hardly accommodated the leanto tent attached to her bed. Only her upper portions visible, she was bravely enduring considerable pain. Strains of *La Traviata* underscored our conversation.

"Olive oil," Gypsy was saying. "Be sure it's warm. Just rub it around the bump and all over your breasts. Twice a day, she told me, and you won't have any stretch marks when it's over."

I grinned. "I'll go to sleep at night smelling like a salad."

She moaned, "Don't make me laugh, please, June, it hurts."

I sobered at once. Under the tentlike sheet you could see that her legs were spread apart with the feet sticking out. There were blinking lights coming from the small machine being operated by a stern-faced nurse. Parts of the machine were inside Gypsy.

"A-a-al-most over," the nurse singsonged.

"Thank God," Gypsy sighed. "Like the Bible says, fornicate at leisure, repent in a tent." We giggled quietly.

"There we go." The nurse was rolling up tubes, turning off the blinking lights. "Try to relax." She was pushing the machine out the door. "I'll be back to get you in a taxi, honey," she sang, unsmiling, then she was gone.

"The personality kid," Gypsy said. She closed her eyes. Her face looked wan.

"Want me to go?" I asked.

"Uh uh." She turned to me with a tired smile. "I'd like to be sure this baby business doesn't ruin all your chances. You wearing that big bra?" I nodded. "Good," she said softly, "and the olive oil religiously . . . If your breasts droop you're going to be out of luck, that's all." I leaned closer. "And be sure they bind you up real tight afterwards, because they don't unless you say so." She was relaxing now.

"I'll remember," I promised.

"The opening night of the opera . . ." there was a smile growing at the corners of her mouth, "I made all the columns. At just the right moment a big car drove up, the doorman hopped over, opened the door, and I stood there with every camera on the street flashing bulbs at me. Ignoring the others wearing the same old things, candles on their heads, frontless, backless . . . And why? I wore a floor-length cape made completely of orchids. I simply stopped traffic." She chuckled softly. "Hear that music? I'll be a walking information center on long-hair music and opera—and see those books? Spinoza, Dante—all marked with just perfect quotes for the right occasion. How do you think I got where I am and to where I'm going? . . . The brain, June."

She lifted her head so she could point the words at me. "Smart. Bright. My guy knows the music, the books, and all about those opening nights at the opera, so I'm learning how to make myself seen and heard. But how long do you think he would consider me so amusing and brilliant and fun to push into the spotlight if

I sagged all over from having a baby nobody wanted?"

I stood up. "I want it!" I almost yelled.

"Shhh . . ." She looked pained. "Keep it down, June. Be quiet."

I sat quickly. "I'm sorry," I said. "Why can't anybody understand my side?"

She shook her head. "Hopeless . . . you just insist on being unbright. . . . Well, anyway, use the olive oil and remember the binding. It's too late to try to help you any other way, so go on, darling. I think I can sleep a little before Dancing Dolly comes back in her taxi for more laughs . . . see you, honey . . . 'bye."

I watched her as she took a deep breath; then as the breathing softened and settled into a deepened rhythm, little by little the strain was erased. I remained there watching the subtle changes. A delicate flush lit the pale skin from within.

"Why am I so stubborn?" I thought. "Why wasn't I born bright like my sister?" But she was right. It was too late for me now. I knew what I wanted as well as anyone. It's just that I never seemed to be able to make myself clear. I wondered as I gazed into the now completely relaxed features, would she worry so about me if I were not unbright?

I didn't see much of my sister during the following weeks, but the mystery of the whispers and shuffling feet turned out to be no mystery at all. There were other tenants, transients like me. We all wore slippers to keep down the noise, but I was the only one who stayed in my room on Tuesday and Friday nights. Then came this one special time. I guess it was inevitable, because here it was.

Mother's meetings had all been noisy but never before erupted into what sounded to my ears a riot. My sister's voice rode above the bedlam, then was heard no more after the building was shaken with a cannonlike door slam. A moment's silence—then great crashes as furniture seemed to be hurled against walls. Shouts of protest, fury.

I listened numbly, wondering if interception was wise. Then Mother's voice cut through the walls: "Stop, thief!" she screamed. "It's all I've got, don't—oh—stop! Stop, thief!"

Pulling my wispy robe over the hulk I had become, I opened the door and stood framed in the light from my room. A few candles sputtered feebly from saucers on the floor. All else was darkness. The sound of panting came from every corner. As I moved toward the light switch, the panting stopped. All present were holding their breath. It gave me courage. I turned on the light.

The cast was huge. A single glance at the costuming and I knew without a doubt that this was not a meeting of the PTA, Equity, or even National Variety Artists, Inc. The battle line sat center stage on a worn settee. She was of mammoth proportions. Wearing a severely tailored suit, she had draped her ample flesh across the settee in a spread-eagle fashion, muscular arms reaching full length to right and left. Beefy legs, wide open, displayed rolled lisle stockings up to a stretch of bullet-proof skin, thence to a pair of workmanlike shorts. Her wilted starched shirt had sprung a few buttons, revealing bosoms resembling a couple of mislaid elephant trunks. Many of the company were dressed in what were termed "formals" in that day. Some were truly exotic, lovely, simple or sweet. A few resembled chorus boys at a reunion of some old musical comedy. The focus was on that settee.

Mother stood dramatically at the front line of her contingent. Realizing the moment of truth had arrived, she pointed a finger accusingly at the behemoth sprawled on the settee.

"That thief has my grapefruit!" she announced.

There was a quivering silence. All eyes were on me. It was my turn. I knew it. I had a wonderful platform here—a role in a situation that any actor might dream of. I had to forget my lack of experience, I told myself. No one knows you don't know how to play this scene, so . . . go.

I turned my attention to the settee. In my best Nazimova-like tones I inquired, "Do you have my mother's grapefruit?"

There was a general lengthy intake of breath, but no action. I knew more was expected of me. I picked up one of the scattered handbags, extracted some change, and moved ponderously into the phone booth, studiously avoiding contact with all faces except one. It was safe to stare at the clock while dialing 0. Mother's cherished, then-in-vogue dual dispenser of time and melody stared back. It stood eight feet tall in the disguise of a grandfather clock. It was deformed, inasmuch as the large head it sported contained a very small kitchen-style face. Not a real clock—a sort of semi-watch. Where Grandpa's vest buttons might have been were a few knobs over several slits, which lit up when its radio parts were turned on to whatever program Mother fancied. I heard the soft strains of Guy Lombardo's beat under all the panting. It underscored the scenario. Vincent Lombardo's voice crooned, "It seems to me that I'm lost in a fog. . . ."

The operator was in the earphone.

"I want the police." Mother had to be proud of the authority in my voice.

"I'll always be lost in a fog without you. . . ."

"Sergeant Murry, police."

I jumped, then found comfort in the plainer-than-plain voice. "Sergeant, there is a very bad situation here, and uh—I—uh . . ." I faltered for words.

"What's the situation, lady?"

I mustn't be intimidated, I told myself. He is only a man. "It's a—a fight—there is a—person here who won't give back my—my—mother's grapefruit." I could feel the room straining for his reply.

"Lady?" His voice was soothing now. "You call Spring 0-6666. Got that? You must tell 'em what you just told me. Okay?"

I murmured my gratitude while dialing. The room was so still it might have been a painted backdrop. No one had budged. Why didn't they run out of the place? Remaining calm and dignified was my only hope. It wasn't easy because I couldn't get all of my bump inside the phone booth. I was standing half in but mostly out. The next voice came crackling clear—the listening tableau simply had to hear it, even over Lombardo.

"Bellevue."

It was as though we had all arrived at our destination. There was movement in the room at last. "Bellevue" had to be some kind of magic word, I thought. I stood a little taller.

"Can I help you, lady?" Coats and handbags were being gathered up.

"There is a bad situation here. . . ." I told my story amidst a scene of orderly dispersal. All but one customer was on the move.

"Lissen, lady, if we rushed out on every call about some lesbo fight over grapefruit, we'd be chasin' all over town forty-eight hours a day. It'll work out. Be patient. They ain't your grapefruit."

I held the receiver close and breathed deeply. "Yes sir. This is the address. . . ." I pretended he was still on the phone. "Right away? Thank you." I hung up and turned toward the departing merrymakers. "They will be here in a few minutes." My voice surprised me.

Finally I was left with only Mother, Kate, and the quarterback, who had removed herself from the settee. I started toward my room. I wasn't sure how Mother would take this intrusion. My legs shook but somehow carried me to the door.

"Wait. Willya wait a minute?" I hung on to the knob. It was the grapefruit thief. "Here," she said gruffly, "here's your lousy grapefruit." She rolled a couple of the prizes toward Mother's feet, then turned to me. "I guess I had a snort too many."

Mother pulled herself into a posture of disdain. "You," she said, "have lost your membership here."

The big girl glared at her. "Membership? A buck and a quarter to get in this ratty setup, and then pay seventy-fi' cents a slug for that cat piss you serve?" She laughed in my direction. "The worst part—she's no sense of humor. You can't run a joint like this if you got no fun in you." Her face sobered. "We were having a little laugh, that's all. Then you showed up and—well, it's kind of a surprise to see how pregnant somebody gets." Her sincerity made her look smaller. "It's too bad and—I'm—I'm—" She was gone.

Mother sat suddenly on the floor. She crumpled into tears. "I can't live on crumbs—that's all your sister has left for me. Crumbs." Kate moved toward her compassionately.

"Rose, Roanie, don't—don't cry, please." I watched from my doorway.

"I had a great career—you know that, June. First with you— my baby, my star—all over the circuits. From the time you were two years old, I made you into something. A star . . ." She fumbled for her big handkerchief. "You ran away from me, for what? Why, I could have made you as famous as I have made your sister, but no, you wanted to run your own life." She blew her nose mightily. "I have to have a career, too. A life. I have no life of my own. Your sister has left me; paying me off with this big empty apartment and a measly allowance isn't enough."

I found my voice. "Why not furnish the place? Or—or— Mother? You could get a job, or—or get married again."

She almost choked. "A job? I can't work with my asthma. I'm not strong enough to work. Besides, punching some clock

I'd go mad and punch somebody's face. . . . And marry? Never, never. I gave up marriage years ago because I hate sex, hate, hate sex. Don't I, Kate?" She clung to her friend.

"Yes, Roanie, yes."

Mother struggled to her feet. "Sex is dirty because men are dirty. It's all they see when they look at a woman. All they think of is what's hanging between their legs." The familiar red spots were spreading upward from her throat. "Too bad you're not as bright as your sister. While you're wasting time watching your belly grow, she's in the very center of the biggest money market going and she gets her share." She slammed the grapefruit into a cupboard.

"Marry again," she mimicked. The doors of the cupboard almost cracked as she banged them shut with her foot.

"What has sex got you?" Those little flecks began to appear at the corners of her mouth. "Don't you dare feel superior to those girls who were here tonight. At least they have the good sense to know they can't get pregnant with spit!"

Distraught, she stood glaring. Out of breath, spent. Suddenly her face crumpled. The small frame bent almost in two with the impact of her surrender. Dry, gravelly sobs tore their way from deep within. She beat the air with her small fists while pounding the floor with her feet. Kate collapsed with her. Between them they stripped a part of my soul I had covered with great care. The wrappings were blown away and I stood as part of a trio. Terrified and alone. Together and separate. Shadows from the pointed bayonets outside laid stripes across the bare floor, across us, across the walls. The last of the candles guttered out, sending a vaporous trail upward.

"Goddammit." Mother's voice was frayed. "Goddammit to hell." I was in her arms, or was she in mine? "I only want you both to escape all the hell and disappointments and loneliness. There has to be something better for you than what I am."

I wanted to conjure up a gift. A delight. A circle of light. But I said, "You have us, Mother, and now you'll have someone else as well." She held me at arm's length.

"Yes?" She tried for a sardonic smile but it was a grimace. "What do we ever do together? Where do we go? Do we even have the same friends? Did we ever? Do we tell each other things?" Her voice was rising. "No. Oh, no. We aren't a family. I don't have children. I haven't got a home. If I run a pickup joint with booze it's not my fault. So don't you march around in that silly rag calling Bellevue every time you hear somebody laugh out loud." The climate was changing with no warning. "Everybody who comes here knows exactly where everybody else stands." Mother's head was high. "No false faces. They get what they pay for and it's as good as I can afford for the price." She was in full command. "Besides," she said, "they're not welcome at normal joints. They simply haven't anyplace else to go."

I cleared my throat. "Well, it's—just—I wanted to help. . . ."

Mother lifted her arms heavenward. "Help," she cried, "if you want to help, get off your fat butt and let's clean up this mess. They're my friends and I love them but they're a messy bunch of freaks." She grinned at first and then we were all laughing. Laughing.

22 ᛉᛉᛉ

After that I felt more useful. First in the kitchen, mixing and serving the pale spaghetti Mother sold to "members." A surprising number were willing to take a chance on the dish. It went for seventy-five cents with no cheese. Coffee was fifteen cents. Canned milk was served in its own tin, of course. Mother's style amused, even charmed her clientele. Mother was "in." The place was always packed, but I never thought of counting the house because I didn't know about working on a percentage—yet.

Someone was needed at the improvised bar. I volunteered. There was nothing to concoct. The liquor was served from large pitchers. All I had to do was pour some of the stuff into the small paper cups Mother liberated from handy ladies' rooms around town. I dotted each with a maraschino cherry. I wasn't trusted with making change, so the girls did that, or they just put the seventy-five cents into the cigar box on the counter. I watched the customers sip or gulp that drink with a queasy rolling in my own insides. When Mother and Kate mixed the stuff in large quantity, the bathtub they used wasn't scoured. Mother said alcohol killed anything. The rooms were all lit with very few candles sputtering in odd dishes. So, even if it wasn't a clear liquid, no one would be able to see. As Mother said, the stuff sold like hot flaps. Who cared how it was made, or from what? It worked. Fast, too.

"Have you got a cup there without one of these anemic cherries?" The girl was a stunning brunette. She smiled at me as though we two were in on some wonderful secret. I poured the drink. She dropped the money into the cigar box. Another girl joined her. Now they were both smiling with me.

"Is it all right to ask how many months you have to go?" It was the first time anyone had mentioned my bump. I was pleased and flattered.

"Well, now," I confided, "it should be sometime early April, and let's see, this is mid-March, so-o-o-o—" I grinned.

"What does the doctor say about your weight?" I looked at them. Apparently they didn't know about these things.

"That's later," I said confidentially. "I haven't been to a doctor yet. I have to wait for the pains to start, you see. Mother explained that a first baby can take days to arrive after the first pains start."

The handsome girl exchanged glances with her companion. Then she leaned over the bar. "Listen to me," she said. Her attitude had changed completely. Even her voice was different. "I'm a nurse. I work for an obstetrician." I must have looked blank. She spelled it out. "A baby doctor. Waiting for the pains is like waiting to thumb down the next covered wagon—obsolete." She wrote in a notebook, tore off the sheet, handed it to me.

"You want a live baby?" My mouth must have fallen open. "Close your mouth," she commanded. "Meet me at this address tomorrow afternoon whenever you can get there." I fumbled with the paper; she took it out of my hand and pushed it into the top of my dress. "You're twenty pounds overweight," she whispered into my face. "If you want to hurt your baby, maybe kill it, listen to those old wives' tales. If not, be at that address tomorrow." They swallowed their drinks in one gulp, turned and disappeared through the door.

The next day I was at that address. "Just like in the movies," I thought, watching my new friend all dressed now in her snowy white outfit, tiny cap bobby-pinned to the coiled brown hair. She wrote all the information being gathered about my condition into a long legal-looking folio. I had been careful to avoid discussing a doctor or my wonderings about a hospital with Mother. She didn't trust either.

"Think of the pioneer women having babies in the ox trains." She loved those tales but I had a growing fear I could never live up to the challenge. Could never hope to take a place among those heroic women because I simply and truthfully had a terror of pain. "You'll forget all about the agony" was a password. I knew I wouldn't forget. I was an admitted coward.

So I answered the doctor's questions with a sense of happy arrival. This was it. Euphoria had been my consciousness level ever since I knew I wasn't going to lose the baby, but now the pinkness enveloped me completely. I was on my own personally conducted tour of cloud nine.

I knew the advantages of not being alone when the big moment arrived, and I don't suppose I would have willingly moved away from Mother on the last eight bars, but my sister brought her love, Eddy, to the apartment. There he was. All the Arrow collar ads rolled into Eddy.

"How do you feel?" He didn't wait for an answer. "You are too big," he announced with authority. "I've had—we've had three kids and I know, so you just stop eating all those goodies. Say! Don't be embarrassed with me, please." He hugged me so hard I yipped. "Here," he said, peeling some bills from a huge roll, "I'm betting on you. No, sir! No back talk. You take this toward the baby." He put the money in my pocket. "Just be sure it's a boy." He took his laughter down the hall. A door slammed.

"A boy!" Mother snorted. She took the money from my pocket, counting it under her breath. She didn't look up when Gypsy returned to the room.

"He-is-nice!" I smiled.

She nodded. "I wish he was mine."

Mother looked up. "Now, dear," she admonished gently, "he is. You have the best of him. She has all the burden. The children and all that. There's over five hundred dollars here, girls. No baby could cost that much."

Gypsy laughed. "Give it to June, Mother."

I started, "No, I couldn't—"

"Why not?" Gypsy said. "Everyone else does."

I shook my head. "Put it toward my rent, then, and I'll—"

My sister interrupted. "Rent?" she asked.

"My fifteen a week," I answered. She looked at Mother, who looked down at the money in her hand. "But I pay for my own food," I said quickly.

"Some plans are too good to last," Gypsy said solemnly. "You pay Mother for your room, I pay Mother for your room, and if she keeps this," she took the wad and held it up, "Eddie pays Mother for your room, too." She shook her head, chuckling as she departed. I departed shortly after.

My sister found Mother's attempts to bunco endearing. "You have to give her credit," she laughed. "It's just not that easy to hit the dinger if you're not a pro." She sobered. "Mother never got enough of anything, June . . . let's try to always remember that, okay?"

I nodded. "Okay," I echoed. But I was glad to be on my own. I found a room at the top of a large building. It felt like living in a penthouse, but the tiny rooms were really there for people in the apartments below who needed more privacy from their servants. I loved viewing the lights of the city from that roof. "Someday," I vowed, "after I have my baby, I'll get back on a real stage. Only this time I'll be a real actress."

23 🌿🌿🌿

Spring was late, but the doctor said I was going to be right on time. Calculated, of course, by the sketchy information I had provided. Eventually convinced that weight measurements and blood tests were only part of what he needed to know, I had offered dates but no detail. The doctor knew little or nothing about his patient. Overweight and overjoyed was about it. He said I was indeed healthy. Strong. Smiling, he squeezed the bulb attached to the band circling my arm. I watched a needle dance up and down a large thermometer in response. I smiled, too. He was writing something in my file. My file. All about how I was having my baby. Details concerning weight, blood, and that dancing needle's report.

"Relax, now, just close your eyes and relax." His voice was comforting. He was good-looking but not pretty. Impersonal yet involved. "That's a fine, healthy heartbeat. It almost speaks." He gave me a slip of paper. "Diet," he said. "You are going to lose some weight." I scanned the list.

"No hot dogs, pie." He shook his head. I smiled back, "Okay, you're the doctor."

He grimaced. "Ow," he laughed.

The outside office was standing room only. Some women with babies in their arms; some, as Mother would say, "with a bun in the oven." I stuck my head in the appointment window.

"I'm fine, I mean, we are," I said. My friend looked up from her writing. "Write down how perfect we are." I turned to go.

"Wait," she called. "How about this one?" She cleared her throat, looking over her shoulder before she read:

> 'Then there's that chick from Peru
> Filled up her bloomers with glue.
> Said she, with a grin,
> "If they paid to get in,
> They'll pay to get out again, too.' "

She was looking at me expectantly. "I just wrote it," she said.

"But it's old," I told her. Then I wished I hadn't. "I mean, it's new to you, maybe. . . . Well, see, you probably heard it long ago and forgot it till now, or . . . or . . ."

She shook her head. "No, I just now put it down on paper. . . . I would have remembered something like that."

I nodded. "Sure," I said, but I wished I had kept my mouth shut. She didn't look up as I pulled on my coat. I found my way through the women and babies and babies-to-be, vowing I'd learn when and where not to talk.

"Second-acting" is easier if you're not pregnant. Actually, your credibility is better if you are pregnant, but there's a lot of standing and even kind of sneaking behind things and other people if you think you're going to be asked for your ticket stub.

I had seen some actors in three or four different roles, different plays, by this time. How wonderful, I thought, to go from play to play. Never to stop. How glorious. Seeing Katharine Cornell as Joan, Juliet, and Elizabeth Browning, Tallulah Bankhead as Judith Traherne and Sadie Thompson—lots of scenery, big casts—I was sure it would all last forever, and if I could just stay on my feet there was bound to be a space somewhere inside all that glory for me. I had even learned the origin of my favorite motto. I couldn't believe my ears. The very same words that vaudevillian spoke into my ear as I stood in the wings frozen stiff with fear of forgetting my new song. Right there onstage at the Music Box Theatre, an actor named Kenneth MacKenna was saying, ". . . in the words of Polonius, 'to thine own self be true.' . . ." I blanked out. It was too stunning. So now I knew. All I had to find out was, who is Polonius?

The end of March was still wintry. Cold. But even in a blizzard I had managed to second-act at Carnegie Hall. I forget the names, but I sat on a warm radiator top because my clothes were wet through. The violin penetrated my very soul as I steamed dreamily. Gorgeous. That night for some reason I carefully washed my hair, which was long enough again to braid into two pigtails. I did my nails and rubbed olive oil in the right places, and I slept. It was dreamless and deep.

I was awakened by a sense of emergency. My heart turned over hard before I realized what had happened.

"Be calm, don't panic." It was my voice, but it worked. I dressed quickly, then stepped into the elevator. Hugging my bump, I heard my voice again: "At last, at last," then, in sterner tones, "Shut up. Pay attention." I pulled myself together, but my hands shook so that I dropped the nickel three times before it finally clinked into the slot. It was two o'clock in the morning so I dialed my doctor's emergency number. Then I listened impatiently to one, then two, then three rings. I had rehearsed what I would say, but the pain came in such a giant embrace I slid convulsively down the side of the booth. "Hello—hello," the doctor's voice squeaked at the other end of the phone. I gathered all the strength I could and hurled it toward the mouthpiece. "Help me—oh— help . . ." It was a puny sound, not at all the way I felt. I was at least ten feet tall. I weighed all my hundreds of pounds in diamonds, just like the Aga Khan. I was in a contest with the pain, but I was rich, the pain was a paralyzing but poverty-stricken hurdle.

"Who is this? Hello—who is calling?" The voice kept repeating the same question. Doctors are eerie, because then, quite clearly he said, "June, is that June?" Perspiration chilled my back and dampened my head. "Can you remember what I say?" I groaned loudly in what I hoped he would accept as yes. "Tell a taxi driver to take you to the Women's Hospital—that's all you say—Women's Hospital, do you hear?" I nodded. "Do you hear me?" he repeated.

The pain had miraculously ebbed into a throb. I took a deep breath. The phone's mouthpiece came back into focus. I spoke into it, "Women's Hospital—a taxi—I understand—you will be there, won't you? I won't be alone. . . ?"

"I'll be waiting—hurry now." There was a loud click.

I replaced the receiver and laughed extravagantly. Oh, wonderful rainbow world, but walk soft—walk carefully—into the self-operated elevator up to the top floor. As the floor numbers passed I thought up a wall against having a pain in that dungeon. "Not here, I may never get out—not here." The dungeon clattered to a halt, the gate slid open. I opened my door and bent over to pick up the small suitcase which had been waiting. I turned to go but this time my legs curled under me as the pain and I clutched each other fiercely. I closed my eyes and tried to count. I got to eleven. Breathing again, I pulled my enormous weight up. Usually one hundred and ten, I now weighed in at a hundred and fifty-two. Even with the diet. I knew the time between pains was what you counted—it would keep getting shorter, until you couldn't count at all.

At the corner I hailed a cab. "Women's Hospital, please," I said. We turned sharply in the middle of the empty street and started uptown. I relaxed against the worn upholstery and opened all my pores to the rosy glow that enveloped me. I put my feet up on the jump seat and hummed softly. "You better go a little faster," I said to the driver. "I'm going to have a baby." The last few words were almost smothered in ecstasy.

"You're what?!" The driver turned around to face me. "You ain't gonna have no baby in my cab," he yelled. His face was puffy and red.

"Of course not," I said. "I'm going to the hospital, I told you—"

He threw up his hands. "Hurry—yeah, of all the cabs on the damn street you gotta pick me. Now, listen, you get out of my cab—I don't want no mess!" He swung out of his seat and opened the door. "Out!"

I thought he had misunderstood me. "I've only got ten minutes between pains and I've got to get to—"

"Out!" the driver yelled. "You got ten minutes to louse up my whole night's take and I don't need ya—I got troubles plenty without ya."

I picked up my bag, then paused. "All this time you're wasting yelling, we could be there!" My voice was loud, too.

"I ain't takin' chances!" he hollered as he drove off.

I stood in the street, dazed and furious. All the things I should have said came rushing into my mind. I mumbled angry sentences as I searched the empty street for another taxi. None in sight. I looked for an officer—"Never one when you need one," I muttered; then I suddenly realized anyone might wonder why I was alone in the middle of the night. Pigtails in red ribbons. I laughed and the sound danced up and down the street.

When the pain began I was unprepared. I looked for a place to get through it. I picked up my bag and started for the corner. I got as far as the street lamp and dropped the bag to clutch myself. "It's like being kicked in the middle by a giant," I thought grimly. In the full glare of the street light I struggled to keep on my feet. "Center stage," I thought, "full in the spotlight." The roar of the hurt drowned out everything and then subsided again. I pulled my hands away from the cold iron body of the lamp post. I wanted to say "thank you."

The street was still empty. I figured I had better start walking, so I pointed myself in the direction in which we had been driving. Hadn't I heard all my life that the pains went on for hours and even then a warning came in plenty of time to let you set yourself for the big ordeal? I had a doctor and I was on my way to the hospital. I wasn't any more afraid than could be expected. Perhaps I would have been if it hadn't been for the joyful singing sound in me. I heard a car and turned quickly to find the comforting sight of an empty taxi. A moment later I was on my way again.

The idea of once more being thrust out onto the sidewalk because of bragging about my condition kept a soundproof shield between my now-familiar next pain and the driver. I doubled up as far as my enormous bump would allow and gritted my teeth, pushing wet palms against my mouth as I tried counting again, but I had lost the control to count. I came out of the pain realizing the time was shorter than I had thought. Panic rippled through my voice. "Can we please hurry—please?" The driver was going through red lights. I hadn't noticed, but now I did, so when he pulled up in front of what appeared to be a sprawling gray castle, I almost laughed out loud with relief. I opened the change purse I had fished from my pocket.

"C'mon and hold on," the driver's head was right beside me. He was a big man. He was grinning into my face as he clicked the purse shut and closed my fingers around it. "Just tell the kid his first ride was a free one." I felt the strong arms lift me. "Here we go," he sang. The hospital was at the top of what looked like a pyramid of stairs.

"But I'm too fat for you to carry me," I gasped.

"Don't worry, honey. I carried my wife six times so far and I like to keep in training." We were traveling up the gray stone steps at what seemed a magical pace. He was only a little out of breath as we reached the top.

"You ain't fat," he said, "only pleasingly pregnant." We started toward the huge swinging doors. "Hope your guy gets here in time. I woulda hated missing any of mine." He was so comfortable. So big and comfortable.

"Yes," I lied. "Any minute . . . I'm not alone." The relief on his face was worth it.

That makes the big scale balance, I thought. A lie to release you from bewildered responsibility. Your kindness to wipe away my earlier experience.

"Thank you." I shook his hand formally.

"Any time," he said, disappearing into the whirling glass doors.

24

The door went flap, flap, flap; then there was silence. Struck by the suddenness of no sound, none of any kind at all, I froze. The floor was marble. All kinds of shapes; mostly diamond figures leading into one another. I stood center of a large circle; above, there loomed a huge dome. At four sides of the circle the marble diamonds separated into single paths. They went in different directions, all disappearing into nothingness. Which to take? One potato, two potato, three potato—no, that would take too long. I closed my eyes and turned. First to the left, then to the right, then three steps forward, open eyes and go. Walking the marble diamonds under the arch, then into the dimness, I didn't even try to resist humming, "I love a parade, ta boom ta ta boom, ta boom boom ta da—"

Ahead, on what appeared to be a small floating island, a woman sat writing. The only light came from the green-shaded lamp on her desk. She must have heard me, for she was peering in my direction. Our eyes met. My mouth must have been stretched into an enormous grin, or so I thought, for I was so glad to see her and there was so much to tell her, but the grin kept growing until my mouth felt stretched beyond all possibility. I didn't like the scream. I was ashamed of the echo dashing against the walls, racing along the corridor all the way back to the dome. She was on the marble floor holding me in a strong, tender grip.

"Don't be afraid," she said. Not until that moment did I realize: I was terrified. There was a wheelchair. I clutched my overnight bag as we sped along the corridors. There were quite a few of us but we were very quiet. The rubber tires glided over the marble. We moved into the biggest elevator I had ever seen, then almost immediately emerged into another corridor. There were only whispers now. As I was lifted onto white sheets in what seemed to be a windowless room, the pain took some words out of my mouth but no one seemed alarmed. My clothes were being removed during the grinding, tearing agony of it. I had a flash of clarity: someone was saying, "It's nothing. Why, I smoked a cigarette all through." I tried to tell the nurse but my voice was still a shrill scream.

Then I saw my doctor open the door. He was looking only at me. Smiling. Into his hand a nurse had thrust a black funnel-shaped thing. He came toward me slow motion, offering the black funnel as though it were a gift. I reached for his hands and pulled them down to my face; at least, as I remember it was I who pulled his hands, holding that funnel to my face. It was a gift.

I whirled into space, but as I went I saw my sister at the door. She held a bottle, a brandy bottle, in one hand and a glass pot of coffee in the other. She wasn't smiling; she was angry. I wanted to stop the whirl so I could explain, but there was no time. From the revolving door to the funnel had been more than three hours in time if you measured time in hours. It would be months before I saw my sister again, but I didn't know that then. I only knew she was whirling out of sight.

"Come to steal our gold, willya?" The voice, in an echo chamber, was directly over my head. "Take this." Searing heat coursed down my parched throat, but I could not move in protest. I was bound. The molten fluid scorched my inner ear, went flaming down, down. . . . The voice now spoke in Spanish. Ah hah. Tricky. How did I get involved in this revenge for treachery? Where was I? Who were they? I opened an eye warily. The liquid gold had spilled. "Let go. Uh uh. Tense up, you hurt." The voice was now in fragmented English. Indian? I opened the other eye. My enemy was a small lady in trouble. The orange juice was all over my face. "Don't like?" She was trying to clean and feed me at the same time. "Oh, yes," I scratched, "more, more . . ." The sweet coolness pampered my scorched throat. I winced.
"Too much scream," she said. "Everybody scream, then hurt." She moved away. I reached to feel for my bump. It was gone. Oh, miracle. I was flat again in the middle. My hand traveled upward, exploring. I was bound tight, rolled like a mummy, and I hadn't remembered to tell anyone. "My baby." The words were blurred even to my ears. "Baby fine. You sleep now." I tried to say I didn't need to sleep but didn't get past the thought. I remember feeling very different when I finally awakened. The dry stinging in my throat and mouth had abated.
I wasn't at all surprised to find the binding on belly and breasts. Ice had been added, however. There were long rubber ice bags covering my chest. I could hardly see over them. Did the milk have to be chilled for the baby? With blurred vision I examined the square pale room. Three other beds. All empty. Various tables, a few chairs. Nothing else. Clean. Very clean. This was the first hospital I had ever seen from the inside. Very impressive, but where did they keep my baby?
"Baby fine." I remembered hearing that. Of course she was fine, I knew that, but where was she? How to get attention in a polite way? The door was open but it was quiet outside. On the table beside me was a stack of little waxed cups. I reached for

them—just made it. Lifting my head as far as possible above the ice bags on my chest, I flipped a cup across the highly polished floor toward the door. It skittered into the hall. Delighted, I waited. No one came. I only had six cups. Each danced merrily through the open door but found no audience. I began to worry. Marooned?

I was about to take a chance on my raw vocal cords, to forget polite, to yell—when I heard voices. Craning to widen my view of the hall, I was rewarded at last. A double-decker cart rolled slowly past my astonished gaze. Lined fore to aft with bundled babies in wire baskets, it went on and on, finally paused before my door. A nurse lifted one of the bundles from its basket and came toward me with the prize. She made a place beside me, a place in the crook of my left arm.

"Don't you want to know which it is?" she smiled. "I know," I murmured, "may I unwrap her?" The nurse laughed out loud. "It's yours, isn't it?" Her rubber soles made squeaking sounds as she walked away.

The tiny face was a blur. Asleep, it looked unborn. Unfinished. I touched the skin. Of course it would feel like that after floating so long. It was adorable, but . . . unreal. Where was the singing I had felt all along? The cloud-high joy? I stared into the little closed face. Now that we are no longer one, I thought, are we to be separate? A sense of loneliness enveloped me. I forced it down as I began tenderly uncovering. There were folds of soft blankets, small enough to layer and wrap and to hold firmly. I examined the minute fingernails. Mother had said never to use a scissors to cut them. No matter how small. No. A mother always bit off the excess nail. Bit it away like the animals do. I had forgotten to ask the nurse how much the baby had weighed. With the poundage I had carried about, this trifling bit could hardly have accounted for much of it. The arms waved slowly. "They sleep at first, twenty out of twenty-four hours," I murmured to myself. The small belly was bound like mine. "Of course," I told us, "the button, you see, like the comic says: 'If the button gets loose, your pants fall down.' "

The body was well shaped, although the legs seemed a bit bowed. I decided this had to be caused by the push of the diaper. They were easily unfolded—there, I held the legs together. Per-

fectly straight . . . what was that between the legs? I froze . . .
no. Impossible. My voice found its way up the scratchy throat
and out. "NO . . ." it wailed. "No, this isn't my baby—take it
away—it's not mine—somebody, please?"

A nurse pattered toward me. Her face was pink. "Shhh, now,
now . . ." She rolled the little boy into his wrappings, then checked
the beads on his wrist. "Stevens?" she asked, then quickly, "Shhh—
it's all right. I'll get yours." She reappeared before I could say
more. "Here," she said. "That cart is so confusing. I'm sure this
is yours." She lowered the bundle into the crook of my arm and
I knew. I didn't need to unwrap or anything. The singing inside
me went wild. I hugged my outside bump.

"Bump," I said, "oh, you are here . . . here at last."

The nurse lingered. "How could you tell?" she whispered.

"Easy," I answered, "that was a boy. Do you happen to know
how much she weighed when she was born?"

The nurse grimaced. "Six pounds, seven ounces."

I squeezed the bundle gently. "Is that much?" I asked.

"Ouch," responded the nurse.

"When do I nurse her?" I asked. "I feel as though I could
supply that whole cart." I tried to laugh. "Ow!" I said.

"Stitches," the nurse confided. "They'll pull for a while, but
it's a wonderful job. You have a good doctor. Lucky. Lots of
women are never repaired," she whispered again, "because their
doctors think Nature's going to do it. I swear, if it was their parts
being ripped, it would be repaired fast enough!"

I tried to take a deep breath. "Why am I in ice bags?" I
wanted to giggle, it was so unexpected and—well, foolish.

"I'll let your doctor tell you that," she said, reaching for
the baby. I hung on. She was firm. "Let go. For now it's back
in the nursery."

I almost sat up. "But isn't she hungry? Shouldn't I feed—
nurse her? I'm—look, I've got all this milk, and—"

The rubber soles squeaked to the door. "Your doctor will
explain. The baby's on a formula. Your milk isn't right." She
put my bundle into a wicker basket. The cart began to roll.

"Wait a minute," I called. Her head appeared over the baby
cart. I lowered my voice. "Do you mean I'm stuck with all—all
of—this?"

She nodded as the picture moved on.

25

I must have needed sleep, because I was only awake for two things in the next five days. Food, and the chance to hold April in my arms. The name just came with the bundle. April was beautiful outside, and even more so in my arms. Sun streamed through my window. At the proper hour it created a golden path, first across my bed, then all the way across the shining floor to the hall. Someone standing in the door would seem to be smack in the middle of a spotlight. That was the usual hour for a visit from my doctor. It was fitting he should be lit that way. His entrance, his exit—always with a smile. This time his nurse, my friend, came with him. She made a fine entrance, too.

"You remember Tina?" He was undoing my milky wrappings. "Albertina," he added.

"Remember?" I said. "I'll never forget. I might have made forty gallons more milk if she hadn't told me about you."

He laughed nicely. "Well, it's giving up at last. Going away. You'll have to wear a nursing bra for a few weeks. Tina?"

She unwrapped a hideous long cotton bra. "My gift," she said. "Ain't it pretty?"

The doctor moved away. He was finished. "Had a few walks, I hear."

I sat up. "And I'm going to learn about the formula, and how to handle my baby. You know, bathe her and—well, like a nurse. Like Tina. I mean, Albertina." The nurse smiled.

"You can call me Al," she said. "I'll wait here, Doctor, if you want to take a look at April. All right?" Doctor smiled once more and disappeared up the hall. "Had any visitors?" she asked. I shook my head. "Didn't think so. Tell you why." She sat at the foot of my bed.

"I don't know many people, that could be why," I offered.

She glanced over her shoulder. "He's the reason. Yes, he is. That night you came here? Well, he called me to ask if you had anyone you might want to be with you during—you know. I said I'd call your mother."

I leaned toward her: "He knows I'm not one of—that I'm—alone? And I'm not really married either?"

She nodded. "He's a grown-up man, June. Well, I called your mother. It was late Friday night, remember? She had a lot of customers. Your sister was there, too, so when I said you were about to become a mother, it was the highlight of the evening's entertainment. Boozed to the gills, about twenty of them decided to move the party to the hospital waiting room."

I lay back and closed my eyes. The brandy bottle wasn't a dream. "But why was Gypsy so angry?" I asked.

"She wanted to run the show. Doctor tells me she knew more about what to do than he did. It got pretty noisy, with you yelling murder in the screaming room, the girls in the waiting room, and your mother and sister yelling directions in the hall."

There was a moment. "Well, actually," I said, and I meant it, "it was kind of nice of everybody to—to want to come here, and—"

She sighed. "Yeah, well, I hear they had a good time. Doctor finally had to call the police." I sat up fast. "Well, you were only in labor a few hours, but they brought their booze along and that can seem a long time if the party gets rough. Anyway, you would have had lots of visitors except for that. He banned them all." I thought it over. "My mother and sister, too?" I asked.

"Nope," she answered. "If they haven't shown it's just that, well, they're pretty busy—and after all they did see the baby right after it was born. That's what did it, I think. Your mother said she was damned if she was going to look through a glass to see anybody. Said you didn't belong in a hospital, you weren't sick." We looked at one another a while. "Want to hear a new one?" she asked. "Lissen:

> 'There was a young pirate named Yates,
> Who liked to Conga on skates,
> Well, he fell on his cutlass,
> So now he is nutless,
> And practically useless on dates.'"

"Very good," I said. "You wrote that?"

She grinned. "Go on, willya? That's old." She made her exit through the spotlight at the door.

I stood looking out the window, my window that caught the

sun like a runway, remembering the story about the man in the hospital bed furthest from the window. He was jealous and miserable because the patient near the window saw all the wonderful things that happened outside. He told about them, too. You couldn't shut him up. All about lovers kissing under the beautiful tree across the street, the birds, and little children at play. The man listening to all the stories was ashamed to realize he was secretly wishing the patient by the window would die so he could have that bed.

Whether it was his selfish wish or not, in time the first man did die, and the nurses moved the other man at last to the coveted bed by the window. He couldn't wait for morning so he could watch all the exciting life that was going on outside; not hearing someone else describe it, but actually to be witness. He vowed he wouldn't waste his breath telling the others. When finally daylight came, he stared and stared out the window. The others in the ward implored him to tell them what he saw, to share the pleasure of the outside world as the first man had, but he was silent. You see, the window looked out at a bare wall. Nothing else.

The storyteller for me was forgotten, but I knew I'd always remember the story. I looked around the room. My few possessions were downstairs where I had paid my bill, and where I would go now to collect April.

"Now is the beginning of my life." It was a sobering thought. A job, yes—a job is the first—but who will care for April? I can't work at a job and still be with her. No, the very first thing of all is to think. I had just enough money left to squeeze a little time for that. "Curious," I thought. I had been frightened. I had been worried. But not anymore. Everything feels . . . right. Even the very last of my calluses are almost gone. That whole part of survival was over. Everyone, every single solitary human with whom I had been intimately involved twenty-four hours a day, for months on end: gone. Washed out in the tide of now with no emotional trace. I had not once experienced any weighable desire to see any certain person arrive at this door. I had longed for, waited for no one.

If I were to peel back one secret corner of my mind, there would be the desire to talk to my sister. Agreement had never been the destination of our thinking, but the trips were always exciting. I accepted my position on her list of priorities as worrisome, but of minimal importance. Perhaps we had enough confidence in one another to vanquish apprehension. Youth is a powerful drug. Given such a world of time, surely all is possible. Yes, I could always use a breath of the rarefied atmosphere surrounding my sister.

But she was busy. I understood.

26 ꙮ

When had I learned there was no nutrition in my mother's company? The deadening had been gradual, the realization so gradual it was difficult to place the point of suffocation. A memory of the sense of loss, of ebbing passion, flashed across the years. I closed my eyes against the sun's presence—futile, because its power lit the blood in my eyelids, recreating the episode in red. Deep red. Dark red.

Sometimes lilacs are pale pink to lavender, but I have never heard of or seen a dark, blood-red lilac. Lurking in the memory, hidden behind that thin blood, they were bigger than life. Lilacs don't grow like that anymore. Banking one side of the luxuriously wide pavement in tall, tight formation, they stood at attention as Mother and her friends ambled along. The hotel manager had been gracious when he told Mother to invite a couple of her friends on the bill to join them at his home after the last show for a little midnight snack. Vaudevillians seldom enjoyed the pleasures of a real home, but a child star was a novelty, so Mother had many invitations to share with the other acts. Strolling with her now were six of The Twelve Mad Chefs, a comedy tumbling act; Ricky Rowdy's Taps and Tricks, hoofers; Bellissima Bella Bay, the opera diva (who was only taking a flyer in vaudeville); and Alonzo the Great. The lilacs were taller even than he, and Alonzo stood six feet six in his frog-costume feet.

Our destination was in sight. A pretty frame house set in a rigidly patterned garden, banked now on both sides by the lilacs, which were oversized and peculiarly pungent. Mother stood still. She sighed a Mélisande that would have wrung any Pelléas. Mother was beautiful then, small and fair, blue-eyed and vulnerable enough to enslave all the Roman armies.

"Lilacs"—she pronounced it "li-laks."

"Old-fashioned lilacs—oh, how I love them. When I was a little girl, about your size . . ." She placed a hand tenderly on the grotesque head of Magpie, smallest dwarf of The Mad Chefs.

He looked up at her in warm response. "Where was that, Rose?"

"North Dakota," she said, "Wapaton, North Dakota. Lilacs everywhere. Not as giant as these . . ." She closed her eyes. "And the scent is—much, much . . ." She swayed just a little. "I'd love to hold them in my arms. All of them. Oh, I love them so." Magpie thrust one short arm into the blossoms. "No, oh, no." Mother pulled him back. "It's all so beautifully planted and cared for. We mustn't pick a single one—not one. Shame on you, Magpie. One like you and we all get a bad name."

She slapped his hand playfully. "How clever you would have to be to pick an armful of them without leaving a bare place. And of course I could not be happy with less than an armful, so I must do with only my memories." Her blue-blue eyes swept by me as she turned and started up the walk. Her voice curled in her wake like the chiffon train worn by Polychrome, Queen of the Rainbow. "It's like a stage set in this moonlight, isn't it? Nature gets away with it—but try to put it on a stage, any audience would say it was faky, wouldn't they?" The door opened, adding a yellow shaft to the blue. The oddly assorted silhouettes moved forward, murmuring soft homilies as one by one the yellow slit devoured them. The door was then closed.

I looked down first one avenue of lilacs, then the other. Mother was right. They were perfect. Only an insensitive lout would disarrange their effect. I wandered toward the rear of the house. Roses climbed over arches, firmly guided by invisible supports. Neat beds of matched flowers, blues, reds, and purples lay grounded in obedient shapes. Laughter rolled out the windows. I circled the house slowly. Mother's lovely voice danced up and down the scale, punctuated by laughter or murmurs of reaction. One didn't need the lyrics; just the music of her tone was hypnotic. Each response from those assembled inside was inadequate in comparison to my own enjoyment.

My step unconsciously fell into the rhythm of Mother's

melodic voice. Everyone loved her—loved her—loved her. Some were ancient, some quite youthful. I was by far younger than any of those adoring so closely. I was five years old and my love was more powerful than all in that house combined. All laughing, all reflecting, all warming themselves in her glow. Smiling silently in the moon's glare, I alone stood in charge of the Forest of Lilacs. Obbligato to the sounds coming from the house was an echoed longing as she said, ". . . hold them in my arms"; the sadness, ". . . when I was your size"; the resignation, ". . . how clever you would have to be to pick an armful without leaving a bare place."

Well, Magpie was only a clown—a man, of course, but a dwarf. Perhaps Magpie wasn't clever enough to fulfill Mother's desire for an armful of memories, but why shouldn't I be? I wasn't a man, of course, but I was bigger than Magpie. I backed away and fixed my eyes on one bank of the lavender beauties, then another and another. One spot seemed a bit full, so I squeezed between to break off the excess spray. It was wet with dew. As I struggled to break the branch it sprinkled me thoroughly. My heart beat foolishly as I stepped back to see if the stolen spray could be disaster to the pattern. No, I could not detect where it must be missing.

I measured once again, then crawled under the bush to disengage a heavily beflowered branch—emerging muddy-kneed as well as wet. Breathlessly I returned again and again, climbing, crawling, wedging between, in and out—always measuring carefully against destruction of the precious pattern. Little chortles escaped me. I knew I was the most clever. Drunk already with the glory to come, I backed away from the last look. At my side lay a heap of lilacs, all mine, mine to offer modestly. I rehearsed the gesture.

My attention was caught by thin spatters of blood on my white skirt, interlaced with mud spots. I traced the stains to scratches on my legs and arms. I raced around the house looking for a garden hose. One lay coiled snakelike under the kitchen window. The conversation within had the ring of departure. I fumbled at the faucet. Panic seized me. Muddy blood and night dew would ruin my moment, detract from my achievement. I washed arms and legs in the icy water, wondering why sounds in one's head reverberate so. Celery crunching or teeth chattering, as mine were now, made one wonder if the skull were indeed but a hollow bone. A human tympanum—different only in that such inside sounds were unsharable with the world.

Mother's party was breaking up. I must hide my gift until we were well away from the scene of the crime, I chuckled triumphantly as I hurdled an entire flower bed on my run to the front of the house. Skidding to a halt beside the towering mass of fragrant boughs, I closed my eyes, inhaled deeply, and basked a split second in the glory of the moments to come. Then I dragged my bounty behind the hedge, where I waited breathlessly.

The door opened. A shaft of light framed Magpie, hat in hand, as he walked onto the path with Alonzo. I thought, "Better to catch them right here after the door closes. Then they must see for themselves how cleverly the lilacs have been removed." Another thought: "Later, at the next corner, I could pop out at Mother with the trophies." Staging the event for the best possible return was uppermost in my mind as I stood shaking behind, in, and surrounded with lilacs. To be drenched in the glory of Mother's approval made any dousing or spattering of one's external being a mere trifle. Mother's joy always fed one's spiritual needs.

I recalled an event the season before this—just when we were to open at the Golden Gate Theatre in downtown San Francisco. My front tooth had loosened, causing my speech to be more than usually erratic. Seeing an opportunity to expand my value in Mother's eyes, I worked all night to loosen the guilty tooth further. It was a tough shag. But by matinee time it hung by one loose thread. Sure enough, on my very first entrance, I opened my mouth to sing and that tooth sprang out like a waiting jack-in-the-box, hitting the conductor smack in the eye. That part was unfortunate. But my song was impaired by only a tiny lisp caused by the gap. The good fairy left me a whole quarter for that tooth after the conductor grudgingly returned it.

I shifted my position behind the hedge. The scratches on my leg had begun to sting. Good. That meant no more bleeding on my skirt and socks. I pushed my wet hair off my face and prepared to step out of hiding for the presentation. Just then Mr. Hotel Manager himself appeared. He touched a switch inside the entry and the front lawn lit up like Sully's Flea Circus. I shrank back. The first sight to appall my eyes was long muddy skid marks I must have left as I gaily leaped over the formal flower beds.

Then a whole crowd of deep indentations, such as only a departing gypsy camp might leave, marked the circles I had made as I tramped around the house.

Mother gasped. It was a special sound—such a sound a Titania might utter to express the depth of her delight at first glimpse of the bewitched beloved. Everyone was smiling because Mother was so happy. Mrs. Hotel Manager stood in the light offering Mother a huge armful of lilacs.

Again strangers moved between me and the moment Mother would have focused every bit of that voltage on me. On me alone. Why? I had been artful, I hadn't been caught. I had heeded the rules. Mother's rules. Like all the times I left the stage soaking wet, gasping for breath, with my reward, that applause, that outside approval, to offer her. To give as proof of my worthiness. Mother! Look what I just won from that audience. It's yours. Here.

But the strangers stood between. Jealousy was internal bleeding, even though I realized that these intruders had no meaning—these or any of the others. These happened to be a simple couple who managed the hotel. Nothing people. With huge shadows.

The next day we moved on. A good supply of the hotel towels, blankets, and sheets moved with us. "Some of the nicest people you'll ever meet, girls. I'm sure they would be happy to know how much we will enjoy all these lovely things." Mother was pensive. "I'm sorry business is bad for them, but all the more reason these extras will never be needed."

I still see the child June turning away, stubbornly silent. Slowly, very slowly, the distance between us had been growing as though we were being drawn backward, one from the other, by some invisible force. Weren't we alike in enough ways? Or perhaps I was the only one nourished fully onstage. That audience embrace has unbelievable power.

Perhaps that made me strong, gave me the energy to believe that whatever it was I disliked intensely enough to reject as a way of being, it was my privilege to reject. Because I had another family, one that stretched from coast to coast, laughing and applauding. Didn't they stamp and shout for me until I finally emerged from the darkened wings and stood bowing and kissing my fingers to them in the flickering light of the newsreel? I stopped the show, I stopped my own act in three different spots . . . or was it they who stopped it? Whoever, it fed me. That was the strength behind my silence. My stubborn silence. I had that amorphous mass of approval. Of noisy love. I was certain it would be there forever. Be there for me. I was only partly right about that. Partly isn't a bad percentage.

April would be ready downstairs. In a tiny bundle, ready. We would return to my rooftop haven. There was an improvised basket on wheels waiting. Bottles, a sterilizer, along with a million instructions, and the time was finally now. I turned to go. The door was blocked.

His face was furrowed. All the features hanging downward, remindful of the pictures of those dogs used to find missing people. A hound. Struck by the aptness of the comparison, I forced back a nervous smile. Any smile could be misinterpreted, and I felt no welcome for Jamie. Although my heart was pounding, my face must have been an open letter. The kind posted by the management on the backstage callboard when the show was closing . . .

He was speaking: "How could you? My little girl in trouble—alone—if you had trusted me I could have helped. . . ." He moved toward me, I backed away. "Cruel . . . trying to find you . . ." His eyes filled with tears. ". . . Your mother finally confessed—" I wondered about that as I circled. Why could I not stand and confront? Speak? State my own truth? "I'll get a divorce now, Jeannie, it's too late to help you any other way." He was in pain with pity for himself. "I want to see my baby." The words bubbled inside a sob.

My voice came. I stood quite still. "We never talked about marriage, Jamie."

His tone leveled: "But in your secret heart—"

The pounding inside me hardened. "I have no secret heart. Whatever we have been is all there was—ever." I couldn't say, "I'm sorry," or stuff like that. How could I be sorry? He was the interloper. It was he who didn't belong and April was waiting for me. "So you see, Jamie, it was over when you went home and I—I—"

His face darkened. The words were accusing, bitter: "When you ran away to hide my baby from me." The door was right behind me. "It's not your baby, Jamie. It's my baby. Please, now, go back home . . . to your wife." I turned and walked—walked swiftly to the stairs, which I took two at a time. The life-size picture of his face, filled with utter disbelief, hung center stage in my mind as I collected my overnight bag, bundled April in my arm, saying goodbyes.

Outside a cab waited. We cuddled in the back seat. We were on our way home together at last. My heart had resumed its steady, firm beat. Then I realized.

Again. I had done it again. No powwow. Dismissal without arbitration. Well, what was there to say? Were there words invented that could clarify the situation for Jamie? Make him understand? And what could he say to me that would change me back into the girl of almost a year ago? This growing up was also growing away. Away with no regret. No backward glance. There was nothing—no one—back there I wanted along with me. I looked into April's sleeping face. "The beginning," I told her, "the beginning of my life—and yours."

27

12 oz. Grade A milk
8 oz. cool boiled water, boil three minutes
Add 3 Tbs. dextri-maltose
Makes 6 bottles
Feed 3½ oz. at 6 A.M. and every 4 hours in the day and every four hours at night.
Boil bottles and nipples before using again.

Got it. April had a fine appetite, but what made that dextri-maltose better than what I had had? Examining my own body, I found no change. No stretch marks at all. I looked forward to telling that to my sister.

Except when we went to market, April and I had no time as yet to realize we hadn't had a single caller. I had washed down every wall, floor, and ceiling with disinfectant. Windows, inside closets, cupboards, and drawers also got the treatment. I sterilized everything that came within touching distance of whatever we used. We were clean, and sanitary too. My hands were red and pulpy but I hadn't noticed until the girl who worked in the market asked me about them.

"An' whattaya gonna do 'bout them?" I hid my hands behind my back. "They don't have to be boiled along with the bottles, you know." I didn't need the brogue to know she was Irish. The marvel of her coloring would do.

"An' how old are ya?"

"Seventeen."

"Me too . . . only I know more, I guess."

"That's easy."

"Sure 'tis, been married since I was fifteen . . . over there he is . . . in vegetables."

"Nice."

"To you nice . . . to me, purfect."

We laughed. She took April in her arms. "Look at the smile on her." She lowered her voice. "So what are ya doin' always in the market together . . . where's her carriage?" I reached for the baby. She drew back. "I've watched ya pinchin' the pennies— yer man out of work?" I nodded. She sighed. "We're both here workin'—he's got a second job and I'm lookin' for a second job, too. Bad times, huh?"

I nodded again. Bad for now, maybe, but I was filled to the brim with hope. As soon as I could find someone I could trust to take care of April I would go out and . . . I looked at the happy pair before me. Perfect. If . . . "Would you . . . could you perhaps come up to my place for coffee? I live right next door." I must have looked awfully eager. She studied my face a moment. "I'm through here in an hour," she said.

Her name was Ann. I paid her a dollar to care for April on the afternoons I did the rounds. I never had a moment's worry, but I did experience a lot of envy. Ann's expertise with life in general was a timely reminder for me that no one is ever alone. A problem can be matched within a hundred yards if you can just spot the other worrier. Ann was, if possible, even more optimistic than I. Her gaiety pervades my memories of that time. It has been my repeated wish that the long road from there to here, gutted, foggy, and hazardous though it may have been, has led her to the same sense of joy of now that I am cherishing.

She found a buggy somewhere. Its wheels had a mind of their own, but it took April to the park. Nude sunbathing on our roof added bronze tones to the sturdy little body. Infant became baby. Formulas changed to semi-food. The grouch bag grew even thinner than my middle. I had learned about headquarters for other would-be's like myself. It was a corner Walgreen's with acres of lunch-counter stools. Gossip as well as tips about auditions ran up and down the snakelike seating arrangement. Hours of trudging from office to theatre lobby to lounge to hallway to a certain spot of a piece of sidewalk in front of a certain building. My marathon feet were useful; so was the old habit of endurance.

It was the growing necessity of doing without food that originally signaled my train of thought toward impasse. Standing in chorus lines, waiting in casting offices, I was getting nowhere. Now and then a club date would materialize, a five-dollar grubstake singing and dancing my old tramp routine to the tune of a hundred clattering dishes at some ladies' luncheon or Rotary Club meeting. But it wasn't good for morale. Occasionally I would pose for an art class: sitting or standing quite still for two hours at seventy-five cents an hour. It didn't add up to much, and even if I had worked up enough courage to accept posing in the nude, that paid but fifty cents more an hour.

"These jobs are all related, aren't they? To what you see yerself doin', I mean?" Ann was always right to the point. "Well, then, what others are the like? Let's look." We pored over a newspaper. "Now, here's a whole line a stuff, hear this: 'Models,' " she read, " 'five feet seven—' " Her eyes calculated my promise. "Look, thir's dozens of 'em, a whole coluyum full." I looked. "Models and actresses, it's the same, sure?"

I shook my head. "No, not the same, but closer than most, I guess." She almost pushed me out the door. "Go now," she said. "You'll be a model awhile and there's plenty a time to be a actress, you'll see." But there were longer lines in the garment center than anywhere else.

"You mean you never modeled before? Well, you don't just walk into it, you know." And then, "Experience? None? You're not a model, dear, until you've modeled." At least there wasn't any union. In show business you have to have the card to get the job, but you can't have the card unless you have the job.

Ann made tea. She boiled the black leaves for ten minutes. Steeped and strained it would have taken the enamel off an elephant's tusk. I loved it. I loved our discussions over the briny stuff. This time Ann was pensive. "I wanta share my good news with ya," she began, "only, I don't know what I'm gonta do about ya after it's told." She sniffed. "I'm to have a child of my own."

I gulped. "Oh, Ann," jumping up, almost spilling the brew, "—just so truly wonderful. Oh, Ann!" We clung together.

"Ya see, now," she held me away, studying my face, "I won't be comin' here ta help out. You got to get some work now, soon, so you can afford to get somebody else—and to eat better, too, so you'll keep strong." Her face was filled with concern.

"I will. I will, it's going to happen soon, now—for sure. You mustn't worry, Ann, not with—well, you have to be happy now, not all upset with someone else's problems." Guilt enveloped me. There had to be other jobs. Perhaps I wasn't trying hard enough. "How long do I have?" I asked.

"Well, now," she sipped her tea, "as soon as you can find somethin' will be good—soon?"

I hugged her hard. "Soon," I promised.

Answering ads, following leads, standing in lines were a simple task compared to returning home empty-handed under the gentle questioning of Ann. The moment of truth was a bad dream.

"There has to be some way to earn a living," I cried. "It's not like I'm asking for something for nothing. I can work and what I don't know I can learn."

Ann smiled. "How do you suppose I wound up in the groceries and himself in the vegetables? Tell me, now, have you got some family perhaps could help?" By now she knew there was no husband in the background, but nothing else.

"No," I said, "there's no one—I couldn't—it would be so hard to ask." I sat down heavily.

"Anything to pawn?" Her voice was soft. "Temporary, of course."

I shook my head. "I haven't enough for next month's rent, Ann." It was a hard confession. I was angry with myself. For being inept. Helpless.

"You can pay family back slow, you know. Not like a bank. You just make a true IOU out for them. Well, you can't go movin' around now. Not with a baby under yer arm you can't." Ann was right again.

"I'll ask." I didn't recognize my own voice. "Right now. I'll phone and then, if possible, I'll go right now while I have the steam. Okay?"

She smiled. "Okay," she said.

" 'A loan,' I'll say, 'just for a while until . . .' " Until what?

What could I use for collateral except my own arrogance?

"The number you are calling has been dis-connected."

I hung up the phone with that same old panic beating against my ribs. Why fly all apart whenever I try placing them and they aren't there? They've never stayed in one place. Neither have I, so why panic? Scolding myself for the tremble I could not control, I dialed my sister's number.

"What a nice surprise, dear. Where are you?" It was Mother's voice. "You sound like long distance, June."

Why did I have to stammer? "I'm—I'm n-not." Very clever answer.

"June? Speak up, dear, don't mumble. Long distance is expensive. What do you want?"

Why couldn't I be that direct? "Can I please come up to—to—see you?"

The phone jingled. "Wait, dear, these wires get me so confused—wait, I'll ask your sister."

I waited. "June? There's going to be a party here, so if you can come right away we can say hello before the guests arrive—all right?" I started to reply; my nickel clunked into the machine. Just before it went dead I heard Mother say ". . . a pay phone, imagine . . ."

After all, I was invited, if I got there fast. Why use another nickel to say I was on my way? In the subway I rehearsed. More than three months had elapsed since I had watched my sister's angry face whirling into darkness. I could tell them how strong, how beautiful the baby was now. Tell about the auditions and some of the people. About Ann. Walgreen's. Tell about the agent who saw me clowning in the hall outside his office. I was doing a cat with a bad head cold walking through a dark basement lined wall to wall with rats. The idea came from the powerful odor pervading the office. None of us were aware of the presence of the agent himself until we were interrupted by his coughing fit. He fought off a few well-meaning huskies trying to pound him on the back, grabbed me by the arm, and headed for the stairs.

"I'm—I didn't mean anything, honest—"

He walked me down the street so fast I was breathless. "Never mind." His voice was fluty, high. "Just remember that routine and do every single bit of it for the man you are about to meet."

Hardly able to believe my ears, I stumbled along for endless blocks beside my benefactor. "Who—I mean, do I know him?"

A nervous smile tampered with the grim set of his mouth. "We all know him," he said. But there was no introduction upon arrival. After he had given the password to the doorman, we were lifted many stories above Fifth Avenue. Another password to a Japanese gent who waved us down a dark hall. My new friend pushed me quite forcibly onto a stool. We waited.

My eyes grew accustomed to the gloom. There were tall lamps that resembled oversized incense burners. Small points of light escaped hundreds of punctures in the gleaming brass. The thickness of the carpeting underfoot made the silence of movement mysterious. Upon examination I discovered we had been walking on a sea of golden dragons. The walls were lined with Chinese figures all created in delicate silk—silk threads. The atmosphere was that of surely the fanciest Chinese restaurant in the world. I looked up to see how much of this was being checked out by my escort, but he was gone.

Auditions. Always in unexpected places. Mostly in theatre lounges, the disinfectant almost choking your words. Musty offices. I looked around at the Oriental elegance. This was the classiest audition spot I had hit. What was that routine on the stuffy-nosed cat going to do for me here? I began to perspire. Why couldn't I be nervous without getting soaked through? Even the roots of my hair were wet. Why be nervous in the first place? I had regaled many a group of contemporaries in many a hallway with one of those routines.

I stood up, shook myself like a dog, tail first. What was that magic phrase for courage? The one that never failed, according to that stagehand in Akron. You had to stand right in the wings almost at the moment you were to go onstage, and in a voice you yourself could hear, you said toward the audience: "You, you lucky sons-a-bitches, you're going to get to see _ME._" Then go out there fast. Never failed. There were some heavy drapes at the end of the hall. Good. "I'll use them for the wings," I thought.

Standing directly behind the satiny folds, I spoke in clear, concise tones. "You, you lucky sons-a-bitches, you're going to get to see _ME._" Taking a deep breath, I waited for the courage to fill my being.

"Is that so?" said a softly penetrating voice. I jumped. "You're supposed to enter as fast as you can after that, aren't you?" He was small, stooping a little, wearing a shawl with a fringe. Carpet slippers. He wasn't being friendly. "Come in, come in." The room was wide and tall. Heavy drapes, huge furniture. "No, no, don't sit. Stand over there." He sat. Almost disappearing into one of the giant chairs.

"Essence." It was a single, flat word. "Essence," he repeated. There was only one interpretation of that word for me. I started forward tentatively. "Essence?" he snorted. "Does the word have any other meaning than the basic soft shoe?"

I added the step, traveling along the length of the room.

"And a fol-de-rol," he prompted. I went into the classic old kick step. A scratchy humming was coming from the chair, then he was beside me.

"Way down upon the Swanee River—" I picked up the tune. We danced. "And a break—slappity—slappity—slap—" We were both a little breathless. He didn't smile, but he looked more friendly.

"There's the morning newspaper," he said, moving toward the monumental sofa. "Get it and come over here. Sit down. Give me your shoes."

I blanched. "I—I—can't—I'm—"

He repeated, "Give me your shoes." Each word was like an arrow. I removed my shoes, but hung on to them.

"You sing, sort of, as well, I'm sure—not great, but you and the audience get along, don't you?"

Tears stung the back of my eyes. "How do you know about— well, all . . . everything?"

His face creased. I guess it was his kind of smile. "We used to be royalty on the road, all right. Don't ever tell legit actors you're a vaudevillian, kid—they're snobs." He reached over the fat cushions for my shoes. "Watch this, now. Don't fold the paper like you did. Nope. The only way to make paper in the soles of your shoes really last is to put it in like this—see? And, this . . . so. Now, try it on." I slid my feet into my shoes. Dry. Comfy. You'd never know the soles were almost gone. "Good, eh?" I nodded.

"Well, now." He leaned back. I thought he looked wan. Some of the timbre was gone from his voice. "I'm trying to do a show—used to just go ahead—do it. But now I'm trying . . .

that's the word. Don't want to start working for anyone else, dammit. Anyway, I can use you." He eyed me—fondly, I thought. "Used to be lots of you . . . no more. The market for you isn't what it was . . . for me, either, I guess. . . ."

His eyes wandered about the room. "Isn't it cold in here?" he asked. "Here, have some hot cocoa with me." Lifting a cozy from a fluted chocolate pot, he poured two cups of steaming brown liquid. "Have some of these." He uncovered a mouth-watering array of sweets. "What you can't eat take with you." He was helping me stash five or six gorgeous pastries into a lacy napkin.

"When do you think you're going to do your show?" I asked.

"Think," he repeated. Then, cradling the empty cup listlessly, he sighed.

I could have knocked off the rest of the cocoa easily, but waited hopefully for an invitation. It never came. The smallish man was asleep. Or perhaps he had died, right there, wrapped in his fringed shawl, wearing his carpet slippers.

I looked around for something to write on. There was a clutter of papers on a desk the size of a banquet table. "I hope you remember me," I wrote. "I'm the one who did the soft shoe in the worn-out soles." I left my address and name. "P.S. Thank you." I also wrote myself a note on a small memo sheet I found. It was to remind me of where I had been and who this man was—who was he? I put the note I had written him on the tray.

I meant to go then, but the rest of the chocolate would just get cold sitting there, so I drank it. There was more than half a cherry tart he had hardly touched, so I finished that, too. I held the memo up to the light. There was some printing in the corner: "From the Desk of George M. Cohan." I stood a long time watching the smallish man sleep. Watching George M. Cohan sleep.

The subway jolted me back to reality. Yes, so much to tell my sister and Mother. I must get off at the next station and walk a few blocks to the Irving Place apartment where my sister lived in the penthouse. If I told them I had met and even danced with George M. Cohan, that he showed me how to really make use of newspapers in my shoes, about the chocolate and the pastries . . . and. . . . That had happened three months ago, almost, and when I asked the agent who had dropped me off about it, he said to forget any of it ever happened.

"The old bastard's always wasting everybody's time," he said.

I decided I wouldn't tell Mother and Gypsy about Mr. Cohan. I knew I had missed an opportunity some way, but how? What would my sister have done in my place? How would Mother have turned that meeting into an advantageous event? I could not figure the manner in which it would have been accomplished, but I did feel certain that Mr. Cohan would not have forgotten them.

28

The subway was almost deserted. The car lurched and staggered to a shuddering halt; its rubber-edged doors yawned jerkily. The platform always sent me into my Anna Karenina fantasy. This time I resisted the dubious thrill of imagining how it would be to end it all under the crunch and growl of those wheels. The train disappeared, taking all its clatter up the gleaming rails into silence. I tried to remember who it was that had so aptly named the subway an animated sewer. Inhaling as little as possible, I started toward the stairs, clutching my newly acquired photographs, complete with resume, the result of a gold mine I had fallen into quite by accident.

One of my sidewalk pals had told me about the Bruno brothers, a trio of photographers who were as broke as everyone else. They were in need of subjects and faces to use for a portfolio they were building in order to make their fortune in the world of commercial photography. They gave useful volunteers a complete set of résumé pictures. A fine exchange. All that was left to do was write in your credits and a little about yourself. You left these at the offices of producers, directors, and agents; then just put your wishful thinking to work.

If it hadn't been for my Norwegian beak, I would have been terribly pleased with those pictures. But then I remembered that Myrna Loy had one blue eye and one brown eye. I had pictures of myself in a wonderful hat staring pensively into a fancy wineglass. Tony said that was a double hook—hats and glassware. Then I sat looking straight at you—mystically, of course—the smoke from any brand of cigarette you wanted to sell sort of curling up between us. My most difficult task had been the physical-culture poses. Tony claimed that the series of back-breaking positions was a shoo-in for a new magazine. I hoped so for his sake. The Brunos were presently my best friends, aside, of course, from Ann. They kept saying they were positive that the world would get around to me. Patience and fortitude were their words.

I knew Mother and Gypsy would be happy with the new friends and all the progress I knew I was making in spite of the bleak present. I hoped there would be time to tell all my news and to show them the startling pictures.

The building faced Gramercy Park, a small, perfectly manicured square of green surrounded with stately black iron fencing. An ornate gate closed or opened if you possessed a key. The park was for residents only. The apartment house in which my sister lived was designed with a Moorish motif. You entered through a long series of arches, walking on a colorful mosaic runner complete with tassels. Much lacy grillwork decorated walls and elevator. It was like being thrust into another world. The doorman wore tassels, too. I had the feeling that he couldn't wait to get to work each day so he could dress up in his gorgeous costume. The elevator glided upward.

I was perspiring. Had they guessed the reason for my call? How could I begin?

I stood at my sister's door. My task was to convince my mother and my sister that I needed someone to go good for me—but just for a while. I would sign an IOU, and repay almost at once, with interest at the going bank rate. I took a deep breath and pushed the button.

Eva answered the door. Eva had begun as my sister's theatre maid, even though Gypsy was dressing with four other girls. It was Eddy's idea, and almost as good as the floor-length cape of orchids. Only stars had theatre maids, and in Ziegfeld's *Hot-cha!* Gypsy was a showgirl. Eva enjoyed the publicity, too. Her main function, however, was running the show in my sister's penthouse.

"You got your track shoes on?" she asked. "We're moving fast up here today! Here, put this in the elevator before the door closes."

I dragged the wooden box by its dangling ropes onto the floor, just as the gates clanged shut. I was on my way down again. A large man wrestled the box away when the gates opened briefly. There wasn't time to inquire if it was intended for him.

At the door again, I tried composing my thoughts.

"Oh, please, June—don't keep ringing the bell. Come in. Do you realize there are going to be dozens of people here in no time? And I am not ready—nothing is done!" She was wearing a filmy negligee. "Look," she almost wept, "I've broken a nail!" The hand she held up was tapering and white, the nails blood red and almost three inches long. "Never mind," she patted my head, "I'm glad you're here. We can talk while I bathe—then, please, June—" her voice dropped to a whisper—"get Mother out of here, will you? No wonder I've got colitis, gasitis and every known itis—here—" she shoved a beribboned box toward me—"put those fruit things in all these little dishes. I'll be with you in a minute."

We could see Mother across the hall in the dining room.

Gypsy sighed, "Wouldn't you know? Look! She's checking the guest list!" Gypsy disappeared in the other direction.

I had just begun on the little dishes when Mother arrived.

"You know, of course, June, that we aren't invited to the party?" Her eyes were wet, her voice very high.

"I'd like to talk to you," I began.

"Eat as many of those fancy things as you can, dear—it's all you're going to get here." Her voice rose. "The ingratitude!"

"Stop it! Stop right now!" My sister returned sans the negligee, wearing only her jewelry. It was gorgeous.

"Oh God, June," she wailed, "I just got that goddam rug up and now they've put it down again—"

I put the sweets aside and reached for the rug. She grabbed the other end.

"Don't just stand there, Mother!" We fought the thing into a roll.

"I'm not asked to enjoy the party." Mother's attitude was regal. "Why should I be treated like a slavey?" She picked over one of the little dishes.

Pushing on, I said, "I have something I need to ask you. . . ." I was dusting myself off.

"Good." My sister examined her nails. "Only one gone— I'll fix that in the tub. Come on, now—we haven't got long."

We followed her into a gold-into-blush-into-red bathroom. Eva had filled the tub with an exotically scented bubble bath.

"The jewelry!" I exclaimed, as my sister lowered herself into the foam.

"Good for them," she said. "I never take any of them off. Even sleep in them."

Mother sniffed, "Only because you are scared to death somebody's going to hit you on the head for them someday!" She leaned toward me. "It'll be one of her dear friends and backers who'll do it, too! You'll see . . . damn hoods."

Gypsy sighed. "All right, Mother, talk to June. That's what you wanted to do, isn't it?"

Mother made herself more comfortable on the little wicker stool. "You know, dear, I am all alone now . . ." she began.

"The curtain's halfway down, Mother," Gypsy prodded.

"How many months has it been, dear, since you left the hospital?"

I sat on the fur covering of the toilet seat. "Almost four," I answered.

"Well, dear, can't you read the painting on the wall?"

Gypsy soaped herself vigorously. "Get to the point, for God's sake, Mother. . . . Listen, June, we had a nice talk after your call. We know it's not easy with a baby and Mother is all alone, as she says, and, well, we want to help. Mother will adopt April and you won't be burdened anymore." She reached for a fluffy towel with a curly monogram. "You can marry some nice man or something."

Mother was holding a flowered box with a blue powder puff on top. "Put lots between your toes," she said to Gypsy before she turned to me. "I'll do for April what I did for your sister and what I tried to do for you."

Gypsy sat at a tiny vanity. She was gluing the missing three-inch nail into place. "Mother lives in the country now, in a wonderful house I found—"

Mother broke in: "I have turkeys, June, at last I have turkeys—not just chickens, mind you. I can look across a meadow and see horses and cows because there's a farm over the hill."

Gypsy put the first coat of blood-red lacquer on the new fingernail. "You don't have to answer today," she said. "Think it over and stay in touch and—"

Eva poked her head in the door. "Do you know there are ten guests already here?"

My sister almost spilled the nail polish. "Oh, God, Mother—you have to use the back entrance now. These people are important."

Mother choked. "You hear that, June? Those bums out there are important—"

Gypsy waved her hand to dry the enamel. "You know what I mean; this isn't just some spaghetti party. If you want to keep those goddam turkeys, you better get the hell out of here so I can be myself!"

Mother snorted. "Yourself? You mean so you can pretend to be that phony-voiced con artiste with the trick French gags and the filthy jokes, and waltz around half naked in all that flashy jewelry Eddy tosses your way, and— Darling, how many times have I told you to wear a bra? No matter how small a bust, a girl needs support."

Gypsy was stepping into a minute pair of lacy panties. "How many times have I explained to you, Mother, that it's too late? Everybody and his uncle knows exactly what my breasts look like, and who the hell cares? Out!" she cried. "Out, for God's sake, and let me go to work." Mother was gone. I looked around for the exit. "Eva will show you how to get to the back stairs, June. . . . Keep in touch." She was gone.

I stood a moment clutching my envelope of pictures. Should I leave them? Perhaps she would have time later to look at them? I reconsidered as Eva crooked a finger in my direction. In the service elevator I suddenly realized I was returning once more to Ann with nothing. I decided not to tell her about Mother and the adoption. In fact, I decided to forget the whole thing.

Looking back all the way, I'm convinced more and more of the strength of that permanent-press fabric from which we were all cut. Oh, sure, there were separate streams of emotions running fast within each of our secret selves. If the most powerful of these streams was affirmative, it ruled. All other feelings were subjugated.

The one affirmative stream was love. Outrage, fury, all other passions battered against it, but there it stood. A wall. One could disagree totally, fail completely to comprehend the other's desire. Demand. Offer. Rejection. But standing pat all the while was the oddball love we shared. The rest was undertow. Above the turmoil ran the stream of our lives, like a healthy surf washing over but not removing the permanent press of the fabric. Not one of us would have considered being another of us for one moment. No one of us ever did anything any other of us wished to be doing.

Now that's a bond. That may have been the answer. You can keep walking in a climate such as that. Keep walking. Up ahead someone will look at the pictures. It won't be the same, but it may work out for the better. Keep walking. Look ahead.

29 ⚘⚘⚘

Moving was easy—all I needed was the baby carriage.

Ann sold my cot and chair at the market. "That sum'll tide ya over for all that lookin' you do."

I slept on a love seat in the living room of the dark walkup Ann and her husband, Paul, called home. April was delighted to have an extended family, but the arrangement was doomed.

"It's the mornin' sickness, darlin's, I can't keep up, it makes me that weak."

For a while the rule was that anyone still on their feet did the cooking and cleaning.

Paul learned prepaternal diapering and baby care with a real live doll. "Look at the practice I'm gettin'," he grinned.

I finally tricked fate. I hung around the ladies' room of a building seething with wholesale showrooms. Admittedly, the first five of my victims resisted me, but persistence won. She was gorgeous. Long reddish hair, green-yellow eyes, exactly five feet seven, and just a little drunk.

"My feet are swollen out of my shoes," she moaned. "Haven't been to bed all night and I'm supposed to glide around in there all day." She plopped onto the worn leather chaise, kicking off her high heels.

"I know how to make your feet like new," I ventured. "Is there ice somewhere?"

She opened one eye. "Think you're in a bar?" She almost smiled. "Go in the office, ice in the big brown box. Aw, Gawd, I'm pooped."

I found a bucket, put in a little water and all the ice right up to the brim, waited till the bucket had frosted, then said, "Up, up on your seat." I pulled her up marathon-style, lifted her feet above the bucket, but before the plunge I said, "This won't feel good for a fifty count, but hold on, don't give up, because I guarantee you'll feel wonderful. Okay, hold on and count. One, two," and on "three" I plunked her legs up to the knee into the icy water. "Three!" I yelped as I sat on top of her in the traditional way. "Four, five, six, go on, count," I commanded.

I thought I heard a feeble voice, but not until I had got up to thirty did I realize I was alone. She was out cold. I don't know why I panicked; perhaps I thought I had killed her. She looked strangely happy. Quite relaxed. Dashing back to the office where I had got the ice I tried to find someone, anyone, but it was a ghost town. "A doctor," I thought. "Surely there must be a doctor in this great big building." I raced down the stairs three at a time, unable to wait for an elevator, to scan the directory in the lobby. No doctors listed.

By now wild with fear and guilt I clutched the arm of the man running the newsstand. "Something awful has happened." I tried pulling him along. "Please come, it's someone—I'm afraid—maybe—she is out cold—"

He looked alarmed. "Sam!" he yelled. A large man in overalls appeared. "Where is she?" asked the newsstand man. He turned to the other. "Another suicide, Sam? Could be—where is she?" He almost shook me.

"In the ladies' room," I said, "but she didn't kill herself." My voice was a wail.

"Shh." Sam took my arm. "Let's go up there—let's be calm." He moved me toward an elevator. "What floor?" he asked. I went blank. What floor had I been on? Looking up at the indicator, I saw with dismay there were thirty-six stories to this building. Thirty-six ladies' rooms. "We don't want the whole place to panic, do we?" whispered Sam. "So please calm down. Now, what floor were you on?"

I took a chance. "Seven," I said. But there was no one resembling my victim on that one or on eight, nine, ten. . . . Finally, Sam lost interest.

Emerging from the twelfth-floor ladies' room, I discovered he had defected. Perhaps I had dreamed the whole thing. Sitting on the stairs in an effort to regain my composure, I heard a babble of voices. I leaned over the railing. Sure enough, there was a lively crowd of girls about two stories below. A line for jobs? I followed the sound. The hall was packed, but I found my way to the end of a line and waited. As desperate as I was, perhaps I could fake my way as a model.

The turnover was rapid. Girls went in a big double door, emerging only a few moments later from a small exit at the back of the hallway. They all looked gorgeous to me. Some wore furs and jewelry. Some were sleek, some fluffy and cute. All wore high heels and silk hose. My shoes were of the serviceable kind. My hose had been mended many times. I began to perspire. Damn. The dress was shabby enough without dark circles under the arms. Heart and gizzard had about hit bottom when I felt myself jerked out of the line and dragged toward the ladies' room. My assailant was the beauteous redhead of the ice-bucket epic.

"You ever done this before?" She wore a divine suit, which was being removed rapidly.

"Uh . . ." I shook my head.

"I knew. Sure. Here, put these on." She kicked the sandals toward me. "No, not with those stockings, here."

We exchanged clothes as she giggled and prodded until a warm thread of confidence worked its way into my blood. "That was some magic trick you pulled on me this morning," she said. "Almost lost my job, but boy! When I came to, that ice had knocked hell out of my sore feet, whoopsy stomach, and even my doom-dome headache. Here, try this color lipstick. Boy, you sure saved my skin. . . ." She backed away to see the effect of her efforts. "Not bad, but now watch. Push in your ass; okay, now make tall, no, just from your neck . . . okay, now lift your chest . . . not out, just up. Follow me."

We walked across the tile floor a few times. Then she sort of dipped and turned. I mimicked. She moved toward a toilet, addressing it in a soft but businesslike tone. "This is a Chanel," she said, one leg slightly bent, arms gracefully held at the sides, "Number 582," she intoned, executing a lovely turn. Then over her shoulder she repeated, for the benefit of the toilet, "Chanel, 582." After which she glided away. I followed.

"Don't be afraid," she said. "They need you in there. You have style somewhere inside there. Good luck. I'll wait here. I don't want to be seen in these duds of yours."

That's how I got the job at Kalman & Morris Evening Gowns

in the garment center. Just in time, too. Ann wasn't carrying well. I hadn't had a moment's morning sickness with April, but poor Ann was now green most of the time.

It was a sunny day when we found the apartment on Columbus Avenue at Ninety-seventh Street. The price was right, and even though the interior was dark, you could climb out a window and find yourself in a postage-stamp garden. Well, there weren't flowers or grass, but it was outside.

"She can get the air out here." Ann measured the space expertly. "Ya see, it's safe to leave the little thing awhile; you can be watchin' from inside." We both agreed that, because the rooms were directly behind a Chinese laundry, it was protected. "You'd never know there was a soul there." Ann approved. So April and I took up residence in what Ann called "the garden apartment." She found a lady who wanted to help.

"Sure, she's gettin' on," Ann said, "but she can watch the baby while you work. Then when you come home, you can do for the family yerself. You can't expect a lady pushing seventy-odd to go draggin' a broom and scrubbin' around, now, can ya?" It was ideal. We were really on our own.

Eyeshadow and a wet, tanned-looking skin. Long platinum hair in a halo braid circling my head. The gowns at Kalman & Morris were shimmery. They floated. Romantic. Four steps to the curtain, a final glance in the full-length mirror, then enter. Instead of an audience, there was a circle of booths in the semi-darkness of the large room. In the booths sat the VIP buyers from all over. All different, all the same. The graceful turnaround and stance, with one knee slightly bent, took place on the lighted platform. These gowns were copies of originals or semi-copies; for the house bought perhaps three details to incorporate into their own version. The announcement, therefore, was legal: "This is a Balenciaga," or "This is a Chanel." Breathe in. "Number seven sixty-two." Pose a second, breathe out, then glide on a tour of each individual booth, repeating the same phrases. Having shown that gown to all, you went back to the models' room for a quick change into something equally gorgeous for a repeat performance. Personality was discouraged; it detracted from the main issue. Any display of humor or wit was instantly squashed for the same reason. You were there because you were a good-enough walking, talking hanger. Monotonous, but understandable from the owner's viewpoint.

After the effort of living up to those demands became routine, my spirits began to break out of my discipline. "This is a Canal," I would lisp, dipping just a bit drunkenly. Or, with the right knee in an exaggerated thrust, state flatly: "This-is-a-Main Boker." It worked. The buyer looked up from fabric to face. Calamitous. A model in the garment industry has no face. The buyer suffered shock. Warnings were heard.

"Don't be noticeable. You want to get fired?" Erin whispered harshly through the flimsy drapes. She was the ideal mannikin: slim, long-legged; her torso curved and undulated perfectly; small, chic head on a long neck. Yes, she was lovely.

"You're lucky just to be working at all, my dear, with those tits." It wasn't disapproval, just clinical appraisal.

The girl who had been hired after me snorted. "I'm not going to flatten down for some job, oozing around in a cloud of anonymity."

The complete one grew haughtier. "You," she said, "are a summer-fall temp. You won't have to flatten down for long." She was right. The temporary girls left as winter approached. I resorted to my best conduct. I didn't want to flatten down, but didn't want to be a temp like Shelley, either.

"Who needs this?" Shelley was packing. "I'm not a statue, I'm an actress."

Gorgeous nodded from her pedestal. "Sure, sure—aren't we all?"

I wanted to say I was an actress, too, but more than that I needed to stay on that payroll. "It's going down to zero tonight, dear. Bundle up."

Shelley turned at the door to fix a steady eye on her opponent. "If you see me billed," she said, "drop backstage? Cold—zero? Remember the name, Winters. Shelley Winters." She smiled at the rest of us. "That's the one who will be okay in the blizzard—whatever she's got is frozen stiff anyways. 'Bye." She was gone. The last of the temps. I still had my job.

There was a trolley that went downtown on either Broadway or Seventh Avenue . . . hard to remember which is which . . . ever— Anyway, a nickel was important money. You could go to all sorts of places on a nickel. You could use the phone, buy a giant pretzel, a tamale—a nickel was important money. If I ate one meal a day, dinner, and pocketed all the bread I could snag, it was easy to nibble through work hours using the proper lunch period for second-job hunting. Armed with the pictures Tony Bruno gave me in exchange for posing for his commercial portfolio, I made the rounds in a whirlwind. If there was a chorus call it was usually midday, so I went even though I had secretly given up, because in perhaps a hundred lineups I had yet to be chosen. The calls for straight plays and musicals were different. They went on and on into the evenings. I managed to get to every one I heard of.

The balm of time stimulates the growth of humor. In retrospect, even monstrous calamity is dwarfed, even comedic. That is, if the negatives match the positives of your own personal battery.

The Belasco Theatre. The end of the rainbow. They were synonymous to me as a child, although I hadn't seen either. Fairytale horizons. The Langwell Hotel on Forty-fourth Street was only a few hundred yards away from the clamor of the raid. I hung perilously from the window of our room to get the best possible view as the cast and even some of the audience were escorted from under the glowing marquee to the waiting Black Marias at the curb. Lights spelled out the name "Lenore Ulric" above and along the sides of the theatre, while the title of the play blinked below: *Lulu Belle.* Grownups raised their eyebrows when mentioning the play or star; whatever went on during that performance was considered "blue" by the vaudeville code. Nevertheless, it was legit. Lenore Ulric didn't ride in the wagon. She emerged swathed in furs, posed in glamorous defiance for the press, then was swallowed by a long black limousine. I tingled, but that was long ago when legit stars came in many shades. Mae West took a few rides, too. Though appearing on the boards of those theatres they didn't seem to be *of* those boards. When the Belasco stage was graced by stars of more subtle shading the picture was in perfect balance. My longing was for thralldom. The tingle was a frivolous side trip.

When told a play was being cast and the call was at the Belasco Theatre, a thrill went all the way to my toes. This time there was no line, no small groups of competition. It was late afternoon. I had hurried from work, complete with wet look and halo braid. The doorman barely glanced up from his paper. "Go out front, up the aisle, through the lobby, down the stairs to the lounge."

The stage was bare. The house slept under the watchful glow of a single work light hanging over what we called "two." First came the apron, one, and then two. The view was breathtaking as I walked slowly from the farthest point of upstage center. When my heart was stilled a bit I walked even more slowly down. Down— I was center of two—then one, finally. I stood right in the middle of the apron on the boards of the Belasco Theatre. Impossible to try for a deep breath, but I did.

Gilt, plush, crystal. The red velour curtain was parted. It had been bagged at either side of the stage in canvas socks. No dust fogged the air. Clean. It was all so well cared for. A valuable. A treasure. Untarnished by adventures (that was then); corrosion wasn't visible.

Up the aisle as slowly as my body would move. Make it last. Stretch this moment. The garnet-carpeted stairs down. As I descended, I fingered the red velvet which covered the balustrade. At last I stood on the cherished tile of the ritual spot. I was in the right place at the right time. The traditional casting cloister. I was in the Gents Room of the Belasco Theatre on West Forty-fourth Street in New York City. The Great White Way. Broadway.

A girl about my age moved toward me. She was checking people in. I drew a photograph from my envelope. She took it, looked at the back, then smiled. She wasn't beautiful. She was beauty. Pale brown hair pinned in a soft knot, perfect skin. Simple dress. Her voice cool, almost caressing. "Your biography?" I blinked. She sat us down at a tiny desk. "I need to know your credits. . . . I'll write them down if you'll give them to me." Pen poised, she waited.

Hold on to that moment. Stretch the time. Each second is nourishment. What was the familiar acknowledgment for a show stop? The vaudevillian would hold up his hands until the audience quieted. "Applause and laughter," he told them, "is food and wine to a performer, and—well, I want to thank you for the nice, big banquet."

Focus returned. The small white hand held a silver pencil. Nails clean of polish with pale half moons. "Any plays at all you have been in . . . school?"

I stared at that little hand. "No," I blurted, "I've never been— done a real play." I looked at her fully. "I'm nobody," I said.

She returned my gaze. "If you really believed that you wouldn't be here." The voice had no caress now. "There are all sorts of other places . . . choices . . ." She almost smiled, then ran one of those cool, long fingers down the length of my face. "Too much." She displayed the finger sticky with residue from my wet, tanned look. Made it circle around my platinum halo. "Jean Harlow imitation? Or whatever is inside those wrappings? If you are confused about who you are, how is some casting director supposed to feel?" The awful heat began crawling up my neck. "Anyway," she said, "there isn't anything in this play for you."

I found a voice. "Is it because—because—?"

She patted my arm. "You are just too—well, too much of everything." She moved away toward another shadow emerging from the stairs.

There were plenty of mirrors available. The models' room was lined with them. They ran along the shelves for makeup. Tall ones at all sides of the room. A guarantee that the gowns were being carried to the best effect. At last there was that tall, wide one at the top of the stairs for the final check. I studied them all. Under the platinum hair was a greenish ash shade. Skin under the tan makeup was olive. Without chiffon and sequins the body was almost athletic. Not muscular, but strong. Proportions adequate but not spectacular. The body carried itself easily and well. What about the mind? Was I, as my sister often said, "unbright"? What did that mean? I was on the wrong track, no doubt about that.

I looked around the models' room. Three other girls very like myself. Chosen for measurements. Two were working wives who worried mostly about getting home in time to clean the house and cook dinner. Erin was hopeful of a career as a photographer's model. They were on the right track. No advice from them would be helpful.

Henry threw a gown my way. "Hurry in," he ordered. "And no comedy, huh? I got a hot repeat."

The gown was flame red. I examined myself again before I stepped onto the platform. Too much? Maybe, but who could tell me what wasn't? "Number 683," I intoned.

The buyer was a squat lady with very thick glasses. "This is the same old rag," she whined. "Every time I sit here you drag out that same dreary old rag." Her voice rose. "I said no before, Henry. I say no now. It's a dull old tatty rag."

Henry smiled. "We got it in blue, too," he said. I glided toward the arch. With the walls papered with Henrys, who was there to give advice to whoever I was? What if I was trapped? Could this be a dead end?

30 ❧❧❧

Thanksgiving, 1935. Overcast, wet, cold.

"There's no sun out in that hole except for one hour come noon." Della was large. Her gray hair wisped from an attempted control in the form of pins and even combs hugging the sides of her head. Her jowls shook when she was unhappy. "Besides, a dog got in between those boards there. He was licking her face."

April looked no worse for the show of affection. She was ruddy and solid. We sat on a blanket on the floor. "We can't move for a while," I explained. "I have to find a steady second job, you see.'

Della's jowls trembled. "Peace," she mumbled. Della was in love with Father Divine. Advice from her would have to be channeled. "I had turkey with dressing today at the meeting." She was dangling a worn teddy bear toward April. "Why don't you see the light? It isn't too late. They're giving out turkey until eight."

I put my arms around her. "Peace," I said. "I'm not hungry, Della, and I need advice about other things first. Honest, I'm okay in the faith department."

April was getting too big to sleep in her wicker basket, but she cuddled into the warmth with a smile. Della lay heavily on the bed with her Bible. "You gotta eat something, child. It's Thanksgiving. Everybody has a full belly. Peace." Her brow wrinkled in worry.

"The Brunos invited me." A small lie would be forgiven. "I'll just walk over there for a while . . . Peace."

The air was getting real teeth. I walked faster. Advice at the Bruno studio would be plentiful as always, but not particularly practical.

Laughter greeted my frost-stung ears as I climbed the stairs.

"Just in time." Tony's arms were around me. "We are celebrating." He led me into the huge room. Two standing cameras with related lights and equipment were the main furnishings. A few odd chairs and tables had been rescued from sidewalk garbage collectors. These were in a circle; the party had settled in. "Guess!" Tony was jubilant. Other faces wore the look of triumph.

"A magazine ad!" I almost shouted. A negative murmur all around. I thought hard. "An—an account from an agency."

Tony took stage: "A whole, complete picture layout." The announcement was stunning. "Joe Bonomo's Physical Culture." The group applauded.

"But he makes candy. . . . I mean, he—he has that factory."

Vic Bruno shook his head. "Nope. He is somebody else, too. He is a muscle builder." I must have looked mystified.

"Used to be a strong man." Tony laughed, "Don't you see? It's work for all of us. We can shoot the series at night. Nobody has to give up a regular job."

Vic held out a large box. "Here," he said. "Celebrate. Mom sent dozens of 'em from Boston." The box was sticky, the cookies wet and red. "Wine cookies." Vic grinned. "Don't get too drunk."

Tony held up a cookie. "Let's toast," he said. "This may be all we eat this year, but next Thanksgiving we might all be rich." We dug into the sweet, gummy squares.

"Use actors, I told him." Tony acted out the scene. "Actors can nearly all dance, and if you can do that, surely you can do those muscle-building positions. So he says, 'Why not?' and it's all set."

We chewed happily for a moment. "We gotta be patient," he added, "because it's all on spec. But a great book like that on anybody's physical well-being has to be a big success, and that's when we get our share."

When the gaiety subsided I got a moment alone with Tony and his brother Vic. They listened attentively while I explained my dilemma. "So, if I don't seem to be what I think I could be because I look like something I'm not, what do I do?"

Vic's face lit up. "Who do you admire most of all?"

That answer came easily. "I don't want to be a look-alike. I want to be my own self."

He nodded understandingly. "Yeah," he said. "Harder. Much harder."

Tony paced thoughtfully.

"I'm not afraid of hard," I cried. "Hard is easy and it'll be worth it."

Tony stopped mid-pace. "Listen," he said emphatically. "Now listen carefully. You remember up near Boston, only a few years ago, your sister was just another one of those naked girlies playing just another one of those flea-bitten burlesque houses?"

I nodded. Gypsy's act then matched the environment. Naked at the end of her number, my sister had none of the wit and glamour that was her eventual trademark. She talk-sang "Minnie the Moocher" in the traditional stripper style. When finally down to the G-string and surprisingly small bare breasts, her bumps and grinds wore the usual blue spotlight. After those shows we always avoided any reference to how we were living.

I was in transit from one marathon to the next, which was to be at Revere Beach in Boston. Neither of us was bragging. The meeting in Lowell, Mass., was especially brief because of a violent brawl backstage. Something about Gypsy's costumes not belonging to the company. Mother kept dragging things onto the sidewalk and stuffing them unpacked into a taxi. Finally she threw a coat over my sister, who was clad only in shoes that glittered eerily on the pavement. As they drove off, the man who had been screaming obscenities at them waved his fist at the departing cab. There was little time for us to discuss "the act."

"I remember," I told Tony.

"Well, June, she found out who she is. That's a far cry she is doing at the Irving Place Theatre from Lowell, Mass., huh?"

Vic chimed in, "Alla those diamonds, too."

Tony shot him a glance.

"Well," he responded, "they're real, aren't they?"

Tony grunted. "What other stripper is doing Dwight Fiske's material on a burlesque stage? It's the Persian Room at the Plaza right down on Fourteenth Street. Sure, she can give you the advice."

Eddy. My sister had said that he had given her someone special to be. The girl in the floor-length cape of real live orchids at the opening night of the Met. The one with the funny French phrases. Quotes. And of course, the evidence of wealth. Penthouse. Diamonds and furs. Champagne and the people who match it. Glamour galore. Dwight Fiske himself out front loving the gag.

"I'll go," I said. "But it's not the diamonds. I just want—"
Looking at my friends I realized what I thought would never wash
with them as truth. No one except those who are addicted can
appreciate the devastating strength of that longing for one special
stage. Not the glitter, but the quiet membership. First the earned
right to belong; then, if needed for any one of all the reasons
that follow, then the jewels and furs and any other adornment,
interior or exterior. Only then. Not as a route. But as a reward,
and only if deserved. Surely someone knew the first step. The
first door. I just wanted to know where to begin.

The Brunos were in the same boat, but we just weren't growing oars fast enough. Youth and inexperience weren't their itch.
Tony had come from California. A failed marriage and a desire
to change his billing, which read: "Bruno of Hollywood." The
name and field stayed the same for them, but when these events
were taking place in 1936 I had no real name. I was still Jean
Reed. The title under which I hid in the marathons. I smiled at
Tony. "I'll go," I repeated.

The doorman knew me so I pushed the right button and
rode the elevator up to the right floor. I hadn't phoned this time.
It was late and I knew Gypsy was through at the theatre. I was
too intent on Jean Reed's future to realize how inept Jean Reed
was in the present.

A tall girl in gold lamé opened the door for me. Music underscored a buzz of conversation. "I didn't know there was a party."
I backed away.

"No," she said. "No party. Just us. C'mon in. Hey, everybody," she yelled. "Look, looky here, Halloween!"

General laughter. I shrank into my skin. "Never mind them,"
she whispered. "They're all on a cloud. Gimme your coat. . . .
Okay, now, what's your poison? You name it, we got it." Her
eyes dilated. Speech was thick but concise. She tossed my coat
onto a pile, partly covering an array of furs and brocades. It looked
like a tarpaulin protecting the goods.

I turned; the girl was gone. Bad timing, I thought, never
get a moment alone at a party. Wishing I had called first, I bent
to retrieve my coat. The belt had joined forces with some kind
of furry tails.

I was working on the problem when I heard the command:
"Don't move. Just put that cape down—go on, put it down." I

dropped my coat and the cape of fur tails before looking up. "Oh, for God's sake, June, what are you doing here?" I held up the intertwined garments. "Who did you come here with?" my sister asked as we disengaged the tails.

"No one," I answered. "I wanted to talk, but I didn't know—"

She waved toward the noise. "Getting on my nerves. Let's go. I'd like a cup of coffee without sound." She started away. I followed. "I'll get some money."

The singing came from the den. But we went through the dining room. My sister continued on, but I stopped in my tracks. The table had a ring of pots and pans filled with water. A group of giggling people circled slowly, stopping at a pan or pot long enough to inhale from a cigarette, blow the smoke into the water, then inhale deeply once more. The game didn't look funny but the participants obviously found it hilarious.

My sister returned; I fell into step behind her. "Your guests, won't they—"

She overruled my doubts. "They'll never know I'm gone." She took the first wrap available from the pile. "God," she said, "look at this. . . . Talk about ostentatious. . . ." She threw the long white mink over her shoulders.

"But just look at those things." I pointed to the wrap composed of ermine tails.

"That's mine," she said. "Come on, here's the lift."

I laughed. "The lift?"

She arched her back in a pose. *"Sois chic, sois gentille,"* she murmured.

It was only a couple of blocks to the restaurant. "Yak a mein," she told the waiter.

"Two, please," I added, "with lots of scallions chopped fine." I inhaled the familiar fragrance of the Chinese cooking.

"You see," my sister whispered, "you can take the girl out of the yak a mein, but you can't take the yak a mein out of the girl." She grinned.

"I'm glad," I said. She emptied a jigger of brandy into her cup of black coffee. "Thanks for leaving your party and the games, and—"

She looked at me over the rim of the cup. "What games?"

I put three sugars in the tea, the rest of the little packets in my bag. "The dining room—" I began.

"Really, June," Gypsy sighed. "Marijuana, dear. It's a better lift that way. Ever try it?" I shook my head. "Well, I had to give it up." She was lighting a Turkish cigarette. "Makes me too agreeable. I'm not giving anything away, I'm selling it. Sweet? Submissive? May as well be a housewife. Nope, it dims my luster, makes me resemble others—that's the worst thing that could happen." She held out the cup. "Now, brandy makes me shine. I don't want my mind souped up or down. I just want my elastic tightened inside and out."

The yak a mein was heaven. Between eating and listening I didn't get much said, but it didn't matter. There was a lot of advice inside the talk. "Sorry I growled at you over those coats, but everybody steals everything from me. I've got to police everybody all the time."

Between swallows I offered some advice of my own. "Why not let Mother help?"

She put down her cup. "Mother," she said, "is the biggest thief of all." She mixed another brandy and coffee. "Everybody thinks it's all so easy. Sure. Mother says I'm the most beautiful naked ass—well, I'm not. I'm the smartest. Look at that." She tossed a newspaper across the table. I read: "Gypsy Rose Lee says her favorite fan sits in the front row at every performance with a lunch box on his lap and his room number printed on his forehead." She sipped her coffee. "If I can keep saying things like that in all those columns I'll be a fad."

I put the paper down. "You want to be a fad?" I asked.

"Of course not." She was patient. "I want to be a legend. A fad is just one step along the way." The pear-shaped solitaire on her finger glittered. At her throat was a cluster of diamonds in the shape of a bouquet of flowers. A few bracelets shot colored lights. "What about you?" she asked.

"All those diamonds," I said. "Aren't you afraid of someone stealing them, too?"

She went pale. "Scared to death," she whispered. "That's why I never take them off. Even sleep in them. Any thief who wants them will have to fight me, fight me hard."

It was indeed a hard fight about two months later, but all the jewelry was stolen. Even the pear-shaped diamond ring. Gypsy tried swallowing it, but the thug rapped her so hard on the back she spit out the diamond, loosening a few teeth, as well. Mother should never have told the insurance people that Gypsy knew the thieves by sight, because there is some clause about that, and they don't have to pay. But all that was later.

"Well," I began, "I'm modeling and doing the rounds and—"

Gypsy finished her coffee. "What about April?" she asked.

"She's beautiful," I answered, "and fat and—"

She chuckled. "Like I was? Don't let it get a grip—you can't hide fat with a blue spotlight." She called for the check. "Think I've got a lovely job coming up, June. It means the road, but you'll be proud of me." She dabbed at her mouth with a lipstick.

"I'm proud now," I said.

"Let's say you're prouder now than you were, huh?" Snapping the compact shut she rose. "Don't forget," she yanked the mink over her shoulders, "Mother's offer still stands about April." I started up the street with her. "I'll drop you here, June."

We stood on a windy corner. I looked up into her face, speaking loudly because of the sound effects. "Nobody wants to have a baby and then let someone else have it. Even if it's your family it's—it's not—"

She pitched her voice against the wind, too. "It's your timing, June. We worry about you."

I choked. "What if it was your baby and I was the one who—"

She moved us against the shelter of a building. "I'll have a baby when I have the time . . . when I have the money. . . ." Her voice strengthened. "And I won't have it by sweetness and light, June, because that's not what the world respects. I'll find the hardest, most ruthless son-of-a-bitch available without strings because my baby won't be a victim of the world, my baby will beat the hell out of anything that gets in the way." She was a little breathless.

"Well, how do you know mine won't?" I was a little breathless myself. The wind howled around that corner. Suddenly I was in my sister's arms.

"Goddam them," she sobbed against my head. "They think everything's so goddammed easy." My own tears began stinging my cheeks. "I wish to God I didn't worry about you, June, but you don't make it easy." She sneezed. "There," she sniffed accusingly. "If I catch cold in this frigging wind, it's going to be all your fault!"

I pushed her away. "Go on home, go inside," I yelled. "I'm fine! Don't worry, I'm going to be okay!"

She looked back once. "Like hell you are!" she shouted.

31

We settled in an L-shaped room at a theatrical hotel on West Forty-seventh and Broadway. April took the sun on the roof, and I could get a five-course dinner and all the rolls I could pocket for fifty cents in the dining room. Around the corner from the Palace Theatre, the hotel had enjoyed being host to hundreds of acts I remembered. I read their billing, ringing the walls in gilt letters, as I ate. Patsy the Horse. Mallia and Bart. Bert and Betty Wheeler. And on and on. A little stage still stood at one end of the dining room, even though the days of beefsteak suppers and fish fries had ended.

The Somerset could boast but a few straggling vaudevillians now. The lobby was festooned top to floor with framed photographs. It was like coming home. Intelligence informed me the Somerset was a suspended museum, to be dropped at any moment into the crevasse, but I snuggled into the environment as though it was endowed forever.

I had just stashed the rest of the rolls, generously buttered, into my bag, when I spotted the hotel manager weaving his way toward me between empty tables. It wasn't only rolls and butter; sometimes I made myself triple-layered catsup sandwiches, too. Could he be on his way over to discuss this? No. He wouldn't be all smiles like this. Then I saw that he wasn't alone. There were a nice-looking woman and a natty man in his wake.

"I'd like to make you acquainted with someone, Miss Reed. This is Freddie Lightner, a great act indeed." I stood up to shake hands. "And his wife, Rosella." Mrs. Lightner nodded.

"Sit down, honey—you better." Her husband's solicitude had an anxious ring.

"I got to put up this picture right away," said the manager. "Yup, all our famous clientele get featured spots on the walls. You bet." He waved the frame, but I couldn't see who it was.

Freddie sat opposite me. "That's some great publicity you got there, and it looks enough like you to recognize, too—don't it, Rosy?"

I wondered where a picture of me had come from. Why? And the manager had said "famous." I didn't puzzle for long. Freddie jolted me out of my seat.

"I got six weeks booked, you see, and—well, the little lady can't play 'em. Can't work for a while." Rosella looked wan; it was easy to see that she wasn't well. "Now, you got all those modeling things you do, and, uh—I can't pay you what you get for that, of course, but you'd look great in the act. It's just until we . . ."

I turned to Rosella. Her face was a mask. "I'm sorry you aren't well," I said.

Her chin went up. "I'm fine, I'm perfectly fine." She wanted to cry. Freddie patted her hand.

"We never had a stranger in the act before this," he said, "but we got to play those six weeks. We can't do the act together now, because we—we're pregnant."

There was a silence. I didn't know where to begin. To yell out, "Yes, yes! Oh, yes! But I'm sorry you don't feel well! But I'm glad, too—how awful! But how wonderful!"

"I could pay a hundred dollars a week," he continued. "You won't have travel expenses, because we go by car."

The Lightners looked at one another, and I knew the stranger in the act would be a personal invasion. Watching the silent oneness brought a rush of remembering. They hadn't altered with time. They had remained the same. Unspoken word for word, a team.

"You don't do much. You see, I'm the act. I just need a pretty girl to bounce a few jokes off of. . . ."

Kalman & Morris surprised me.

"When you hit the big stem, I'll be out there in the first row, rooting." Mr. Kalman meant it. "And listen—that gown you been 'borrowing'?" His eyebrows danced up and down like a comic's. "Take it—keep it. Use it in the act. It's an old number, anyway."

I not only wore it in the act, but for the next few years that gown was my theatrical wardrobe.

We left for Atlantic City in a blizzard. Sitting in the back seat, I could guess the extent of Rosella's nerves. Freddie was at the wheel, but she was driving, too, pumping away at imaginary brakes, shifting invisible gears—it was dual driving and it scared me to death.

Sliding up to the unloading dock of the theatre at last, I saw Rosella's face. It was gray. They went about their usual tasks, while I wandered into the theatre alone. There it was, waiting. The pinkish smells, the cathedral-like silence. We were very early.

No one tending the castle but the old doorman dozing at the stage door. Wandering onstage, I rolled myself into the velour arms of the house curtain, and whispered my joy at being home.

"Home." That word conjured up visions. Visions that were ever and always right behind my own reality. I could see, smell through or beyond whatever restaurant, furnished room, hotel, or upper berth happened to be the temporary shelter of any particular sliding moment. Somewhere, over some rainbow, was H.O.M.E.

But theatre itself was always the consummate reality, needing no superimposition; the one permanent structure in life. Theatre. The true meaning of the word "home."

Many words have lost the impact they carried when I was part of that time. For instance, "charm," "forever," "elegant," or "lady." The blockbuster word then was the word "mother." Whether in song or rhyme, that word was synonymous with sainthood. A word with clout, power. The power of tradition. Tradition—now there's another all but obsolete word.

What I mean is, anyone's half a century—give or take a little—tends to squeeze a point of view into the size of a pinhole. Values shift. Long ago, certain terminology was certain magic. M.O.T.H.E.R. could easily move an audience to tears. Naturally, there had been some of this popular narcotic woven into "Dainty June and Her Newsboy Songsters."

Among those "songsters" had been a small Italian boy. Mother called him John. He was one of seventeen rickety offspring, hatched by an illiterate father who picked slate from piles of coal in a dark, starving town that clung to the side of a scraped-out hill somewhere in Pennsylvania and a mother who was no more than an exhausted little animal with no mind at all. John's family huddled together in an abandoned hut, slept on straw, ate scraps. Miraculously, they sang, all eighteen of them. The most persistent singer was John; his voice was strong, clear, and true. Although speaking in a contrived equivalent of English, they thought in Italian; consequently, they sang in Italian.

John sang in the street in front of the theatre we were playing.

Mother collected him as we collected stray dogs. Bathed, fed, and dressed, John appeared in the act. Mother moved him gently onstage in the darkness. A small spotlight focused on his face, just his face, because John's small frame was warped. Mother didn't want the audience to feel compelled to pity, so she created a tableau behind him to keep visual attention elsewhere.

Mother's dramatization was simple: a rocking chair; a traditional mother—graying wig, lavender, and lace—reading to her children, who sat adoringly at her feet; soft lights dimming in, then slowly fading to dark, the dark that covered John's shuffling exit. Thus it was that John's voice dominated the moment.

John loved his song; it had deep meaning for him, and he sang with a full heart. "EM e cosi milione m' 'a dato" (M is for the million things she gave me), "O significa h'invecchia" (O means only that she's growing old). . . .

It was the right emotion at the right time. It wasn't only the audience who responded. I responded to John's passionate homage to "Mother." It stuck somewhere deep inside my tissues, for a long, long time. Along with behaving like an elegant lady with charm forever, who was of course a virgin.

Mother had been gallant about taking care of April.

"When you see how much better she is after being out in the country air with me, you'll make a deal, I bet you."

Parting from April had tempered my joy. Mother found a high chair; April sat center stage in the heavily trafficked kitchen, watching the bustle with shining eyes. Mother was making root beer.

"I know this isn't permanent, June. I keep reminding myself I'm not a mother again, I'm just a convenience." She sniffed. "Store your things, leave your responsibilities—believe me, if I was in the business of holding other people's forts, I could charge a lot more than five measly dollars a week."

Instead of the five, plus picking up the food bills, I figured it was wiser to pay a flat fifteen again. I was going to be too far away to check those bills.

Mother had other paying guests. Mostly leftovers from the spaghetti parties—"lonely, unhappy lost souls." She didn't need much help to run the farm while they resided there—"Busy hands make busy minds." There were a vegetable garden, fruit trees, turkeys, chickens, and ducks. For eggs only, of course—"Only a cannibal could eat a friend." There was a great deal of pickling, preserving, and jelly making. "A wholesome nest is all anyone needs to mend a broken life."

Poor "little Mary," "Raymond," and "Pete" were the shifting cast of characters in Mother's productions.

"Poor Walter" was one of Mother's saddest examples—a misdirected youth who had wandered too far from the fount.

"He meant well, which is one of the worst things you can say about anybody, I guess." Mother's eyes misted at this point. "So generous—always giving me gifts, lovely things for the girls. Just twenty-two years old, mind you. A cavalier. Beautiful smile, nice teeth. When the police came, he was in the kitchen, enjoying a mug of homemade root beer." She was genuinely saddened by the memory. "When those men told me that Walter had paid for everything—all the lovely meals, gifts, everything—with money he got from forging checks, I nearly fainted. 'Why, he is like my own family,' I told them, 'thoughtful and kind and generous.'"

The cops had been very sympathetic. "Most forgers are," they said.

"I asked them to give me a little time alone with the boy before they—well, they did have positive proof. He really had to go to jail." After a second, Mother continued. "Who could ever guess that little Walter knew so much about crime? Why, he had swindled successfully for three whole years before being caught."

Mother leveled with Walter. "They have you cornered, dear. Society demands you pay. How on earth did you ever do all that forging, Walter?"

He showed her exactly how. It didn't take long.

"And then, dear, what did you do wrong? Show me—what was it?"

Walter was considerably sobered by the presence of the cops in the adjoining room. "I just don't know, Roanie," he confessed. "I can't imagine how they caught me."

Mother was pensive. "Tsk, tsk," she clucked. "You see, dear, you should have learned what not to do first of all."

After that advice, and a loving pat on the head, Mother said goodbye to Poor Walter, and called in the cops. This was the hardest part to tell: "He asked me to write to him in prison,

and I meant to, but the address was lost somewhere on the road."
She always had to fight tears telling of Walter.

"Even I can't finish what God didn't begin," she would murmur in conclusion.

After Atlantic City, the Lightners and I played the Earle in
Philadelphia. Freddie was very funny onstage. It was hard to keep
my laughter silent. After all, I was "straight woman." I fed him
lines for his gags, sang while he clowned, and at the end of the
act we exchanged jokes while dancing a soft-shoe routine. Gentle
comedy, popular then.

Rosella spent a lot of time with me, helping with my makeup
and costume, showing me how to let the audience know I was
amused and charmed with Freddie, without ever getting in his
light. It was Kalman & Morris all over again, except that now it
wasn't a gown, it was a comic.

"That's a giggle you're getting, kid—a giggle on a feed line
is bad structure. A hole in that bag of grain you want to deliver,
see? By the time you get to the yok, you've spilt your oats slow,
no good. Don't clutter up the road with titters when I'm on my
way to a five-minute belly." Freddie's every word was money in
the bank for later.

Loew's State on Broadway was one of the few remaining
eight-on-a-bill big-time houses. Still straight vaude. The band
wasn't onstage behind you, it was still properly down in the pit,
where it belonged, so you could work to the conductor and the
boys. Subdued by the four weeks out of town, I played straight
woman as well as I knew how.

A few days into our run, Freddie knocked at my dressing
room door. "You decent, kid?"

Properly draping a makeup towel over my bra and panties,
I called, "Yup!"

His face was drawn, eyes red and swollen. "Jean—just for
the early show—can you take the song? And maybe the pan gag,
too? I'm . . . it was a boy—perfect—he would have been tall,
the doctor said—he had a lotta hair, too. . . ." Freddie collapsed
into a chair. "We weren't meant to have kids, I guess. . . ." He
looked at the mirror. "God, look at me. We're on in a few minutes." He got to his feet shakily. "Rosy says don't worry, she'll
be up and at 'em in no time—but for this early matinee, take
the song, willya? I'll be okay after that."

Just like in the movies, someone important just happened to be out front. I got a new job with the St. Louis Municipal Opera. My contract said I was general understudy, but the real title of my position was H.A.P.—translation: Half-Assed Principal. I was in heaven—booked for the entire summer! The Lightners went Midwest to play ten weeks of "interstate time," I went back to the Somerset and Kalman & Morris until summer and St. Louis. But first I went out to collect April. She was fat and sunny.

Mother was adamant. "You can't drag that baby out to a Godforsaken hole like St. Louis, June! Do you remember the heat?"

It wasn't easy to forget. The plains vibrated under a torrid sun all summer. Even during the commonplace thunderstorms, the temperature remained in the hundreds. I remembered wading in a torrent of rainwater—it was as warm as a good bath.

"Three months is a long separation," I said.

Mother sighed. "Look, June, I'll take her for ten a week, no strings. Your own mother's instinct should tell you it's one hell of bargain."

I hesitated.

"You have a couple of months to decide what's best for your baby, but I can't do it for less." It wasn't the money that decided me in the end.

My rehearsal schedule arrived with the contract that changed my name. Knowing Jean Reed and I had to part, I had started to sign that first-of-all contract with my real name, Hovick. I had just put down the H when I realized my sister had been forced to use that name. In Hollywood. It seemed that film censorship had stepped in. The powers who had bought Gypsy Rose Lee were forced to agree that the name was too hot to handle, so for the movies she was to be Louise Hovick. . . . My hand dribbled the rest of the letters onto the dotted line. It came out as Havoc. June Havoc. I didn't like it but didn't know what to do about it. My schedule read:

Rehearsal 9:30 A.M. to 5 P.M. One half hour for lunch.
2 Matinees a week at 2:30 P.M. Evenings at 8:30.

With eight shows a week, that meant playing one show while rehearsing the following show. I thought seriously of leaving April with Mother again. That's when events changed my mind.

168 ೫

Spring, 1936, at Kalman & Morris was autumn of the same year. Wearing the forecasted gowns was like skipping the intervening months altogether. Outside, in the real world, my life was beginning to take on direction. Fear of dependency had compelled me to stash every unworking penny inside the grouch bag. The small crocheted purse fastened with a snap. Still pinned securely to my bra. It would be a long trip to the meaning of the word *bank*. Grouch bag was interim security without interest.

My workaday costume was improved by a small brown hat rimmed with reddish flowers, the wet-look halo effect abandoned for a more relaxed parcel. Lunch hours still were used for scouting moonlighting jobs. Daytimes were work investments, with early morning and evening hours to delight in April. At eight P.M. she slept. The work part of my routine was a solid run. I don't recall experiencing fatigue of any kind, but my feet complained most of the time. I blamed that on the peculiar use of them: Toe dancing at two. Dance, dance, segue into seven marathons. Go directly from them into modeling, which is a long, long walk of a different kind. No, my feet had a right to complain.

At this point we ate fillet, lamb chops, and chateaubriand because my dinner dates came from the silver spoon variety of male, who, upon graduating cum laude or better from one of the fur-lined universities reserved for affluence, seemed to wander into advertising. My pictures and I became regulars at these shrines. I never got to be a Rheingold girl, or struck a Lucky, but I did enjoy a few gorgeous dinners. I had graduated to asking for takeout bags, which I insisted on packing myself. This practice didn't discourage the young men who dotted those spring evenings because they were competitive repeaters. On reflection, they were all strangely familiar, perhaps because they were all emerging from the same backdrop. Eventually I could tag the old school tie at fifty paces. If I was an amusing novelty to them, they were the equivalent of a sideshow to me. They referred to one another as "professional college men." That meant using one's school ties and undergrad equipment excessively. Going to the grave, as it were, in the costume used in the act. Harvard, for instance—the very close-cropped hair, known by the brotherhood as a "whiffle." Brooks Brothers shirts and underpinnings. The white suède shoes with red rubber soles for all occasions. Tattersall waistcoat–Harris tweed combo, a pipe—presto! An animated George Apley. Regulation equipment included boyish charm and a varying amount of wit. With a huge capacity for booze.

My workaday routine was relieved by glimpses into the wonderful world of exclusive restaurants. Hansom rides in the park. Even cocktail parties. All new. All thrill. I observed with delight. I didn't examine or even query, because for me it was all another temporary ride. I was on my way somewhere else. This whole picture was part of the passing scenery. There wasn't any single person different from the rest. Not yet.

My sanctuary of the lone room was comforting with its bubbling life and promise. April bloomed. Her appetite and joy at each tiny discovery were the center of all revolving events. I hadn't cared for any of my new friends enough to confide or share dreams, hopes, or even desires. All this I kept within the tower of the hotel room. Outside I was an observer. Inside I participated fully. The very old woman who shared our spring was content. She rarely left the place. "I've seen everything out there," she would say, rocking April in the sunlit window. "Look here in this little face, now. Something new every second, see?" That something new was being recorded by Tony Bruno. Fascinated with April's beauty, he insisted I bring her each time we added to his portfolio. After the work sessions, April was the center of the lights while Tony clicked away. She was delighted.

"Dark brown eyes, pale golden hair," Tony marveled. "If only she was a grownup I would beg her to help with the commercials."

Tony was earning a fine reputation in show business, but he couldn't seem to dent the industry of advertising.

"Your sister was in for some pictures." He spread a series of proofs on the table. "If she wasn't so rich I'd ask her to pose for that big mural ad. Boy! I betcha I'd get the account." The proofs showed my sister posed in various attitudes. Dignified as hell, she wore only high-heeled glittery shoes and a portion of white fox fur.

"Is there that much money in an account like that?" I asked.

Tony grinned. "It's like an inheritance," he said. "But it's naked art." He stopped grinning. "I can't ask any pals to help this time, and I haven't got the big money for a naked-type model." He waited.

I looked at the last of the proofs. They were all gorgeous. "She's going to have a hard time choosing," I murmured.

Tony gathered them up. "What if I told her she could have them all? For no fee. That is, if she would pose for that mural? A swap?"

I considered. "Well, I know she loves dealing . . . and . . . and bargains . . ."

Tony grinned once more. "And the best is, nobody will ever know it's her. The artist only uses the picture as a sort of pattern, you see—"

I stopped him. "She is a star in the Ziegfeld Follies. Going on to be a big star in Hollywood . . ."

He looked perplexed. "She did the same number, the same strip as she did in burlesque," he began.

I shook my head. "If you were Gypsy Rose Lee in the Ziegfeld Follies and then in the movies you got there because that's who you were and who everybody wanted to see because you were famous doing that number . . ." I paused for breath, then finished my thought, "Would you pose for a mural that couldn't be recognized as you?"

Tony frowned. "Anonymous naked, no jackpot, huh?" I nodded. "I understand." He sighed. "Hell, I could have moved to that big studio upstairs, even got that new lens for Big Bertha, here." He patted the hood of the camera. "I'm just never gonna get out of this trap, June." Tony slumped into a chair.

My heart was heavy, too. I slumped in the chair opposite him. "I'm sorry, Tony, I know she wouldn't. After all, she isn't doing her strip in the movies."

Tony sighed. "She isn't going to be Gypsy Rose Lee in the movies," he retorted.

"Well," I said, "there really isn't anything I can do."

Tony's head shot up. "Oh, yes there is. You could pose for the damn mural. Lissen, June, nobody would ever know it was you but that artist, and he won't even know your name." I stood up, he followed. "Wait a minute now, you can pose yourself, alone in here. I won't even see you except through the camera. . . ." I looked away. "Oh, dammit," Tony almost shouted. "It can't ever hurt you or your future, nobody will ever know it's you, don't you understand? And I can have the big studio, the lens, and if we get the account you share the money."

I looked up at him. I was remembering all I owed to him. My jobs, really. The dozens of free pictures that meant I could go into an office as a pro. The recording of April's babyhood. The wine cookies, even—the affection and friendship.

"Can I hold those flowers in front of—of—" I stammered.

He lifted me in the air. "You can hold the whole damn bouquet!" he yelled.

Every time I pass that giant monstrosity of a so-called mural now, I think of that painful session. Picking up props, stepping into the lights so carefully prearranged, calling that I was ready, then burning with three shades of magenta until I was alone again with the flowers and that silver ashtray bowl I overturned to stand on.

Anyway, Tony got the job, the studio, and the lens, and I got over the goose bumps.

32

That year there was more than spring in the air. There was a feeling of family in the corner room of the Somerset Hotel. Hope was squeezing between doubts. Confidence layered over fear. I was working, paying bills. We were bubbling with energy. There was even a real opportunity waiting in the wings. It was a good time.

My most persistent gentleman caller out-whiffled his competitors. His understanding when I confided secret hopes and plans, all those deductions arrived at along the bumpy road, was comforting. Here was a corresponding heart. He too wanted freedom to pursue secret dreams. He was about to fulfill his promise. All through Harvard he was the editor of the Crimson—the wit, the intellectual homerunner of his class. All he needed was the nutrition of peace and quiet to turn out what he called "the Great American Novel." There were no doubts. Just the natural roadblocks of life.

As we talked and talked those roadblocks became a challenge. Looking at Donald Staley Gibbs—sandy short hair, puddinglike form, broad smile, which closed the small blue eyes further—one would never believe he would someday exert the self-discipline that produces the fulfillment of that desire to write for a living. To produce the words upon words, thoughts upon thoughts—in short, to materialize as that world-renowned novelist so clearly defined in his own self-image. Alas, one would be quite right. The belief, however, was a bond between us, the pact very clear. My part was to become an actress. He was the writer. With this foundation a genuine friendship was formed.

It was quite a while before I learned of the table which Gibbs had designed for himself. It was a writing table of perfect proportions. There had been Mediterranean cruises resulting from the frustration of looking at empty pages day after day, surrounded by the perfect creative atmosphere. Vermont in winter. Snow and solitude. Money was no problem. There had been a comfortable legacy. When Gibbs was an infant, his unloving male parent deserted, never to be heard from again. The deserter's parents took in abandoned mother and child. The mother's passion centered on the only memento of her life. He was eleven years older than I. His education was dazzling. Even his temporary work seemed admirable. He was, of course, in advertising. But it was quite a while, as I say, before I knew very much about him really, and by then it was too late.

First a wash basket. One you could carry easily. Then a bathtub. What safer crib can be found for a baby? A playpen made up of chairs with some blankets covering the hotel carpet. This was the baby equipment I had seen used all my life until Gibbs pointed out pink and blue painted nursery furniture in store windows. There were dozens of special things available for baby care. Sunlight and cleanliness had been my only requisites. I began to think of April surrounded by these pretty accessories.

One could walk for miles in Central Park alone and unafraid in those days; walking from the Murray Hill section, where all the Gibbs population seemed to live. I always peered into windows, looking for the kind of home that had produced these self-assured people. It was the first serious examination of other private worlds available to me. A matter of choices again, spying into windows I didn't feel any great surge of need for the carpets, furniture, plants. Not for myself, then, but—and the but covered miles— was it unfair to April? Would a child fare better surrounded with all these trimmings? How long would it be before I alone could offer her the nice things? If I remained true to my design, avoiding my avowed legal entanglements with men, could I be certain to avoid the rubble of Mother's private life? I remembered her tearful face, "I hate sex, June. Hate it, hate it—don't I, Kate?"—the woman so addressed nodding gravely, "Yes, Roanie, yes." How many episodes had it taken for that anguished denial?

How many other women have lost faith in the search for a man to trust? Mother told me about a girl who was in a car parked in the alley, very drunk, so drunk she didn't know she was in the back seat of a car. "We were striking the act fast to make a train." Her eyes were very dark blue with the memory. "Someone said the girl was unconscious, said to get a doctor." Her voice lowered. "Later we saw the men laughing in little groups, and the truth was they had taken turns going out there to force themselves on that dead-drunk girl." Her mouth hardened. "Those were men we know, June. Fathers and husbands—they thought it was funny."

I had never told her of the "uncles"—men she had liked temporarily who had put my hand inside their trousers; who cuddled alongside me in bed, rubbing a huge penis against me. Nothing had come of any of this. Just my five-year-old disgust. No rape or forcing. I had dismissed it as the male behavior Mother spoke of so often. We had laughed together at the man across the court at the hotel who had cut two holes for his eyes in the window shade so he could see the reaction of the people opposite as he swung his member to and fro, ending the routine by peeing out the window.

We hadn't laughed when a famous violinist on the same bill with us had interrupted our after-the-show ice-cream party. His wife and two children were present, along with Mother and most of the kids in my act. He was very drunk. Eyes red. Blood around his mouth and saturating his collar. His trousers were open, revealing bloody underwear and matted hair. Careening into our circle, he bellowed, "Ice cream! Ice cream! That's all you want!" His wife tried to drag him into the bathroom. "I want more," he yelled. "I can't get what I want at home so I get it from a tramp!" The door slammed. "Shut up, shut up!" the woman commanded. But his voice came through the door clearly. "If you'd let me when you have your monthlies, I wouldn't have to go out to the streets. It's your damn ice-cream mentality!" There was more, but we were following at Mother's heels.

In San Jose the stagehands had pinned up a large picture of three men found guilty of rape by a posse of other men. They were hanging from a tree. It was a peculiar angle, as they hung very low. Not from their necks, but by their penises, which had stretched almost to the ground by the weight of their bodies. Mother was grim. "How can they decide who is guilty among themselves? Why is rape the thing that infuriates men the most? Look what they have done to each other—and remember the very man who is smiling at you so sweetly may be either one of these who hang there, or one who did the hanging."

Mother's conclusions had stifled any belief that among males there could be found a single man to trust. She simply resigned from any effort. She turned toward her own sex.

At the time I was preparing to make the journey to St. Louis, there were six women living on the farm in upstate New York with Mother. Then, suddenly, there were five. That was what decided me against leaving April with Grandma.

"I didn't do a thing." Mother was earnest. "She took the shotgun out of my hand, put the nozzle in her mouth, stepped on the trigger, and pow!"

I guess my speechlessness compelled more detail.

"I didn't actually offer the gun, don't you see? I just had it, that's all." She shook her head. "You should have read the crazy lies she wrote in that diary, June. She was deceitful and—and bad. With your sister trying so hard to be a Hollywood star, and that fool girl blowing the whole top of her head off." She sighed. "Well, the studio put the lid on any big publicity, if that's what she was after, although I don't understand this censorship business. After all, living and dying is life."

Mother's mouth hardened in contempt. "I've never been able to stomach a poor loser. I never told her she was moving in with me." The violet eyes were wide. "Why would I clutter up my life with a wild tramp like that?" She was making herself angry.

"Does anyone know you burned that diary?" I asked.

"Of course not!" She was furious now. "What do you think I am? That stupid girl was renting a room here, and that-is-all." She turned to the huge pot of bubbling fruit juices on the stove. "I'm tired of getting into other people's muckups, just because I know what loneliness is." She lifted the huge pot from the flame.

"I hope you never have to suffer the way I have, June—abandoned, ignored. Sometimes I think I'd be better off dead, too. I told her that, I did. I said, Why not just check out if you're that unhappy?, and there was the gun, and—well, I think she knew what she was doing." She lifted a spoonful of the jam to her lips. "Dammit," she said, "it's too late to add more sugar, now. When will I ever learn not to try to do too many things at one time?"

All in all, Mother was too busy to take in another tenant, so April spent the summer with other babies who had working mothers, at an outdoor nursery on the Palisades. She was tanned and fat and joyful when I came back to claim her that autumn.

My summer of 1936 at the St. Louis Municipal Opera was another learning time. Set in a sprawling public park, the amphitheatre was surrounded by greenery. Indomitable greenery, because it withstood summers of shimmering, waterless heat—heat that was more intense at night. And when it did rain, the water was boiled before it fell. Heat that dried the skin and fried the mind.

The St. Louis Municipal Opera is an outdoor arena seating more than ten thousand people, who refuse to budge in a storm, who simply open umbrellas. We did thirteen full-scale musicals and/or operettas. The huge pit held over forty musicians. There were a ballet corps, and male and female singing and dancing chorus. A company joke was that it took five minutes to cross the enormous stage. I was awed by the three towering trees whose roots were beneath the boards of that stage. They were fed gallons of olive oil. They were a living backdrop for every set.

New stars arrived for every show. Most featured players were signed for the entire summer. Then in another category were three others: one a fine singer, one great dancer, and me, the actress. Not chorus, not principals, we were relegated to the bits and pieces remaining when the budget refused to import more talent. It meant doubling and sometimes tripling. The "in" term for our category was H.A.P., meaning, "half-assed principals." As the season wore on, the singer got married, the dancer got pregnant, and I got all their bits and pieces, as well as my own. I was in heaven. I sometimes played four roles in one show. By never admitting I couldn't do something, I always got the chance to at least try.

"You enter turning, turn, turn, turn to the center, then the boys lift you, and they turn, turn in the changing light, see?"

I nodded mutely. When the choreographer had said "bacchanale," I wasn't going to let on I didn't know the word, so here we were. Turns made me sick, dizzy and sick, but I wanted to do that lovely number in the changing lights. I nodded. The rehearsal piano began. I could imagine how the music would sound when all those pit instruments played it. The dancers whirled and leaped. I swallowed hard, and waited for my cue.

There it was. I hurled myself from the wings, turnandturn. I was almost center, turnturn. Elated, I felt the boy dancers lift me, and we began the spin.

I don't know how many turns it took to make me sick enough to let go, and even though I didn't miss a turn, a few of those dancers never spoke to me again. The ones I hadn't hit thought it was funny. I was grateful for their humor. The music mercifully stopped. I squatted on the floor, miserable, waiting for the verdict. The choreographer stood over me.

"All right now?" she said brightly. "Fine, let's take it from the top—places, please."

I looked up in surprise.

"You'll get over being sick if you don't stop." She was smiling. "Wash up later—it's bound to happen some more."

I couldn't believe it. I was back in show business for sure. I only lost a few more friends before the dizzy sickness stopped and I was spinning to the beautiful music with the whole orchestra playing. That was a milestone week.

It's a true theatre adage: "Work brings work." All the people with whom I toiled then were to figure importantly in the months and years to come. All but my idol.

You will understand why she must be nameless. Beautiful, in the ladylike Norma Shearer tradition; elegant, porcelain-princess style. She used a dainty filigree lorgnette to read her words. When she sang, the heavens swayed in ecstasy. I was the privileged one, to sit at her feet on the apron of that magical stage while she sang the haunting theme song. When the lights slowly dimmed, I was unable to see the cue lights because my eyes were filled.

My heart also. During the scene change in the dark, it was all I could do to rouse myself and carry on. I was a number-one fan. I trailed her worshipfully, and when on opening night the vast audience acclaimed her, I felt the world was indeed in its orbit.

I rushed to her room, clutching a tiny nosegay I planned to present, along with a carefully rehearsed speech. Choking back waves of grateful joy at the response to my knock—"June, yes, dear. Come in, come in"—I stumbled through the enchanted door. She was standing on a square of sheeting, her maid undoing the heavy costume, which would be removed and carried off in a drop sheet.

I began my speech, extending my bouquet to the queen of the world. I had managed to garble the first words, when the dresser undid the last hook and that costume fell. The beautiful lady wore no underpinnings above, just a tiny band at her waist, and, of course, the petticoats. A listening, gracious expression lit up her face, but I caught that part in a fast glance. My eyes fell on her bosoms, and could not be torn away. I heard my voice grind to a scratchy halt, the bouquet dropped. I stared for what seemed an eternity at those small, quite normal breasts, except that ringing each nipple was a circle of very long black hair, stiff, wiry black hair.

I've forgotten my exit, but instinct tells me it must have been what my sister termed gauche.

The last event of that memorable season came on the baking stage during a rehearsal for the final show. There was an impressive small building at the rear of the upstage entrance, emblazoned with red crosses on all sides; its billing stood out in block letters: HOSPITAL. Dancers in particular were inclined to fall over during rehearsals. Some collapsed during performances. It was an ordinary sight to see them scooped up and hauled off to that cubicle. I was proud that the only time I was inside was for an emergency treatment for a dog I knew. That doctor has to be closer to salvation for every stitch that saved that mutt.

Emerging from the relative coolness of that structure, I thought I saw a shadowy being moving like a mirage through the shimmer of heat; down the endless mile from the very back of the seating came this figure. It was vaguely familiar. The costume was strange for a morning rehearsal in St. Louis. The creature swayed as though dizzy, sat awhile, then resumed its journey toward the stage. By about Row AAA, I recognized the hungover, rumpled person of Donald Staley Gibbs. Swollen eyes squinting in the chalk-white glare of the sun, he was looking for me. I didn't know if it would be more politic to hide or to claim him.

He looked so vulnerable. It wasn't hard to guess why he was here, or that he didn't want to want to be here. Whatever amount of courage he had fortified himself with was backing over him now. He looked awful.

"You shouldn't have come all the way out here, you just . . . shouldn't. . . ." I eyed the rumpled dinner jacket, limp white shirt. "Perhaps," I said, "if you had gone to bed last night, instead of getting on a plane . . ."

I meant to scold, but my voice was soft. We looked into each other's faces for a long, long moment.

Unidentified vibrations had tried to forewarn me, as I watched his entrance down that mile-long aisle. He didn't remember that I would not be found out front where the audience arrived, and he never did learn why. The mysticism lay between entering a theatre where he felt comfortable, where he paid to be audience, while I entered by the stage door, where I felt comfortable, where I was paid to meet him across the footlights. A tiny difference? Uh huh, such as between the house variety and the tsetse fly—tiny but deadly.

These negatives were not discernible in the bright white sun of then. As yet I had no doubt that Gibbs's longing to be a writer was made of such stuff as would send an archaeologist to Tibet, or a chorus girl to ballet, singing, acting, and diction classes every single day, or someone like me to St. Louis. It took years for either of us to realize that, in vaudevillese, Gibbs just talked a good act. In the advertising business he was understood. "Mañana" wasn't just a song, it was a way of life. Meanwhile, there were jingles, phrases, and catchwords to write; at day's end, or even in the middle, there was the Harvard Club to wrap around the hurt.

In spite of the novelty of being the only Vermont Democrat I knew, Gibbs failed his promise to himself. He didn't even try to write. But I persisted in the certainty that we were marching along together. Too busy to examine those empty pages of his, to realize the occasional collaborator was only a pal joining in on a talking spree, I began to outpace my partner. The bulk of my efforts represented an inexorable, if stumbling, march toward a goal.

One of the differences between the dilettante and the pro seems to be a willingness to suffer for the win. To wade through insult and hunger with that secret hope intact. Not even slightly unraveled. It's a force that won't accept less than recognition from enemies, unrelated sources. A nod from way out there in the very unfamiliar deep. No platform will suffice until you stand on that suicide square. Security is contemptible. Lead on to the cliff. No alternate route appeals to the soul that is pietistic. Logic is the caboose. Like an empty belly let fear and caution ride at the tail end of the parade.

Because of this theory, I said no to the first suggestion of marriage with Gibbs. I hadn't included the possible comforts in my war manual. Security could well mean the quieting of my starting bell. I had to think about it. Gibbs returned to his rounds of backgammon and sherry flips. I revved up for my onslaught on the big city. Back to the Somerset. To the rounds of auditions.

Men were in abundance. Actors who shared my waits in outer offices, agents who shared my frustrations. A few young writers and directors. Even a hopeful producer or two. The cast included befrienders as well as detractors. We were all so intent on our goal, so purposeful, that nothing resembling the taken-for-granted privileges Gibbs enjoyed were enviable. We talked nothing but dreams. Gibbs sidestepped into other worldly items such as sports, politics, world events. . . . My mind kept drifting to the dumpy figure, the close-cropped hair, ever so plain face—he was lovable. In his own Vermont way, even glamorous. Harvard sophistication mixed with Green Mountain wry. Endearing. As I plodded along my own upward hill, my mind kept drifting to Gibbs. When it did, I think I smiled, and it felt good.

The motherly old girl on pension was waiting for April. We were a trio once more. The baritone obbligato Gibbs added was sometimes comforting. He was a great audience, too. He found my stories of the job-seeking route hilarious. He guffawed when I told him of the forty-five-minute song and dance audition I had done for some young producers. They were using the huge Martin Beck Theatre. All sorts of musicians, actors, and odd types crowded the wings. The usual very short stint with a quick "Thank you" dismissal was prolonged to a forty-five-minute variety act. It went on and on.

"Do something else?" I did everything I could remember. They laughed and laughed out there. Until I stood soaked with death sweat, unable to think of one more song or step.

"I—I think I've run out of material," I gasped.

"Come on down here," they invited. All smiles, they greeted me like a buddy. "You're gonna do fine," they said. "Funny, funny girl. Yeah!" I stood tall, overjoyed. "We can't use you, of course, but you won't be around loose for long, you bet." I sagged. "You can't—you don't want me?" It was a squeak. "You didn't know?" they asked. "We're gonna do *Green Pastures,* you see." Gibbs laughed till he cried.

With autumn still young I ran into the meaning of it all. During daily auditioning on any corner, any Nedick's, I was offered a comedy lead. Cold. The producers had seen me in St. Louis. I was dizzied with the luck. A Broadway show—strong brew.

No fast flashes of super glamour invaded my drive. Not then, not now. Not ever. I was nothing more than a mapless traveler trying to get home. If I could find my way back to where I belonged, perhaps I'd blend into the backdrop and become a natural part of the scenery again.

The route would have been clear except for the figure of Gibbs. More than anyone I had known so far in my life, he represented the rewards of surrender. The end of effort. Relinquishment of one environment for another, where anonymity meant peace. Serenity. Where April would be safe from the fateful headshake, "Too much—you are just too much." In his world there were fireplaces, gardens. Viewing those temptations from my aerie at the Somerset Hotel, I wondered which emotion ran stronger inside me. The heart-fluttering challenge of the new show I was about to tackle, or the low, warm flame of comfortable joy I felt when spying into real homes where there was no half hour at 8 P.M. Which was the more valuable? Which would make a better life for April? Was she like the me I had believed myself to be: all show business, all work? Or the me that became intoxicated with the scent of woodsmoke?

It never occurred to me that I was capable of attaining any or all of these worlds by myself. I was convinced the world of Gibbs could be entered by one route only, the passport being

181

marriage. Like any other foreigner obtaining citizenship.

I filed these questions as rehearsals began. Suddenly realizing how young I had been when I vowed never again to marry. How many ages ago was that? How could that girl imagine a Gibbs when her knowledge of men had been limited to a Bobby and a Jamie?

33 ꕥꕥꕥ

"The old saw about life being 'stranger than fiction' had a new thrust to it when a small girl stopped the musical 'Forbidden Melody' for two encores opening night."—New York *Herald Tribune,* November, 1936.

But out-of-town reception had been promising, too. Enough so to bring the first word from Mother since that summer's beginning. "Urgent," the message said.

We were to open at the New Amsterdam Theatre on Forty-second Street. Ziegfeld's private theatre on the roof of the big house had been our rehearsal space. The vibrations of what that house had been were still strong enough to stop my heart. I walked and worked in a haze of fulfillment. I only had one number, but I stopped every show with it. It would never have been so prolonged a stop if the stage manager, Jerry Whyte, hadn't delayed my return to the waiting spotlight. His method was simple. I made my exit dancing, the audience applauded, I took a bow or two, then Jerry held me by the seat of my pants. "Let's see if they really mean business, kid." At first I was aghast. "Let go, I gotta take another bow." I even slapped at his hands. "Wait till the music for an encore starts," he growled. He was right.

Word got back to the big city during our out-of-town tryout. *Zit's Weekly:* "June Havoc is the find of the season." The dance was first cousin to all the comedy routines done by Dainty June. Still working. The audience reaction was a transfusion of life-giving substance.

The family meeting took place just before opening night. Mother sat at the end of the familiar long table; Gypsy, in the middle, was concentrating on a cobweb of shiny gold thread.

Mother began at the top. "We know you are on dinner break, dear, so I'll be quick." She beckoned me to a chair. "You know, dear, no one ever expected this freak reappearance of yours. I made this big success for your sister, and of course we needed interesting things for her background—the interviews and all of that—she had to have someone to be, so it was the most natural thing in the world. We used the baby, then child-star vaudeville background. It's been very successful. That's what everybody believes, now, so you can see it's too late to try to take any of the stories back, dear."

I studied the flowered carpet. "You mean I can't ever say I was—I am . . ."

Mother helped me. "We never said you weren't there, too, June. Only, if you are going to actually be back in show business with us, dear, you must find someone else to be. Just find a good story and stick with it."

I stood. "But I am someone," I blurted.

Mother smiled. "That's a start, isn't it?" She moved toward the elevator. "We'll get together, and maybe some part that hasn't been used can be twisted back for you." She pressed the button. I looked toward my sister. She was still knitting. "There's a lovely story tomorrow, dear," Mother was saying. "It's very dramatic, and will stop a lot of silly talk before it starts." The elevator arrived. My sister held the door open with her foot.

"June," she explained, "what Mother means is that up till now you really haven't existed. Tomorrow's story will close that gap. If you stay in show business, I mean. It will put you on the map." She held up the tiny gold-threaded thing. It was beautiful. She fitted the shiny thing onto my head. It turned into a tiny gold cap. Almost like a baby's cap. She stood back appreciatively. "There," she said. The elevator took me down to the lobby. I walked onto the street. There was so little weight to the golden cap I didn't realize I was wearing it.

The next day I read the newspaper story that ended my solo flight. "Stripper's Long-Lost Sister Found." It was the first of a couple of decades of fables.

Fables: During the decade called the 1940s, I was an in-person ear to one fable. Looking into the face, hearing the voice of Ben Sonnenberg, who had no idea that Gypsy and I were sisters, or that it was possible any of the present company even knew Miss

Lee. He felt free to regale us with his story. "I was invited to this weird house she owned in Brooklyn," he began (Gypsy never owned a house in Brooklyn). "I was there and I met the girl who writes for her. Her ghostwriter, and . . ." I got up and left because I liked the other people. What would I say, anyway? Gypsy, only Gypsy could ever have written in the style she used. The language was uniquely her own. The story about someone writing for her was a healthy fable.

Fable: The taxi driver reading a magazine article on Gypsy. "You busy?" I asked, opening the door of his cab.

"Naw," he growled, "just reading fairytales, that's all." I settled into the cab, giving him my address. "Looka that." He held up the garishly colored picture of my sister wearing a few beads and a lot of feathers. "There she is." He was angry. "Gypsy Rose Lee . . . yeah, that's what she calls herself. Gypsy, yet. Cheez . . . what kinda face you call that?" I looked. He slipped into gear and barreled down Eighth Avenue.

"I'd call it a Nordic face," I said, "long bones, long neck, and—"

We had stopped for a red light. "Long phoney," he sneered. "She looks pretty, she don't look pretty—she's a little Jew kid— why don't she admit it? What's she so ashamed?" He turned and looked at me. Eyes cold. "Don't let 'em con you. She's Gypsy Rose Levy. I know. My cousin lives next door to her whole family in Flatbush."

Fables: This one is actually billed a fable. The 1959 musical *Gypsy* that meant more than anything or anyone in the world to her. "It's my monument," Gypsy told me. "It doesn't have to be factual, it only has to be big, exciting, and—and a smash!"

Our viewpoints on the importance of identity were the greatest difference we shared. "You were never a pathetic Cinderella," I said. "You have always been strong and positive and—"

"They can't make a musical out of that, June." She was positive now.

I went on, "The real Gypsy couldn't have been hidden in the rear end of that cowskin, and you know it. Her spirit was too great, she—"

Gypsy's eyes sparkled. "To hell with spirit!" she yelled.

I went on again, "You wouldn't sit at the same table with Bobby, let alone be heartbroken that I ran away with him—you disliked him intensely. And as for Mother, she was never a nosy, vulgar calliope, she was—"

Gypsy stamped her foot. "Can't you understand?" she exploded. "I don't give a damn who or what they put onstage in that show; it's my monument."

I persisted. "Okay," I said, "you want the world to believe that your credo says to hell with craft, with talent, with integrity, 'all you gotta have is a gimmick'? Is that your message? Do you really believe that?"

Her face softened. "Listen, June. You're the one trusts all that craft stuff. I tried it, didn't I? Nothing worked but my gimmicks. That's what they bought, that's what they wanted. Wouldn't I be a stupid son-of-a-bitch to disappoint them now?"

I turned away. "What about me?" I asked. "It's all untrue, and it makes me a heavy. An untalented, whining kid who grabs and runs."

She put her arms around me. "We know it's all a fable. It's going to be billed like that—a fable. Please let me have my monument."

Well, Mr. Taxi, and all the rest of you who "know," I am putting it all down before I pack up, because I am weary of my own silence. As for you, I have watched, listened, and read your versions, your "I know," and I am ready to shout it: you don't know. You don't know because you weren't there. Whether it's Levy or Flatbush, Brooklyn or a cow's behind, or any of the rest of the fables. The only one who was actually there is me. I won't sit still anymore for your versions. Fable time, gossip time, and make-a-buck-with-a-gimmick time is over. It's documentary time now, and if this bothers any of you self-styled experts, you can fold it up and tuck it into my cremation kit. . . . It can all go with me. In peace at last, because the record will be straight. It may not get laughs or win the cute prize, but it will be basic.

The season of 1936 boasted over three dozen premières. Only a few revivals. Directors, actors, playwrights, and producers of that time could open and close as many shows per season as there was time. Failure was a percentage, not a death sentence. A personal success in a hit was the rainbow. Knocking critics and audience dead in a flop was only a pass into the arena. I was oblivious of the condition of the track or the odds.

In a very short time, *Forbidden Melody* was just that. My memories are of Mrs. Carl Brisson's earnest efforts to force the director of the show into the realization that he was blind. "All over Europe Carl Brisson is an idol," she yelled. "Women fight over his tossed-away cigarette stubs. Scream love words under his window. Why?" She stood her ground. Strands of hair escaping the picture hat, lipstick smudged, eyes ringed with the hopelessness of being understood even in the three languages she mixed freely. "You cannot fail the women, you have him too much facing front. No good." She finally erupted. "Let the fans see his ass!" she hollered. "It's the most gorgeous ass in the world! Turn him around, you fool!"

The other memory? The plushy feeling of being center stage, doing something that was working, followed by the empty lostness when it was all over.

There was no wedding, just a marriage. We moved the scant furniture from the bachelor digs on Murray Hill and my few belongings to an antiseptic two-bedroom, two-bath apartment near the East River. There was a personal all-around cook-homemaker who had cared for Gibbs for years. Her name was Ogena Jackson. April's room was filled with pink and blue furniture, stroller, rocking horse, and swing. All the drawers were filled with chubbies, woollies, and toys.

Just for the holidays our telephone table was directly behind the Christmas tree. Little lights seemed to grow out of Gibbs's face and head as I watched from the dinette. The connection was poor. There were snowstorms hovering in the atmosphere. "Good morning, Mother." Gibbs was businesslike. "Merry Christmas." He listened awhile. The smile faded. "But, Mother, I'm married now—yes, but—" The small eyes widened. "It isn't that, Mother. You know I'm—I—" He almost whispered, "I love you, too."

Embarrassed again, I moved into the bedroom. The love-hate relationship between them was painful to witness. I closed the door softly, remembering his panic when finally backed against the hard evidence of the wedding ring on his finger. He had no choice but to phone Jessie. To tell her at last that he was married. "Yes, Mother, married." Hoping for no response, he rushed into the tabloid. "She is an actress and she has a baby and I love her, so don't say anything, Mother. Don't say anything that you don't mean, because—because—Mother? . . . Mother?? . . .

MOTHER!" Jessie had fainted after the first eight bars. Gibbs frantically called a neighbor, who rushed to the rescue.

That was for openers. Came the holidays, which to me meant one thing only: an extra matinee. To them, a whole set of others. Jessie couldn't understand how he would consider even a part of Christmas without her. Her devotion smothered him. Humiliated him. He had put off warning her about his involvement with April and me because he knew there was no way, there were no words—it was never, never going to be possible for the twain to meet. That's what he thought.

Jessie was dumpy and gray, a chip the size of a wood shingle on her shoulder. She had more opinions than the *Reader's Digest,* but she was honest, and she loved with every fiber, every drop of her Yankee blood. From where I stood, Jessie was truth personified. I couldn't understand why Gibbs didn't respond to the open adoration. How he could be so casual. Diffident. I figured that anyone lucky enough to have backing like that could lick the world.

I stood at that time at the very edge of illiteracy. Why wouldn't I be dazzled, even infatuated, with erudition? With easy, fine manners, self-assurance. Jessie knew everything. Her vocabulary was like music. She was the real thing, all right; you had only to beware the thorns. A very fair deal. I wanted her approval more than anyone's I had ever known.

Jessie brought distinction to snobbery.

"Never knew a Smith girl didn't drop her underwear to the floor, step out of it, and expect someone else to go picking up after her."

A half point in my favor. I was certainly no Smith girl, and I picked up my own underwear as well as everyone else's. I didn't smoke or drink. My cussing vocabulary was modest. I didn't fit the picture of an actress as she had always imagined one. Another half point. When she told me she had always hand-washed all of her son's clothes right through Harvard, I was impressed. Her reason was that she couldn't endure the thought of his clothes being washed in the same water used for all those strangers. I wanted more of Jessie. I loved her. She was an original.

Through winter of 1936 and spring of 1937, I took unrestrained delight in being mother, wife. The mysteries of home unwound slowly for me. After months of wonder at the intricacies of place setting, window treatment, and closet arrangement, I was hooked on a lifetime hobby, more engaged by a book called *How to Clean Everything* than by any novel. These delights came in the same package as Gilbert and Sullivan and "Ladies Are Invited for Sunday" at the Harvard Club. However, the Harvard-Yale train to and from the great games left less than a desire for repeat performances. Noisy and very, very drunk. Then the game itself, I felt, was poorly staged. Almost as much noise from the stands as I remembered during a heat in a marathon. To improve my amateur standing with Gibbs, I stood up at one point, yelling, "Go, Crimson!" I didn't regain consciousness until the half. Gibbs had failed to tell me he could only get tickets on the Yale forty-yard line, so the Yale guy who silenced my Crimson cheer with a bottle was within his rights.

Way before winter's end, my new look was established. No makeup, now. Natural ash-green hair. Cardigan sweater over a blouse and skirt. Saddle shoes. I was a mess, but I fit into the scheme. A stranger would never be able to tell whether I was educated or not. I was on my way.

I learned about such things as excursions. Weekend trips and cruises. I had always wondered what kind of people made all that so profitable. Well, Gibbs took me to Bermuda. Vermont. Southampton. The most memorable was the ski trip. There were four of us on this merry jaunt. Gibbs and I didn't ski. We drank hot buttered rum and rode a sleigh. Our friends skied like fury.

Returning in a howling blizzard, I was secretly complimenting myself on how well I had faded into the backdrop. No oddity protruding to expose that I wasn't Vassar, that I was Keith-Orpheum. . . . My reverie ended as the car skidded to a snowy halt. A blowout. It was a frostbitten hour before we discovered that I alone knew how to change the tire. It took me only six minutes for the operation itself, but the damage was done. It was a big mistake. Like the indelible error I committed that time I locked myself in the kitchen with the live lobsters because I couldn't bring myself to drop them kicking into the boiling water. Those guests looked at me then in the same way. It was an uncommon expression. I recognized it later in Vermont on the family pier over Lake Champlain.

Gibbs was out there happily fishing with half the colony of that exclusive enclave. Jessie told me to go out and get him as there was a phone call. I dutifully tripped along the shore to the pier, nodding my way past the tea-drinking ladies under their silk parasols; along I went, past the fishing neighbors until I reached Gibbs. My message relayed, I turned to go.

"June," he called, "hold this line. I'll be right back." I demurred. "Come on," he urged, "I've been here two days, haven't had a nibble."

Assured, I took the rod. He had no more than turned his back, wham! A bite. My hands froze. I stopped breathing. The possibility of killing anything terrified me. "Reel it in, reel it in!" Gibbs was shouting. He grabbed the pole, reeling madly. I stood in shock as he pulled a glorious, shining fairytale creature from the glistening water. It was fighting hard and it was strong, full of life and the determination to hold on to that life. Gibbs reached down, picked up a twelve-inch log. . . . He beat the beautiful thing until it lay still and spiritless between us. I came up from my shock like a loose spring. Grabbing the dead fish, I whammed it across his face, left, right, and front, until we both were covered with bits and pieces and I could no longer swing what was left. We stood swaying, glaring at one another. Oblivious of the audience on shore and along the pier.

Jessie stood among them. "Dear?" she called. "You have a phone call. Didn't June tell you?"

Gypsy had married, too. Sort of a command job because the studio felt anything that could make her "more like everyone else" would help keep the Ladies' Temperance Leagues quiet. Her husband was a civilian, too. In some ways we had followed the identical pattern. Bob Mizzy was unexpected. Almost a shock. Resembling a lean, hungry wolf in the Disney tradition, he cast a sweet-sour-comic-evil shadow. They were married in a manner that would yield the best publicity, not once but twice, for fuller exposure.

The second shot took place on a small boat just off the shore of the California island of Catalina. "In true Norse tradition," Gypsy was quoted as saying. Some of the stories were colorful enough even for the bride.

Bob's real name was Arnold. " 'Arnold' doesn't fit his personality," Gypsy explained. "How would it look in print? No." She was firm. "It's bad enough he is in dental equipment. Now, be honest, you'd never guess that to look at him, would you?" I

₩ 189

had to admit it would be hard. "He has the most intriguing frown when he growls," Gypsy said fondly.

Mother was less enthusiastic. "A convenience again." She shook her head. "I just don't know where you girls find them."

That summer I was invited to appear as ingénue with the Starlight Theatre in Upstate New York. April went with me. Jessie was worried. As autumn arrived I was cast in the Chicago company of *The Women.* We rehearsed in New York before we hit the road. April went with me. Jessie was aghast. We were home before Christmas. I hadn't impressed as a siren. Max Gordon was kind and fatherly when he explained, "You got no sex appeal in that bathtub scene, kid, sorry." I could have told him that.

Undaunted, I got together a few songs, a dance—enough of an act to play the few weeks left of vaudeville in some supper clubs.

Christmas saw Jessie, Donald Staley, April, and me as a family. Talking Gibbs into moving into a real home instead of an apartment was not easy. Talking him into making room for Jessie was a triumph. It was a good time for all of us. The little house was an easy trip from the city. Once there you could imagine yourself in far-off New England.

April thrived. Jessie thrived. Gibbs sat in his Veritas chair behind his specially built table, smoking one of a collection of pipes. He read a lot, but there was no writing. In between playing home I played every date I could get. Summer stock. Winter stock. Club dates. Supper clubs. I was even in a forty-five-minute version of *The Desert Song.* Back to four and five shows a day at the RKO in Philadelphia. No one cared. The Starlight called. I had won the "Most Promising" award—would I play a few specially chosen one-nighters? The roles were Raina in *Arms and the Man,* combined with *Mary's Other Husband.* We played eight high school auditoriums, a few Grange halls, three firehouses, and six mental institutions.

The route toward my destiny was well known, well trodden. Stopovers that involved actual lights, an audience no matter how small, and something new to learn, or someone new to be, were nuggets. Pure gold. I cherished each step because I knew I was on my way. This was the right direction.

Summer, 1938, I was Irene in the Jones Beach production of *Sally, Irene and Mary.* The girls playing Sally and Mary were wonderful. One sang gorgeously, one was a real ballerina. I couldn't outsing or outdance them, but I wasn't afraid of the water. The stage at Jones Beach was part of the bay. Across a lovely lagoon the audience watched the show from a respectful distance. A sound system magnified voices a hundred times the size of actors onstage. I sang the "Irene" number but did the funny dance I was beginning to be known for. As conclusion, instead of making my exit dancing into the wings, I danced right off the edge of the stage into the lagoon. Coming up for air, I bowed into the water, then swam for the back of the stage. It stopped the show. I changed rapidly from wig over bathing cap and dripping gown. My dry reappearance only a few moments later garnered more applause. It was a little heady, especially since the whole business which had gone over so wildly had been a dark secret until showtime. Our producers, Messrs. Lee and J. J. Shubert, were back on the double at the end of the show. Filled with a glorious sense of achievement, my friends and I eagerly watched their approach. Mr. Lee spoke. "Whose costume got wet? Yours or ours?"

34 ꮍꮍꮍ

The Starlight Barn on Route 22 near Pawling, New York, was the sole interest of an aging character actress with six children around my age. She had trouped all her life. Played every large and small stock company known. It would be perhaps seventy-five years ago now that she began as a young and vital dreamer of the bright lights. Somewhere in the Southwest she was conquered by a gentleman Indian. The liaison produced the six children but no permanent ties. She took her brood with her from stock company to medicine show to Chautauqua. She was at last stranded in Pawling. The tiny house she lived in sat on the top of Quaker Hill. It gazed at more than four counties. The house had been made from scenery crates. You could read such directions above your bunk as LYCEUM THEATRE—RUSH or SHUBERT—BOSTON. The first winter she had beaten into submission; they had lived in a tepee. The hill was now their own and the children shared the love of the land they farmed with the love of the theatre instilled in them by their mother.

Her name was Mary Verne Jones. She had bestowed romantic

names on her family, such as Isobel Rose, Starr West. These actors learned their lines while milking cows or tilling the fields. I was dazzled. One rose with the bell at 7 A.M., washed in cold well water, appearing at the refectory for breakfast at 7:30, rehearsal promptly at 9. Mrs. Jones was demanding, strong, a little fanatical. A good director.

"We do not teach acting here," she would say. "Please go to the box office and pick up your fare back to the city." Dread words. The worst was you were never told what your offense had been. "The theatre is like the Navy in one respect." Mrs. Jones's tones were elegant, perfectly placed. "As in the Navy, there is no excuse, no alibi." The puzzled actor usually departed in a haze. A replacement appeared like magic.

We watched such a removal during rehearsals for a murder mystery called *Spooks*. Mrs. Jones had engaged the up-and-coming son of a renowned actor whom she knew and respected. Stopping the scene with a gentle tap-tap, she said, "Please go back to the letter business." We exchanged nervous glances. The young actor repeated the business of signing the letter, licking the flap of the envelope, being stricken, then dramatically dying. There was no opportunity to slip him the answer to his problem. Mrs. Jones quietly directed four repeats of this beat as we grew more and more apprehensive. Each time he moved into a repeat he cast appealing glances toward us, but we dared not move, such was that lady's command of her company.

At last the curtain dropped. "Please go to the box office and pick up your fare to the city." We then had a break.

It was only proper to extend regrets to the bewildered actor. "What is wrong?" he whispered hoarsely. "I did it five times just as it is in the script."

The old actor who was a fixture with the company shook his head. "That's right, son." He patted the younger man's arm sympathetically. "But the text won't ever impart stage secrets. One does not die with one's feet toward the audience. Never."

The young actor's mouth fell open. "I died like that?" he asked.

"Five times," the old boy intoned. "Which is interpreted in the world of professionals, my child, as rudeness." He moved away in sadness.

During the season of 1938 I was called to the office of J. J.

Shubert. He sat at a huge desk facing a tray of food. "Come in, come in. Sit down. Down." I sat opposite him. "See this?" He waved a pudgy, beringed hand over the scrambled eggs and toast. "Hate it." He looked over his shoulder craftily. "You hungry? . . . Here." Turning the tray toward me he whispered urgently, "Finish it fast. Go on. Nobody'll ever know I didn't eat their rotten damn food. Go on." I enjoyed the repast while listening to his tale of horror.

"If you say I told you this, I'll tell everybody you're a liar, see?" I nodded. "So," he continued. "Saw you at Jones Beach for us. Three shows. Now. You will go on in case this bitch I'm stuck with tries her tricks, see?"

I looked up from the marmalade. "Understudy?"

He shrugged. "More like a standby," he said. "She's already got five understudies right in the show."

I dunked the marmalade muffin in the oversized cup of coffee. "Why me, then?" A perfectly logical question, I thought.

"Because," his whisper was impatient, "she isn't afraid of them, see? They're showgirls in the same show. Beautiful, beautiful showgirls."

I finished off the last of the scrambled eggs. "I don't see what—"

He pounded the desk; the dishes rattled. "She knows how great she is, she knows those gorgeous girls can't do her numbers—nobody can. You can't either." He looked at the empty dishes. "You hungry? Want some more?"

I shook my head. "Well then, Mr. J. J., if nobody, if I can't do her numbers—"

He sucked his teeth conspiratorially. "Shh. It's imitations she does. She—is—great—at—it. Now, if she won't go on some show, I don't think such a great imitator should be imitated. You see my point?"

We stared at one another. "No," I said.

His eyes rolled heavenward. "I got a surprise for them." He spoke slowly, almost menacingly. "I got somebody who goes out there and does her own number in case of fire, flood, or riot by this bitch, and I have outfoxed her, see?" I sat there considering the strange proposal. "You won't have to do understudy rehearsals," J. J. went on, "just work with the stage manager alone." I hesitated. I had heard of people who got caught in the standby image and never got out. "Listen to me," J. J. was saying. "You walk right in any Shubert house in town, every night, see the shows, free. Or stay home. Just so we know where to get you fast. Lissen, you get a bonus on top of your salary if you go on, okay? Okay?"

I guess the freedom to see all those shows whenever I wanted to did it. "Okay," I said.

The bonus, when I unexpectedly did go on, wasn't the money. J. J. was right about not imitating. I did my own dance, but sang Lupe Velez's songs with and without Clifton Webb. There I was, magically transported to the apron of the Winter Garden Theatre. Libby Holman sang in her sultry voice. Jerry Whyte was stage manager. This time I waited in the wings for a nod from him before I took the encore. He never again had to hold me by the seat. I had graduated. My bonus was the line in Walter Winchell's column: "June Havoc went on for Lupe Velez with twelve hours' notice. P.S. She stopped the show cold." Not only my own dance, but my own costumes, courtesy of Kalman & Morris. The old gown I loved so and a few things put together by the wardrobe mistress were all I had, because Lupe had a special lock on her dressing-room door and a powerful Katinka standing guard. It didn't matter. I was on my way home.

Then it was early spring again. My sister was back from Hollywood. "To hell with Louise Hovick." She was angrier than I had ever seen her. "All that garbage, censor this, censor that. Well, I am Gypsy Rose Lee from now on, and the Ladies Mutual Admiration Society can stuff it up their noses." Her speech wavered because a masseuse tugged and kneaded her throat. "Ouch! Goddammit, why does it have to hurt so?" She glared at me. "This is the family chin, you know, June. You'll get it sooner or later. Oow!" There was no coffee and brandy now, because she had been told in bold letters about the nervous condition in her stomach. A condition that was foreboding enough to frighten even Gypsy. So the new tea cozy sat astride a pot of Lapsang Souchong that could be mistaken for condensed ham fat. Like hot glue, it burned the whole route downward, slowly, slowly. It was consumed all the waking hours. Even though forbidden, the chain smoking continued.

"So tell about you." The masseuse was now attacking Gypsy's middle. She clung to the bedpost, legs spread, feet making impressions in the flowered carpeting as she struggled against the mauling. "Go on, talk," she ordered between clenched teeth. "It makes this almost bearable." I told her of all the club dates, the four-a-day *Desert Song,* Lupe Velez. About Jessie, Gibbs, and the home April and I had now.

"Great," she grunted. "You know what I've got? Ouch! Ah, God . . . well, I've got zilch. Oh, sure, Mother has that house in the country, but I don't know when I'm going to work again." The masseuse was kneading Gypsy's buttocks.

"What about Mizzy? I mean, Bob?" I asked.

My sister sighed between groans. "Another zilch," she said. "Nobody believed a single damn minute of all that romantic crap."

There was silence except for some rhythmic slaps. "Where is he?" I asked.

"Oh, he's still around somewhere. Nothing worked. With him, with Hollywood—zilch." She sniffled. "By God, I tried everything in the book, too. That whole marriage was the most legitimate publicity I ever had."

I couldn't watch the beating she was paying for, but I looked at her now. "But you're a Hollywood star, now, and you—"

She interrupted. "I'm a Hollywood floppo, that's what I am, June. God alone knows what's next. Look over there—that's all I've been offered since I came back covered with glory." There were a couple of scripts and a few letters. "Wait a minute." She pushed the masseuse away. "There's a great song there. The writers are wonderful, June. Here, look at that." She held up a sheet of music with lyrics. "They don't know I can't sing this, and I'll be damned if I'll prove I can't in public . . . why don't you do it?"

That's how I got involved with Theatre Arts Committee. TAC. At the same time, I managed to get myself into the show at the Greenwich Village Casino. A family supper club. Wonderful audience who really appreciated my rendition of Milton Berle's entire act.

TAC was composed of thoughtful theatre people who felt strongly about sharing their political viewpoints. The satirical revue was popular. This group hired huge halls for the shows they did. Harold Rome, Saul Aarons, John LaTouche, Sylvia Fine, Marc Blitzstein, Allen Rivkin wrote and performed; Hiram Sherman, Walter Coy, Beatrice Kay, Dorothy Bird, Max Liebman were among those who managed, directed, and also performed. I was a ringer. On the envelope of my first invitation to be present for a newspaper discussion, Gibbs had scrawled "To be opened by Lefty."

There were recordings of some of the material, including my effort, which was titled "Swing TAC." My sister did come to the hall to see me do that song, but not to any of the other places. Later, when the *Red Channels* rag was on the desk of every producer as well as in the drawer of every Senator, I learned that Gypsy had attended classes at the New School, donated money to various so-called fronts (many later proved as "rears"); that TAC was suspect, too.

In all the time I sang my funny song in those smoky, crowded halls, not once was I invited to join the Communist Party. No one mentioned that card. When I found out later that membership was two dollars, I was sure of the reason. No one thought I could afford it. I also found out, years later, how appearing with members, even though you yourself may be among the non-, can put you on those lists of undesirables drawn up by the inevitable lunatic fringe. It was early dawn for that set of McCarthys, but they were crawling out toward the sun even then. Who could foresee the carnival to come? How to guess that playing a few popular cause benefits could in time put a huge, untouchable signature on an otherwise blotless career? In short, when you're on the open field without a program, how do you distinguish friend from foe? Past maneuvers help us understand how armies have destroyed many of their own men. Confusion isn't reserved for the enemy alone.

Hiram Sherman ("Chubby" to his friends) called me one day. "Can you come to town, June? There's a chance of something good for us in the new World's Fair." A small group of us found our way to Michael Todd's small office in a big building on Broadway. Chubby told us how this man was going to build a whole Globe Theatre right in the middle of the midway.

I was worried. "Shakespeare? I'm not ready yet, Chubby."

He scoffed, "It's a breeze. I'll show you. Ah! Just think, our own company." Such reverie kept us sitting quietly.

In time the secretary covered her typewriter and closed the door as she left. The office building was quiet. We huddled together. At long last the inner door flew open and there was Mike Todd himself. My first impression was of squareness. His jaw appeared to have been sliced by a cleaver. The neck short, beginning directly under his ears. Not a tall man, anything but fat, yet his sturdy body gave me the impression of as much width as height. Spotting us, he opened his mouth in bigger-than-life surprise. Flashing back, the connection hits me now. He was Dickensian, or perhaps someone from the other side of the looking glass. He held a foolishly large cigar. The fingers on his hands appeared to be all of the same length.

We stood up as one. Before Hiram could voice his introductions, Todd slammed the door behind him. "No!" he boomed. "Oh, no, I forgot all about you. You are . . . uh—?" He slapped his forehead with the flat of one square hand.

Chubby quickly offered our names with his own stuck at the end. Todd stood nodding at us. "Shakespeare, eh?" We smiled, glancing back and forth at one another. "Actors," Todd sighed. We beamed. "A drug on the market," he said softly. "Tell you what, I'm gonna eat. You want to come along?" The move toward the door was general.

Mike Todd took us to Lüchow's. He ordered a splendid feast. He opened his secret heart to us and we were overcome with his gentle humanity. The dinner was good, too.

"You gotta understand, Shakespeare is a luxury. It's like the nuts and the whipped cream on top of a banana split. To produce . . . to act . . . it's a goddam luxury." We sat musing on this wisdom. "You see," he went on sincerely, "One hand washes the other. I gotta give 'em the kinda 'drop-the-pants' show in order to pay for your 'Alas, poor Yorick' crap." He sighed. "Hell, I like class as much as the next poor, starved bastard. It's just— it's gotta be paid for up front." We munched thoughtfully.

"I'm the guy dreamed up that 'Moth and the Flame' act, you know?" We didn't. "Well, this dancer all in wisps of stuff gets closer and closer to this fire—took a long time to get that fire stuff to work—so she burns off this and then that, finally you get a really good look. Lemme tell you, I burned the hell out of a lot of dancers to get that one right, but it paid my way here from Chicago." We tried to look appreciative. "Then that black *Hot Mikado* gimmick? Was all mine, you know, that wasn't any pile of chopped liver." He sighed. "This one's tougher. There's nobody around like the dame, say, who put that Chicago World's Fair on the map. The one with the fans and the blue spot—Sally Rand, yeah."

A light popped on inside my head. "You mean you want a Sally Rand?" My tone was cautious.

He nodded dejectedly. "A lost breed," he mourned. "The Little Egypts who were like the Pied Something-or-Other, you know, brought out the hicks like that Pied Whatever brought out the rats. Big business."

I looked at the others. "There's Gypsy Rose Lee," I said.

"Oh, sure," he poohed, "there's Gypsy Rose Lee stinking up Hollywood."

I bristled. "She looks beautiful in those movies, and you—"

He stopped me with a wave of his cigar. "Lissen," he said strongly, "that's a no-talent broad worth a million bucks on any midway. She's baking dead clams now, but that don't mean I wouldn't give my right ball to get her into a show of mine."

I exhaled. "What kind of a show?" I asked.

"I'd build a whole trap around her—aw, hell, she's out there. Forget it." He sank into his coffee cup.

I gathered myself up. "Ladies' room," I murmured, as I headed for the pay phone.

"How do you know he isn't one more fink?" my sister asked.

"I don't," I replied. "But you said you didn't have offers— well, maybe people think you're too big. He does, and the World's Fair sounds good. . . ."

Her voice was weary. "Ah, God. Another runway."

I jumped. "He says you are worth a million dollars on that midway. . . ."

I could hear her thinking. "Did he mention money?" she asked.

"Not actually," I replied. "But he said he'd give his right . . . right . . . ball to get you," I blurted.

"Great," she said, "that's worth a nickel of anybody's money."

I gave Mike her number. They met the next day. It was money at first sight. Most people know about the partnership that ensued, but I wonder how many know it was financed with Gypsy's cashed-in annuities. Good at business, she bought eighty-eight percent of Todd. In time it added up considerably.

Lost somewhere in the Hollywood scramble was Mizzy. Gypsy was free again. Well, almost. She told me she had been infatuated with Bob Mizzy's upbringing. "Think, June, the same two parents all along the line. Mother, father. Just lovely people. I'm going to miss them."

It would be soon that I would miss Jessie, too.

35 ꕥꕥꕥ

The early winter of 1939 that turned into late winter of 1940 was memorable for the whole world, not just me. Events whirled about us like leaves in a storm. Too much was happening. Warning voices were lost in the wind. The strength of opposite opinions diluted evidence. Even an untrained mind sensed impending history. I wept at newsreels. At half-grasped meanings in strange streets. Witnessing muddied deaths, the sense of epic, real-life drama permeated my being.

I listened. I watched, but I had no vocabulary for discussion. The truth was dawning. I was ignorant. So ignorant. In the time wasted disguising that bumbling lack of knowledge, I might have learned how to sharpen the mind hidden under the clown cap. Somehow, the chance went by unrecognized. I played the fool well. It was too easy. Evoking laughter became my crutch. Moves extended into grotesqueries. Facial extremes masked the hidden hope, the desire to know. To learn. It was more urgent that I make use of every second now, count costs later.

It was much, much later that I discovered how little respect I had for that merry madcap I had created. The instrument had been viable enough to play itself, mindlessly. The trick was going to be to master my own abilities. Without guidance, how does one develop selectivity? Disregarding for the moment innate sensitivities, how does one avoid choices that leave lifelong scars? Self-destruction? Shame? Regret is like the Chinese torture, in that it eats away at its target insidiously.

During that period, my outward appearance had settled into total nondescript. I never looked at myself. It wasn't important. Within the Floating Waif Society a small group had formed. Two writers gathered some of us who sang to audition their revue material. We were supposed to be the money-raising element. Large, sometimes small audiences heard us to evaluate whether the show might be a good investment. We performed in penthouses, hotel rooms.

Then, in spring we were offered a place of our own. It was

called White Roe. A rambling series of buildings on the top of a mountain, once again in New York State. A picture-book lake mirrored the sky. There were a miniature theatre, a nightclub, and a social hall. Lots of remarkable food served by singing waiters. A stable of horses. Tennis and golf.

To the trade, it was on the Borscht Circuit. To me, it was a marathon of a different color. Monday we were a choral group with the concert, monologues to music thrown in. Tuesday there was a water carnival. Many prizes. In the center of the lake I did comic dives from the high board on the float. Wednesday, nightclub time. We did an entire bill of acts written for that milieu. Thursday, drama. We resorted to Odets—a straight play, full length. Friday, presentation. The band onstage, it was updated vaude. Special material. Saturday, the big night. Our writers had the opportunity to strut. We did a musical comedy. All original songs. Sometimes a revue. Usually a book show. Sunday, poetry readings.

Rehearsals were all day. Every day. And if you happened to get caught in the shower with some of the guests you had better have five minutes of original patter.

This time April stayed at home with Jessie and Gibbs. Home in summer was the Victorian cottage on Lake Champlain. I began each season on the broad porch, helping Jessie beat the rugs, remove the mothballs from inside the upright piano, and air the sunny rooms. One of these busy times I had been rummaging through a dark closet. Jessie appeared silhouetted in the door. "Why are you in here?" She spoke in a hushed tone. "Nothing here, June. Nothing."

I returned a few blankets to the shelf. "Is there a light?" I asked.

"No. This place belongs in the dark." Her reply had been too swift. Tense.

I stared through the gloom toward her. "Jessie?" I put my hand on her shoulder.

She crumpled in my arms, weeping convulsively, the sobs ripped from her depths. I held her tightly. The moment passed. We stood together in the small stuffy cubicle. Finally she pointed to a toy trunk. "It's all in there. All of it. I can't even remember the things or the actual words anymore, but I remember the pain—when my heart broke." I stared at the little casketlike box. On its lid, written boldly in Jessie's precise hand, were the words "Memories that sear and burn." Whatever lay fading to dust in that secret place was all the voice there was left to speak for the one time Jessie had loved—all, of course, but the issue. The baby. Child. Boy. Man? Gibbs. Jessie's one proof of existence. Donald Staley Gibbs. Other proof, such as "With this ring I thee wed," a small band of gold with no inscription. A few dusty documents. Legal words to the effect that there was a marriage.

"I look at the papers, at the ring he put on my finger." Jessie's eyes closed with the pain of remembering. "Every single word of that ceremony haunts me." She was whispering, staring down at the little trunk.

"Jessie." I tried to make my voice authoritative. "Burn that memory. Put the important papers in some bank like you do the good silver, and burn the rest." Her jaw dropped. She stared at me. Her head moved from side to side. "Oh, no," she breathed, "if I do that I won't have anything, anything at all."

So Jessie clung to fragments. To fragments and her child . . . man? I tried clinging to the plan. Working my way through the maze of ladder bottoms. A veritable forest, rungs everywhere.

Coming home to my co-dreamer. "Did you get to the book?" I shouldn't have prodded. I guess I wanted to share. To swap stories. Gibbs receded further and further.

Our friendship, born at the gate of the upward path, was encountering all the monsters lurking along that route. If they were no surprise to me it was no doubt because I had met them all before. However, I was beginning to suspect that a formidable difference existed between putting down words on that empty page, between the football games at Harvard and that empty page at the typewriter sitting on that specially built desk in front of the Veritas chair in the little house by the side of the road.

Writing as a subject was taboo. In this case, frustration didn't make good conversation. In my world, however, frustration was the mode. It was the school tie of my gang. The constant search for something, anything to forge into even a self-destructing rung on the invisible ladder was a way of life on the way to life for us. Lunch was a hot dog on the run. Lunch to Gibbs was a three-martini trip of waste space. Excursions, cruises, and social loitering on the way to the main events made Gibbs miss his own entrance. This observation is not shared by those people who get in the ring too late for the bell. If all the excuses for not writing were piled together, Busby Berkeley could choreograph *Stairway to the Stars* from his spot in heaven downward all the way to hell, and back.

In my case, lack of communication eventually eroded the early interests. The college humor which had dramatized my everyday efforts soured, became cynical. However, if the climate at home was unproductive, it didn't rub off on me. I looked over my shoulder in sympathy. But I kept moving along.

End of the season at White Roe was the start of rehearsals for a new play for me. Southampton, Long Island, supported a small, exclusive theatre. Mr. Lee was trying out a Shubert possibility. I took April to the beach. The play wasn't as much fun as sand castles, but we were edging along.

The White Roe gang called. "Let's rent an empty theatre, invite all the producers in town, and show 'em all the great stuff they missed." Fine idea. We gathered under the lone worklight. Our shadows fell over the empty seats out front in streaming lengths. The composer was in despair over the ancient piano. "It hasn't been tuned since *Blossom Time!*" he wailed.

After we had mopped the crusty scales off the stage, shaded the lone bulb so it wouldn't blind our important audience, and swabbed the toilet for them, we waited.

Among us there could not have been a single eye that would recognize any of the producers we hoped would arrive. When enough of the dusty seats were filled with bodies, we would begin our show. Through a peephole I searched the house for Mr. J. J. The atmosphere was so grimy and dark I half hoped no one would be out front to watch. The other half of my heart, the part composed of old pieces of juggernaut, was wishing away with the old fevered affirmation. Eventually enough seats were miraculously occupied. Whispered queries expressed the fear that there were no known impresarios among the arrivals, but then, the whisperers shrugged, how do we know? As the fateful hour struck, no old pro was needed to recognize the office boys and receptionists who comprised our audience. "Well," we sighed resignedly, "with luck they will tell the stenographers, who will tell the secretaries, who just may tell the boss."

The composer pounded out his melodies on whatever was working on the keyboard, and the show was on. During the nonstop hour that ensued, I sang high, low; danced fancy, plain, tap, adagio, on point; did dramatic scenes and comedy sketches. I changed shoes five times. Trembling with exertion, soaked with cold sweat, panting and puffing, we took our nods, then flung ourselves to the floor backstage. Our main objective achieved, whatever was to follow would be garnish.

The house emptied quietly. We gathered up our shoes and the few props we had felt were essential. Gloom descended. Why did it all have to be so mysterious? The abandon, the thrill of performing bits and pieces tailored to fit our individual talents had abruptly ended. Confidence doesn't linger. The warm breath of hope must fan it constantly or the embers die. Consistency is rare. Technical performances are either good or great. Seldom awful. Inspired performances, on the other hand, are either great or truly bad.

Some artists are born with an unquenchable flame. Lucky. Hardy, too. They usually are indomitable. Then there are the plodders. A magnificent technique develops along the way. They study. Learn. They too are indomitable. Finally, there is the happy freak. Ignorant of the meaning of the words "technique" or "inspiration," untouched by textbook or planned method of work, they burst into a spotlight in such a frenzy of joy to be there at all that an audience responds as though discovering a secret self. I enjoyed that confusing category. My love affair with the audience, almost any audience, was my lifeline. My security. Even dark and empty, a theatre was an impenetrable fort. A safe haven . . . It was only when you stepped over that threshold into the artificial light of day, onto the unreal street, that doubt crept in.

I was wiping my face with a terry cloth when the man's shadow fell over me. I cried out in sudden fear. "Didn't mean to startle you," he said. He was as tall as anyone I'd ever met. "Can you come up the street with me?" A few of the gang looked suspicious. "To the Barrymore, I want you to audition." I looked down at my crumpled skirt. Under the arms of my jersey were dark circles that extended all the way to my waist. Even my back was wet. "You look fine," he said. "We have your music. Come on." Lew the composer walked ahead with the tall man. I followed, happy for an extension of the wonderful feeling.

At the Barrymore Theatre, my benefactor disappeared into the audience, Lew into the pit, and I into a horde of aspirants.

Within minutes my name was called. Moving through the waiting crowd felt good. The tall man had to be somebody.

Center stage. Dim outlines of people out front in a small cluster. Lew's face glowing in the light of the music lamp. This piano had all its keys. Lew pounded out the intro. The clammy wet of my clothes warmed to the heat of my body. I heard laughter from the orchestra seats. It worked on me like a transfusion. I clowned. Danced. Sang. Overjoyed with "Do something else" instead of "Thank you, next." It went on and on. "Do you know any popular songs?" Lew's face clouded. I shook my head. "Play 'Tea for Two,' " the voice said to Lew. "I'll throw you the words." The smiling man was Richard Rodgers, but I didn't know enough to recognize him. Or George Abbott, Larry Hart, even the author John O'Hara. But I picked up the words and sang along with Richard Rodgers.

The show was *Pal Joey*. That wouldn't have struck one of my bells either. Then the party was over. For the first time I experienced a terrible letdown. I realized fully that some rare opportunity had come my way. "Did I do enough?" I asked the tall man. "More than enough." He laughed. "What can I do now?" I wanted to hold on to the moment. "Nothing," he replied. "I want to tell you that ever since you've been in town people have been trying to sell you to me and I've never let you get past the waiting room." The chance was there, then. I should have asked him, "Why?" but I stood staring up at him dumbly. "Well," he said, "if they want you, they'll let you know." He gave me his card before he was lost in traffic. It said he was with the office of Dwight Deere Wiman. It said that he was Forrest Haring. Neither name meant anything to me then. It was years before I remembered that I had failed to tell him how grateful I was. I didn't even say thank you.

I went home numbly. The house was empty. I slid off my clothes and lowered the aching bones into a tub of warm bubbles. The tears came. What did I always seem to do that was so wrong? The four years since *Forbidden Melody* were crammed with trying. All sorts of auditions, endless effort. Whenever I could get to an audience there was no doubt of my effectiveness, but the trip there was not as successful. Was I still "too much"? If I had asked "Why?" of Forrest Haring, the answer could have been cruel. Painful. Had I been cowardly? Stupid? I let my weight float in the warm water.

"Yoo-hoo." Jessie had brought April home from kindergarten. There was a knock on the door. I washed away the gummy tears. "Come in." April held a large card proudly. "She won first prize, June. Look at that." Jessie's voice from the hall was muffled. "I'm covered in bubbles," I cried. "Come in." April's drawing was explicit. "Oh, that's good," I said. "It's Jesus," April explained. Jessie looked worried. "An—an interesting subject, isn't it?" I asked.

"It's just that—" Jessie hesitated.

April looked from one to the other of us. "He has a large belly button," she said gravely.

"Well," I studied the picture, "if that's all he has to worry about, he's lucky, huh?" We laughed together until I saw Jessie's face in the mirror. She had often told me that she was afraid for April. For me. Afraid of what life was going to do to us. We weren't going to escape, she said.

36 ﹠﹠﹠

Pal Joey began rehearsals in November. I was thrilled to vertigo as I received my contract. It said "As directed." We rehearsed in two theatres. On the stage of one the actors worked with Mr. A., as he was carefully called. The other stage was noisy and exciting. That was where Robert Alton worked with the dancers. At the first reading I had sat in the circle with Mr. A. and the actors. My part was very small. I didn't appear until the second act was well under way. That was at first.

The magic circle began with the creators of *Joey,* then continued with its star, Vivienne Segal, its star-to-be, Gene Kelly, then on to lesser lights. Leila Ernst was the lovely ingénue, Jack Durant a blackmailer, and Jean Casto a reporter. Among the chorus were Van Johnson, Stanley Donen, and Amarilla Morris. Best of all, the production stage manager was Jerry Whyte. First to arrive, last to leave: June Havoc. The name of the character I was to play was simple "Gladys." But I was restless. I prowled between the two theatres, burning for more to do. To be. To at least try. I began working behind the dancers as they learned the beginnings of Robert Alton's intricate choreography. There were two numbers planned for Jack Durant. In them I was supposed to be a sort of second banana. Neither character appeared until the second act. Not in the beginning, anyway.

Managing to insert Gladys into the first act became a crusade for me. I frantically tapped my way into Alton's sight line. He installed me into a marvelous comic routine up early in the show. "Go tell Mr. A. O'Hara has to find a way to get you on for this." A tiny scene was written to establish Gladys so she could do the number. Oh, wonder.

A few days later, after rehearsal was over and the company had departed for the evening, I watched from my hiding spot in an upper box. Rodgers had brought in a new song. He played and sang. Everyone laughed. "Tomorrow," he said, "find a funny voice who can really move, okay?" Auditions were planned, the golden group departed. I emerged from my secret place, pouncing on Jerry Whyte. If he hadn't snagged a copy of "Terrific Rainbow" for me so I could work on it all that night, I could never have beat out my competitors at the auditions the following day.

The next event: same set, same cast. Rodgers played them "Flower Garden of My Heart." It went over big, too. "Find a tatty soprano tomorrow."

Auditions were set. That night, after blessing Jerry again, I blessed the vocal coach who had given me a few five-dollar lessons. That investment had liberated a high B-flat I hadn't known what to do with until now. As extra insurance, I sang in my high voice while on point. Oh, joy, I got the number. I now had five spots in the show, starting from the very first moment. Each time a new number fell my way, John O'Hara wrote something to get me onstage, so by the time we opened in Philadelphia, I had five songs and a nice fat part. I sang high, I sang low, I danced fast, slow, and on point. And, for the ending of my first number with Jack Durant, I carried 180 pounds of blackmailer offstage while we sang the last sixteen bars of "Plant You Now, Dig You Later" in harmony.

Pal Joey was my overnight stardom that took all of my life since the age of two to reach. It was the best of times. It was the worst of times.

The twenty-eight-hour day of one hundred ninety-five percent absorption during rehearsals. The unavoidable physical debilitation, emotional spin were trade facts, but myths within fantasies to Gibbs. There really are people who believe the show is made up as you party along.

Finally, in the usual state of breakdown, we opened. A smash. Publicity began. "This is it!" I hollered. "*Life* magazine is coming to do a whole story on me—whoops!"

Gibbs and Jessie stared. "You surely aren't going to let them inside the house, are you?"

I stared back. "They're here, they're here!" I moved toward the door.

Gibbs blocked it. "This is going too far, June," he said.

The much-discussed dream—as reality—became a nightmare. An intrusion on the dreaming. The comforts of non-achievement were threatened. Pictures, interviews, benefits to play, appearances would follow. Some of the people who lived in the little house by the side of the road were uncomfortable. We were no longer talking the act, we were right out in the light doing it, and it was going over big. I plunged forward; this time I didn't look back.

April and I danced too much. Sang too much. Enjoyed success too much. There was a gradual lowering of the boom. The little house darkened.

Then there was Mother.

I was called to Mr. A.'s office one day. Worried, I tried to use the nice pay raise just received to ward off fear of being fired. Tall, blue-eyed, fair-haired, Mr. A. was also Scandinavian. Cool. Some considered him cold. "Tell me about your mother," he said. I went blank. Where to begin? How?

Looking at Mr. A., his cleaner than clean skin, clear as clear eyes, I doubted that someone of his impeccable backdrop could ever fathom . . . Mother.

My sister had put an end to the closeness of their relationship after Mother had chased Mizzy around the Malibu house with a gun. That episode had been part of the Hollywood saga, which includes the time Mother got dressed in worn shoes and the old coat Gypsy said they used to wear on cold nights when milking the cow back on the farm in Highland Mills. She had added a white makeup for the desired effect, then called on Mr. Zanuck. He listened as she told him how weak she was from long privation. Had asked him for a bowl of hot soup. The way my sister told them, the Mother stories were all hilarious. To the press, to outsiders. When she told them to me, however, it was a little different. "She wouldn't let go of you, June, remember? Until you ran away. Closed the door completely." Back then, Mother had done that identical routine with a gun. Held it almost touching Bobby's chest while she pulled at the trigger. An automatic—the safety catch was on. We often wondered if she understood that. Also, if the rifle she used to chase Mizzy was purposely unloaded. It was funny in a surreal sort of way, because it was almost impossible to credit. Funny Mother stories.

The stories were basically true. The guns weren't stage props. The events weren't fiction. In spite of that, as the reels unwound, all near tragedy or high-to-low comedy emerged as unreal, unbelievable. Something had to be done to make it all credible. So Gypsy applied a coat of humor. It came out funny as hell in the reruns. At parties or in interviews everybody howled. "Keep it funny, June," my sister advised. "Nobody buys a subplot like ours. Make 'em laugh or you lose the audience."

I got over big with some funny Mother stories of my own. The one about the mean lady playing on the bill with us who kept insisting that Dainty June was a midget.

Mother's eyes clouded. "She needs a lesson—a good scare, that's what she needs."

We huddled over our coffee. "She's mean," my sister said. "I don't think you ought to tackle someone so mean."

Mother smiled. "Tackle? Oh, no. I'll write. I'll write a letter she won't forget. I'll say, 'Someone is following you, and within two weeks your body will be found floating in the river.'" We shivered. Mother's voice had lowered to a dark, menacing tone.

"But that's evidence." My sister looked worried. "She'll see that you wrote that letter and then she—"

Mother stopped her with a snort of contempt. "Do I look D.U.M.B.? You think I'd put my name on a threat? No. I'll sign it miscellaneously."

Then there was the time we were traveling by car. The long overnight jumps left me limp with fatigue.

"It's all going to be different, darling." Mother was jubilant. "You will sleep like a little queen on the long jumps, because I traded in the car for a real luxury boat."

The boat was long and black. Mother sat in front with Elias, who drove but who was actually a very good eccentric dancer.

The rest of us shared the extensive flat surface usually reserved for a coffin. Bundled in stolen hotel blankets, we viewed the passing landscape through delicate leaded windows. "They threw in the curtains, girls, so you can have privacy." Mother's experiment was doomed to failure, but the story was always a boff.

Drama was Mother's forte. Unloaded guns and dead cars were part of her own personal reality. It was all quite contagious. The truth was so close and yet so far. Fact was an honest kaleidoscope. Wonderful material for funny stories until the girl at Highland Mills died of gunshot. Suddenly there was a real gun. A gun that was loaded. The kaleidoscope jammed. Its complex pattern was clear now.

"Around then," my sister said, "I had to figure losses." Gypsy was playing nightclubs when *Pal Joey* happened to me. We hadn't seen a lot of one another in the years between *Forbidden Melody* and *Joey*. But we wrote letters, we phoned. I had seen Mother not at all since my sister's warning.

"Get a lawyer if you can afford one, June. She won't stop getting in the act until you do." Gypsy had a big important lawyer who was the go-between for her. I couldn't afford one so she shared her lawyer's advice with me. "As long as she writes letters, it means she isn't going to show. You're lucky." I hadn't had a letter for a very long time when Mr. A. called me to his office.

"What was she wearing?" I asked him now. He stared out the window. The skyscrapers looked like painted scenery. "She looked pale—sad, shabby. She sat in that chair and wept. She says she doesn't understand why you and your sister are so distant."

Where to begin? How?

"She asked me if she could stand in the back of the house to watch you onstage."

I swallowed. "Did she say anything about—about hot soup?" I asked.

He turned and looked at me fully. "That's right," he said quietly. "And it was a very good getup, too, old coat, worn shoes—good." My mouth must have fallen open. "Only one thing," he continued. "It's old. Been done by every stage mother in the business." He grinned. "Disappointing—no new twists." Later, I wondered why Mr. Zanuck hadn't been as wise. Hadn't grinned.

Mother saw part of *Pal Joey*. She came late, then after the intermission didn't return for the second act. She was with a friend.

That's when the letters became important. Before *Melody* failed there had been a few. Then silence. When *Joey* opened a world for me, the letters had begun again. There was no mention of what I was doing. Of April. The theme was so plaintive that I sent the first of a collection to my sister.

"Is Mother ill and poor?" I wrote. "Tell me what to do."

The answer was immediate. "Don't ever reply," she wrote. "Keep the letters, but don't write back." She said they were almost identical to the ones she received regularly. If there had been less similarity my resistance would have melted. Not because of Mother's words, but because part of me was experiencing hope. The impulse was to share.

But inside the letters I found no reference to either of us. Either one of us or the other as people. Women. There had been no recording of us as participants in a struggle toward survival. No questions regarding the effort or result. No recognition of the fight toward a goal. There was no goal. No struggle. In essence, we did not exist except as money funnels. Only variations on the same theme. "God will punish you because . . ." "My teeth . . . I need . . . Can no longer see well . . . I need . . . My asthma, can't breathe . . . need . . . must have . . . cold, no warm clothes . . . lonely, a radio at least would be some company. . . ." The needs were endless.

"June," Gypsy's tone was strong, "I warn you, June. She has radios. I have receipts. Radios, glasses. Dentists. You name it. Close your eyes, I'll give you a picture of our mother mailing those letters—ready? She alights from her car—oh yes, June, her car. You know she has never learned to drive. There is always a friend. A friend who lives at the house, drives the car, who used to work—but nobody needs a job when an annuity pays the way, do they? So, she leaves the house that Mother owns—yes, owns— and look! She mails the letters. She is wearing a lovely mink coat." There is a pause to let it sink in. "Where is your mink coat, June?" Gypsy told me that Mother had everything she kept begging for. All the material things. In an interview she said: "Material things always fascinate Mother. Why haven't I said more about her? I'm saving her for a book. If you had a mother like mine you wouldn't go around handing her out to everybody. She's one of the wonders of the world, like the Hanging Gardens of Babylon or the Colossus of Rhodes."

To me Gypsy said, "You take care of your child, I'll take care of mine." She meant Mother, of course. Gypsy repeated the formula many times. "I stay away. I send money. I get receipts. I do it all through my lawyer."

Newspaper people had a special love for Gypsy. She was a symbol. She was also good copy. The stories Mother sent to reporters were often rerouted to Gypsy in mysterious ways.

"I've warned you, June. Read this and then tell me about Mother's letters."

She tossed a sheaf of penciled manuscript toward me. We sat at a corner table at our favorite Chinese restaurant. The writing was only too recognizable—the spelling confirmed.

Gypsy grinned. "Mother's answer to my interview last week. I made some reference to her. By now I should know better."

I riffled through the yellow sheets.

Gypsy went on, "It says such godawful things about me the paper wouldn't dare print it." It was sordid stuff, all right.

"But, this is so—so—" I looked up. Mother's manuscript held secrets, dark secrets.

"Mother says she made me the most famous naked star alive." Gypsy's eyes clouded. "Do you think she has earned general admiration for that motherly feat?"

I pushed the yellow pages toward her. "But she is so short-sighted she doesn't understand that if this ugly stuff was printed, it would cut off her own paycheck."

She shook her head. "Even if I had no friends, even if all those poorly spelled shockers were true, one thing—just one, mind you—makes the whole enchilada yesterday's tabloid."

I was hanging on every word. "What is that?" I breathed.

Gypsy folded the papers neatly. "You are new here, June." She put them in an envelope. "Mother isn't. The main thing that makes her funny to the outside—funny and different—is my way of presenting her to the world. Without my wit, Mother is just one more corny song with a boring lyric. Add that to a bad performance, and it won't make it till the end of the week."

We sipped our oolong. "So don't you get into the act," she continued, "because you don't know the music." I was only too glad to stay in the wings. "Someday," my sister said, chuckling, "it'll all pay off. Meanwhile, I'll do the thinking on this problem." She put the envelope in her bag. "Just to be on the safe side," she added, "keep your letters, keep everything. Don't look so worried, June." She put her arm around my shoulders. "I've had a lot of practice at this. I'm real good at crapping the crappers."

After that I read Mother's letters over and over whenever they came. I wonder now from this distance if the searching could have been for a clue, something that would explain my own reaction to Mother. Some remnant that could help untangle the solid wall of knots and weavings standing sky high between us. Reruns of the most vivid events stored in my recall vault are instantly available at the touch of an emotion. A scent. Pictures of Mother are almost all of the face contorted in fury, eyes spilling tears, mouth twisted, the corners spitting wet. Mother being canny. Mischief in the voice and manner. Indulging in the sneak stealing that had a name unknown to me as a child. Mother standing small. Face appealing. Voice artificially pale. She is lying. Talking her way out of paying or giving something owed. Getting away most of the time. Mother gloating over the escape. She always looks beautiful in this shot.

Where were the missing closeups? Lost somewhere at a very early stage in our lives together were the sepia-toned pictures of her face gentle in repose. Aglow with tenderness. Warm in serenity. They were lost. Gone. Only the conviction that they must, must at one time have existed. It remains impossible to conjure up a single moment that puts the lie to my dread of what was Mother.

It wasn't until later, much later, that ordinary people recognized such things in one another as marks of illness. Of disintegration that might be healed. It was, and is even now, later still for the ignorant, the unaware among us.

But nothing then was recognized as pitiable. Fearful, yes. But it takes knowledge to embrace a falling wall. To know how to avert the crash. To employ grace and compassion as bandages.

No, I could find no memories of Mother as she may have been to me so long ago. Before Baby June. Before my sister appeared in our lives. Dainty June, Gordon, the Newsboy Songsters. Long ago when she was a girl. Slender, with long, softly curling hair. Velvety eyes that changed from violet to the hues of an evening sky. We had been alone together at first. We must have been close. Did she ever hold me? Smile into my face? Perhaps I had snuggled against her, clung to her, been kissed. Loved.

I remember no touching. The recollection of that girlish Mother refuses to move out of these photographs I hold. A stranger may have known her as she was then. I never have. There were to be opportunities to know her better, much better, later. A too-late later.

37 ❦❦❦

Later than now.

Now was winter, 1940, the winter of *Pal Joey*. Rehearsals had begun in November. I'll never know how a Scorpio kept a birthday quiet, but I told no one. I was twenty-four. I was in a big show headed for Broadway. I was on my way to our first confrontation with an audience.

Philadelphia was the initial date, and my sister managed to be there in person. The audience was glittering. The City of Brotherly Love adored its premières. The theatre rang with laughter and applause, and I was part of it.

From my first entrance, Gypsy sobbed with such gusto that Dick Rodgers left his position at the back of the house, walked down the aisle quietly, and brought her back to stand with him.

"Cheer up, Gypsy," he whispered.

"Cheer up?" she replied, swallowing hard. "I've never been so happy. Look at that—nobody, including me, ever expected to see her on a stage again." She hid in the manager's office between acts, where she could really let go with her joy. Then we wept together when it was all over.

"Two show stops, June, do you know what that means?"

I blew my nose happily. "Sure," I answered, "I've got some wonderful numbers in this show, and—"

She sniffed. "You always stopped the show, June. You used to have to go out in front of the damn newsreel to take a bow, remember?"

I remembered. Oh, yes, I remembered. The strength of that sound in my memory was the wonder drug that made it possible for me to scrounge gaily all the way through the funhouse. Past the hall of mirrors. The wind trap. Down the fiery slide and over

Devil's Hole. That laughter and applause had been my vitamins, meat, and potatoes. My Caribbean cruise. How much glowing pleasure and pride can you squeeze into a hundred-and-twenty-pound tube of skin?

At the Ethel Barrymore Theatre it was the best of times; at the little house it was the worst of times, and I didn't know how to stage-manage either location. The quick transfers from the hot pink of the theatre to the icy compress of home were thinning my blood. If only I had had an arsenal of illustrative answers to the deflating queries that weakened me.

"Loretta Young has always been a lady," Jessie held a lovely picture of the film star dressed in black, "otherwise she wouldn't be playing saints and nuns." The Sunday magazine section held other evidence. "Just see Irene Dunne, June, never a hair out of place. Never a questionable word or gesture. . . . Class will tell." Musical comedy was déclassée. I had no reply. "I'll wager Helen Hayes never shook her you-know-what for a laugh." My big moment was less than prideful to them. My success a failure here.

One response to what I was doing matched my own enthusiasm. April came to see a matinee of *Joey*. She sat in the first row center so the conductor could keep an eye on her. That was the idea, anyway. It would have worked, too, except he gave her a chocolate lollipop just before overture. Between entrances, all of us backstage watched her as she reacted to the show. She laughed, applauded on cue. A great audience. Until she became bored with the lollipop. Not knowing what to do with it, she found a place that no doubt was logical for her. She leaned forward and ever so carefully pushed the remains in the conductor's ear.

Oh yes, there was light in the forest. I even had an agent now. There were offers from places I hadn't stretched a thought to. Hollywood. Hollywood! Scary. I didn't know anything but the stage. . . . "Films and theatre are the same." My new agent was talking, encouraging. But oh, my long Norwegian beak. What would I look like on the screen? "You'll look just like you look in the mirror." I changed agents and forgot about Hollywood for a while. Onstage I didn't have to worry about how I looked. Mirrors weren't important.

That was the year Bobby lost the game. He was master of ceremonies in Ottawa. On the marathon floor, being very funny.

Pal Joey, *1941*.

Tony gets his mural.
BRUNO OF HOLLYWOOD

BRUNO OF HOLLYWOOD

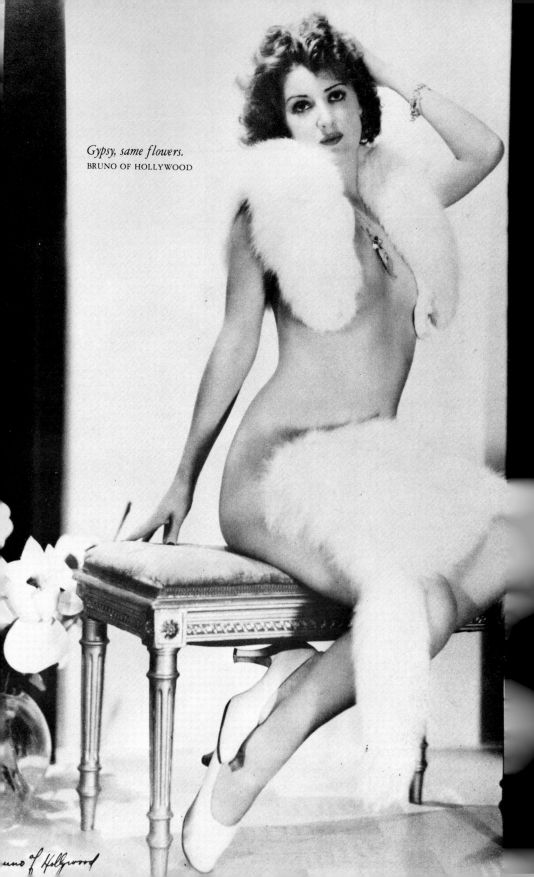

Gypsy, same flowers.
BRUNO OF HOLLYWOOD

More for the Bruno portfolio, 1940.
BRUNO OF HOLLYWOOD

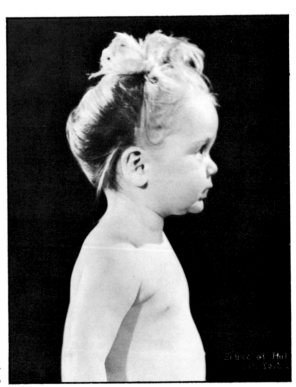

A Bruno study of April.
BRUNO OF HOLLYWOOD

April and June,
Mexican Hayride *time.*

The fingernails.
MAURICE SEYMOUR

Gypsy Rose Lee, circa 1935.

Mr. and Mrs. Staley Gibbs.

Gyp and June on a Circle Line
tour of Manhattan.
ELIOT ELISOFON

Clowning.
JACK ROBINSON

*At 20th Century-Fox with
Betty Grable and Jack Oakie.*
20TH CENTURY-FOX

June in Gypsy's bed, 1944. ELIOT ELISOFON
Hollywood (inset). PARAMOUNT

The contestants had gone to quarters for the rest period. Some fan threw a handful of coppers—the big pennies that are no longer popular. One struck Bobby's glasses. They splintered. "His eye dribbled down his cheek just like a soft-boiled egg." That was the report I got. There was more. While hospitalized, Bobby somehow touched an infected part of his body, then put those same fingers near his eye. The hospital said they were not responsible, as they had not been informed that Bobby was syphilitic. The disease overtook the mind, the brain. . . . My letters that year from Bobby were stamped by an inspector. They were sent from an institution. The scrawl was gibberish.

Hard to believe, but Jamie died. He too was on the marathon floor. Being funny. He simply toppled over. That was the report I got.

All those letters would stop coming now.

I closed my eyes, making an effort at visualizing the familiar dance arena . . . rest quarters . . . the ringside people. But I could hardly make out a full picture. Perhaps it was too soon to remember. Perhaps I didn't want to remember. It was over for me. I would never go there anymore. Never see Bobby or Jamie again.

Jessie? I had lost Jessie. If only my triumph had been more acceptable. If only I had managed to secure a spot at the Metropolitan Opera, say, as a super. Achievement without glory, with hope only, would have fit the pattern. The jigsaw with just enough hidden pieces. The game that was such a pleasure because it was all planning, no completion. Passion that fires and fires, my passion, was to Jessie's timid soul vulgar.

I lost Gibbs in a similar way. He considered theatre my lover, his jealousy probably the strongest emotion of his life. Not, however, with enough power to counterbalance the downward sliding of his ambitions. He slid and slid, finally settling between a pitcher of martinis and the 4:58 commuter train to ranchville. Safe at last on another planet.

Gone. They were all gone. I had failed each and every one. Failed to materialize as whatever any one of them had considered it possible for me to be. Wanted me to be. Needed me to be.

If I suffered a sense of loss, the duration was too limited to record.

One realization began to dawn.

So far, there had been no one in my life I wished to emulate. No parent. No relative. Lover. Husband. Friend. There had been no life that filled me with a longing to parallel. No guide. There were many warning figures. Some mute with pride. Some with fury. Some with love. Jessie: alone in an expensive hotel room. Snuggled warmly in her silver fox collar. Alone. Lunching, being prompt for her shampoo and set. Waiting for a summons, any summons from her child. No. Many times no.

Mother? Whirling in a fantasy world, waiting for a moment, any moment of triumph. No.

My sister? Climbing a rainbow. No hands, see? Moving within a translucent skin that hypnotized all onlookers, while the rarefied air of that height suffocated the creature deep inside who struggled for light, for air. Who would in time surrender to the weight. Indeed, in less time than was acceptable to the world. To me.

Older people were the most frightening, for as yet there had been none, none at all, with any independence. Any life of their very own. They were victims of flabby planning. Why depend on one's offspring to cushion the sores and aches of age? Where is all that wisdom one is supposed to acquire with the years?

Looking at April, I vowed never to be beholden. To be a burden. That was part of it. Beholden . . . never. Another realization: marriage was something I must avoid. I didn't have the talent for it.

The resolve distilled: From here on in, I'm in charge of my own life, right down to closing, and even a bit after that. No planting of these remains in some lonely hole. No one to be beholden, to feel ashamed for not bringing flowers, for not standing, kneeling, speaking to the space around the lonely stone. No burying at all. Freedom then, freedom now.

Now was a time of change. Of choice. It was a time of introduction. There was so much to ingest. Choices needed to be clever. I knew I was not stupid, just ignorant. There is a difference. Ignorant can learn, but there is no cure for stupid. Could I learn?

38 ≋≋

New York was a Juicy Fruit dream for a learner. Even an ignorant learner. "Maybe now I can find out about arithmetic, spelling." I told myself that I was one up on many of my peers: at least I knew I didn't know anything. I was ashamed, of course, in moments of exposure. As when expected to know what that ten percent commission for my agent amounted to . . . In time I could guess. My sister was encouraging.

"You can always hire someone to work out those sums. And it's deductible, too." Then she taught me the most important lesson of all. "Now, here is a pie," she made a circle with her hands. "When we cut it up, it goes like this: one piece for your agent, one piece for the government. Okay?" There it was, right in front of my eyes. "Half the pie is all you ever part with, understand?" Her hand was fanned open in the middle of the imaginary pastry.

"This half has to be yours, because only half of this half matters, see? The one half you need to live on, but—" her tone lowered—"this half of the half that is all yours goes into a secret account that you forget you have. Forget!" She pointed the word at me. "Nobody's ever given you freesies so far, have they?" I couldn't remember receiving any gifts along the way. "I'm not surprised," she said. "Also, you never borrowed from anybody?" I shook my head. "Try to keep it that way," she said. There was a moment for digestion.

"One more thing," Gypsy resumed. "You are a business. Remember that. You don't go into somebody's store and ask for free shoes or furniture, or whatever the hell they're selling, so when those civilians ask you for passes to your show, sit them down and explain that you too are a business. No freesies, June, you're a pro. Hell, I won't even take off my gloves unless I know what the money is." She sniffed. "Of course, you're so glued into this starvation legit thing, you'll never see any real money. God, just think: at the Irving Place, walking through my strip number, I made four times over what you're drawing at the Barrymore, busting your lungs and feet as usual. Well, never mind, honey." She hugged me. As I responded to the embrace, I was enveloped by an extraordinary fragrance.

"Oooh," I inhaled, "you smell good."

"Enjoy it, baby," she said. "It's the closest you'll ever get to that scent, because that's the most expensive perfume in the world."

I pulled away. "You're joking," I said. "You mean you pay all that money for—"

She grinned. "The most goddam expensive stuff going— only," and she pointed this at me as well, "I don't pay for it, June. Nope, somebody else always pays. It's got to be a reverse freesie, or you're just one more amateur. Don't you understand?" She sighed. "It's all so clear, June. Why do you—?"

I interrupted. "I do, I do understand," I lied.

"Well," she looked dubious, "if you don't, it's your behind to the Indians, not mine."

She was looking into my face with a trace of hope, but mostly exasperation.

I was a little exasperated myself. We frowned at each other.

"All right, all right," she said finally, "let's avoid the wrinkles in any event. Let's relax our faces, June. It's all part of whatever money we'll ever have in any bank."

Tumbled among the losses of those years was Eddy. All the beautiful jewels my sister wore to bed were gone, too. Stolen in a too realistic reenactment of the bad dreams. There was no longer a need for attention getters such as the full-length cape of orchids, the funny French; no, attention was focused quite firmly now. Eddy could gaze at the creation of Gypsy Rose Lee, from wherever he had been permanently deposited, with quiet joy. As partial molder, he could rest in pride. The job was well done. A masterpiece.

New styles, sounds, attitudes—social, political, even criminal—would roll softly in and out, or come crashing along like the ever-changing sea, but the veneer of Gypsy Rose Lee was of one piece. She walked in shoes identical to the original camouflage. There were dozens—in different shades, some with toe bows, some plain, but all alike, because she wore size 10½, and she knew that a simple shoe didn't draw attention to her feet. She was right. Camouflage. "I'm not in the feet business!"

Gypsy's torso was long. It was a family torso, Big Lady said.

218 ⚘

Even I was long-bodied, but our legs were long, too. Instead of viewing these lengths as handicaps, she shaped them into assets: "Miss Lee's legs are of such gorgeous length she must have her hose specially made," went the publicity.

A sewing lady (such species now extinct) made Gypsy's tiny panties. Pure silk or satin, lace-trimmed with her name hand-embroidered at the left hip. They stayed up with the help of one tiny pearl button, the buttonhole hand-sewn in matching silk thread.

A petticoat sometimes, but it too would be closed with a minute button. Gypsy said zippers were common, also abrasive. Beribboned, thin silk elastic went around the waist. Four petal-like matching ribbons fore and aft. Lace rosettes concealed soft garters, which held up those extra-long silk stockings.

Gypsy's skin was silky. A natural brunette, but without the usual excess of body hair. What little there was she removed easily, but with her usual economy.

"Watch this, June, and remember: the only secret is speed." She squeezed a tube of pasty substance onto one shapely leg, smoothing the stuff flat with a small wooden spatula. The leg covered, she leaned back on her chaise, inhaling the ever-present Melachrino.

"Thrift," she smiled. "Never use more if you can do the job as well with less." A few moments later, she lifted an invisible hair gently from the gooey shin.

"All cooked, okay? Now, for the fast part." Scraping deftly, she removed the depilatory from one leg to the other.

"Da daaa!" she sang. "Two for one, see? You can bet they don't put this method in their ads!"

Impressed, as always, I was reminded of a romantic story Van Johnson had told me.

"What if you are very brunette, and . . . well, you have a more . . . a bigger job for the depilatory people. I mean, Van said his girl had to—well, she shaved."

Gypsy's eyebrows went up. "Shaved? Her face?"

"No, of course not. Her legs, and . . . and . . . well, up."

"Up?"

"Uh huh. The hair went up her legs—way up."

My sister thought for a moment. "How did he know about all this?" she asked.

"He was in love."

"So?"

"Well, he did the shaving."

"Well, naturally a man would enjoy all that, but . . ." she ran two long fingers along the smoothness of one leg, "a dark brunette can't afford such attentions, no matter how well or lovingly intended. Mark my words, June, that very same hair is growing out like porcupine quills by now. Shaving went out with foot binding. God, who wants legs that are as bristly as a man's face?"

Traveling upward: Gypsy's waistline was unpredictable. Without warning it could spread a good two to three inches. She was always being pounded and squeezed in this region.

"A low waist is sheer hell, but can you imagine what those no-neck, short dumpies go through, June?" I tried imagining. "Another good thing about us," she continued, "pear-shaped behinds don't have the dreaded future of flat butt."

"Flat butt?" I repeated

"You know," Gypsy explained, "you've seen those middle-aged, once-beautiful rears, the ones that, when young, sort of bubbled out like falsies?"

I was trying to remember noting same.

"Well, when you see those spectacular rear elevations, just remember my words. That's the ass that flattens right down the back of the leg in no time, and it just hangs there. Be grateful yours is long and born low."

Gypsy didn't believe in alteration.

"When I think of the disasters I've seen." She shuddered. "Strippers, with perfectly adequate equipment, letting some quack pump silicone into their breasts so they could display forty-two-, forty-six-inch bosoms," she shook her head sadly, "have to sleep on their backs the rest of their lives."

I missed the connection. "Why?"

"Because, June, those boobs are hard as rocks and twice as heavy. Do you remember that man—that one I told you was such a wow at those circus parties?"

"You mean the one who . . . never got tired?"

She wore her wisdom expression now. "Money in the bank as long as he was natural. He could keep a hard-on for hours— do all those acrobatic sex gigs, and still go on and on—but was he satisfied? Oh, no! He had to go and get that damned silicone pumped into his penis, so he could be even more spectacular. So where is he today?"

I shrugged.

"He is through, that's where. O.U.T. Because he thought he had to gild the lily. Too bad." She sighed. "He wasn't satisfied to be a natural star."

"Gypsy?"

"Uh huh?"

"How did he sleep the rest of his life?"

"I was just wondering."

We pondered.

Gypsy didn't actually wear a bra—it was more of a soft bandeau matching the panties. It didn't push or press against her breasts, and it most surely wouldn't dare lift them. No. It simply covered them softly. She said the reason she wore size 36 was only because she had "broad Norwegian shoulders."

"As long as I'm broader anywhere above, rather than below, I'm safe."

Her arms were beautifully tapered, flowing into long, slender hands. The fingers were strong but delicate in appearance. She wore artificial fingernails at least two to three inches long painted a dangerous red.

Considering how she used her hands, the longevity of this artifice was a miracle. Gypsy's hobbies were twenty-four-hour-a-day occupations. Delicate stitchery, lace appliqué, embroidery, tiny silk-thread sewing. Beading, collage, knitting. She made argyle socks while watching movies—in the dark.

She put together all sorts of colored glass, creating lovely light fixtures. Sewed all her curtains and drapes—bedspreads, too. These things had an originality about them. All the things she produced were as identifiable as the self-produced clothes she wore.

I was certain the fingernails were doomed when Gypsy taught herself to type, but no. She used the two-finger system employed by newspaper people, and those two fingernails never touched the keys—only the under part of the forefinger. I'm not sure how many words an hour, but more than enough to make the system enviable.

Only once do I recall those nails giving way. Gypsy was in the wings with me at the Capitol Theatre in New York, where I was making a personal appearance. The orchestra had begun my introduction, but the cabbage roses on the back of my costume had not been finally secured, so Gypsy was on her knees sewing madly on the damn things.

The last note possible sounded. I said, "I gotta get out there, Gyp. I'm sorry—" and I made a dash for center stage. It's a good thing the spotlight followed me away from the first entrance, because my sister sprawled onstage, spilling scissors and thread. She crawled backward, in sort of a crablike movement, until she was out of view, but I did the whole act with needle hanging from thread among cabbage roses. When I got offstage, the crew were trying to help Gypsy find one of her precious long fingernails. I joined the search, but it wasn't until we were back in my dressing room that we found it—impaled on the needle she had been using; it too had hung from my flowered rear all during the act.

But I get ahead of myself. That was later—more than a whole decade later.

I am attempting a description of my sister as she was in the very early 1940s.

Before Gypsy learned that the patrician beauty of a long neck is most desirable, she also made attempts at neck camouflage. Later, the opposite was true: she featured the elegance of her long, graceful neck in all ways possible.

Gypsy's head was small but in perfect proportion. The pale brown hair was darkened by Bandoline in the early days. Applied almost like glue, it not only darkened but fastened the curls or disobedient strands to wherever you wanted them. It had a sweetish odor. Gypsy's face grew pink as she applied the stuff, because she held her breath.

"Damn baby hair! Won't comb, won't curl, can't even get a permanent!" It was true; her hair was very, very fine.

"In Hollywood, June, everybody wears wigs. Wigs and hairpieces. Nobody has to go through this. Dietrich has dozens of wigs, even for the street. Men, too—not just toupees, mind you, but bits and pieces to cover a bald spot here, a thinning spot there—they call them rugs." We giggled. "And the little pieces? They're called doilies."

She could not endure a shampoo or manicure, so early on she learned all the beauty parlor tricks so she could make her own magic right at home. She slept sporadically—three or four hours—or twelve. Even an aspirin was dangerous to her system. The cool facade was misleading.

When she was eleven, Gordon—the man in our lives at that time—took us to the first dentist we had known. Big Lady didn't approve of such indulgences. "Why, they are only little kids, Rose. That man has them brushing the enamel off their teeth twice a day just like they were sick or something."

Big Lady was overruled. We did go to the dentist. The results were: Mother needed almost all her teeth removed, an entire redo; I had ten cavities; my sister as many cavities, plus two fanglike incisors which were growing out of her upper gums. She also had trench mouth.

Panic.

But Gordon had seen to the overhaul of Mother's mouth and the filling of cavities. The fangs were painfully removed from my sister's gums, and a daily painting of her mouth with iodine was suggested for followup on the trench mouth. The condition worsened, however, leaving new problems after each new doctor along the road. The problem was never solved, so that later in her camera-conscious period, when Hollywood was her secret dream, the fear of a coveted closeup revealing crooked teeth became a nightmare. A small impediment of speech turned into an electronic boom in her ears. The efforts to correct these defects never ceased. Each time she signed for a film, some emergency repair job took priority over all other preparation. One such effort had to be completed within twenty-four hours, in order to make the deadline for her departure. The doctor's pronouncement was that all of Gypsy's teeth must be filed down for caps—all.

After the first marathon session of eight hours, she slept a bit, then took the Novocaine needle in her own hands, because, she said, "The hardest part is having someone else stick that needle in my gums."

Another ten-hour session and she was ready for the trip West. She told me she slept that time for the whole journey.

People remarked on our extremely small ears. Mine were too little, but Gypsy's were almost invisible. Both of us tried piercing, because earrings were as important in those days as gloves. In the long run, the only way we could wear the popular bauble was to conceal a thin, thin wire that circled the whole ear and was doubly secured by a piece of flesh-colored tape.

Lace, ribbons, and expensive perfume were a part of the Cinderella syndrome. At that time, movie stars were considered royalty by the fans. There was a responsibility toward one's public; supreme effort went into a public appearance. I think that such heavy work—yes, work—in living up to the image so carefully designed is a full reason for the contrast in private. The public shell was purely external. A coating. And, in many ways, it was fun. Dressing up and pretending. It was more fun for me—easier. I could step away from my creation; leave, go on to another, right in front of everyone. The only escape Gypsy had was behind closed doors. The audience who caught my sister in private retreat was very, very small. She was a creation of her own publicity to the world, but in private she was her very own person.

Gypsy slept in long, almost topless, sheer chiffon nightgowns. If there was any chill at all in the air, this floating wisp was worn over baggy-kneed, butt-sprung woollies. She hated removing makeup at night, so if no appointments with the outside were scheduled for a few days, possibly a week, the mascara and other remnants remained comically on her face. She said it was unpleasant combing or brushing her too fine hair, so it straggled disobediently in the uncertain grasp of one huge hairpin. The fingernails were permitted a rest, as well, so they chipped, cracked, and fell off until there was a professional reason for repair.

She didn't launder the cotton housecoats she wore. When the paint, glue, food, or whatever gathered enough to make it uncomfortable, she simply threw it away. The same applied to the tattered scuffs that seemed to enjoy life everlasting. I know every single detail of the "at rest" costumes worn by my sister, because it's a luxury we shared down to the last unsavory rag.

It wasn't the unsavory "at-home" look that anyone imitated. It was never the interior person anyone quoted. It was always some stranger's inventions superimposed on Gypsy's own invention.

Zippers were common, she said, abrasive. She never wore zippers. The notion was useful, though, so there was a funny song in *Pal Joey*. Jean Casto, in complete mufti of sweater, tweeds, lisle hose, heavy oxford shoes, horn-rimmed glasses, played a hard-bitten newspaper reporter doing a sardonic burlesque on a burlesque queen. The song was titled "Zip." All during the action of undoing imaginary zippers over the heavy clothes she wore, Jean sang of the philosophy of a stripper—finally naming

Gypsy. The song was brilliant and wonderfully well done. But zippers? Zippers used by Gypsy Rose Lee? My sister swallowed hard.

"Just as long as they spell the name right, honey."

If you are famous—for whatever it may be—how does it feel to see yourself "interpreted" by others, who have, for their own purposes, created a set of circumstances and a character totally outside of any reality? Any truth? "As long as they spell the name right, honey" was a sentence as unreal as the accepting smile. Again, the exterior spoke. Again, and again.

The imitators all must have heated those secret acids until they rioted, burning and looting the fibers of the sensitive inside of that cool exterior.

From the Rodgers and Hart lyrics at the Ethel Barrymore on Broadway to the saloons along skid row, imitators removed elbow-length gloves . . . rolled long silk stockings slowly down a leg—wore curls atop a sleek head—or wig if a female impersonator. They had a field day being what they, each one individually, thought was Gypsy Rose Lee.

Everybody and anybody is certain—no, positive—they have all the inside information on whomever they put their fix on. It's one of the things that make journalism so interesting, so provocative. Such creative opinionating—

Yes, Eddy would have reveled in all the gradations of his original concept. His masterpiece. It was heyday time for the unoriginal.

"Money in the bank," Gypsy said. "Thank God I'm not among the carbon copies—double thanks I am the original."

Gone, along with Eddy and all the orchids and jewels, was the special framework for that work of art: burlesque had been outlawed, but only on its own turf. The product was transferred briefly to a main stage.

During that period, musical comedy picked up the brassy glow. Then the shadings altered again, replacing the midway blare with folklore items. All-singing, all-dancing war. Eventually, drama complete with foxholes onstage, bombs and fireworks offstage. Marching to glory became popular, followed by . . .

Somewhere inside the funnel of the early forties, just about when I had settled into my one-room unfurnished apartment for the duration of *Pal Joey,* the professional climate of my own life changed.

39

Gypsy put aside the script.

"Well," she said thoughtfully, "just remember what happened to me in Hollywood." The film offer that tantalized me was from RKO. "Of course," my sister continued, "you wouldn't have the fringe benefits of Mother chasing Mizzy with a gun, while she wasn't doing her white-face act for Mr. Zanuck. No—you won't have the censors screaming to change your name, either."

I picked up the script.

"It's a funny role," I said, remembering the advice offered not that long ago from one of my idols:

"Don't get stuck playing one character too long." That's what Gertrude Lawrence had told me. I went on, "This part is a sort of first cousin to Gladys, isn't it?"

"What's wrong with that? She gets the laughs, doesn't she? She's brought you a ticket to Hollywood, hasn't she? Ye gods, June, you finally have found someone to be, and it only took you one show—one role. Look how long it took me to invent Gypsy Rose Lee."

"But I don't want to always play one person—to be just . . . well, an actor plays all sorts of people. An actor—"

"Actor, hell. You want to be an out-of-work actor or a working character?"

"I want to . . . I'm going to be a working actor. I am . . . or else I'll . . . I'll . . ."

Gypsy's face softened. "Sure, sure." She nodded. "Just because I didn't come up winners doesn't mean you won't, does it? Only—honest to God, June, it hurts . . . I mean, to try so hard and . . . well, nobody, just nobody seems to want you to make it. Like one of those screaming nightmares, where nobody hears you? I killed myself learning that damn play, remember? You saw me—you never said what you thought. Be honest. Why?"

"I . . . I didn't think you were ready. . . ."

"Ready? I was just the most quoted, publicized, photographed, most—"

"I mean, to act."

We regarded the floor that stretched between us.

"Tell me the truth, June. You saw me replace Ethel Merman, and you never did say what—"

"You couldn't sing." The silence was thick.

When Gypsy spoke, her tone was even. "Well, you see, June, if you are Gypsy Rose Lee, you don't have to act, you don't have to sing. All you have to do is keep up your strength so you can carry your money to the bank."

"I didn't mean—"

"It doesn't matter what you meant, June. I knocked myself down in money to do both those shows, took less than I get in any saloon in the country—why, the publicity alone was worth my salary to those ungrateful producers. . . ."

"You asked me to be honest, and all that doesn't matter."

"People pay to see *me,* June, not the character I'm supposed to be playing."

"But you can't step outside the play and go talking to the front row as . . . as yourself, Gypsy. In a straight play, you're supposed to—"

"My audience expects more from me, expects something personal. You have to give the people out front what they pay to see, and my audience isn't interested in some cockamamie character they can't recognize as me. Hell, I only throw in a little footnote here or there."

"Like tossing a garter to some baldhead down front?"

"I can't see the baldheads further back, can I?" She grinned. I laughed. We both laughed. I always believed then that we were both laughing. Laughing together at the same thing.

I poured myself another cup of the dark, brown tea, and my sister lit a new cigarette from the glowing butt she was finishing. I watched the smoke suck away to a vapor as she inhaled deeply.

"Anyway," she said, "now I'm a writer, to hell with acting, huh?" The smoke puffed from her mouth and nostrils with each word. It had made a circuit, finished a tour.

What instinct made me watch that smoke with such loathing? I had parted with cigarettes after my first introduction at the age of ten. I disliked the hot, black taste, ashes, smelly butts permanently in a dish.

"Move over there, June. The smoke won't follow you." Gypsy's voice was laced with annoyance.

"Three packs a day—it's ridiculous! If someone ordered you to smoke that many—"

"Three tins of fifties, dear—that's a hundred and fifty Turkish cigs a day, and one of the few pleasures of my life, June. My God, I gave up brandy, didn't I? Black coffee and brandy, one of my—"

"You were warned to quit, to stop! You didn't give them up!"

"Why are you so furious? Hell, nobody's asking you to give up one of the pleasures of life. Just move over there and the goddam smoke won't follow, because it likes me best."

I did move away, but the sense of fear, of outrage, was always present. It stood on my face like a large, twitching second nose when the room filled with smoke and the ashtrays filled with butts. We argued about it a lot, for years and years to come. Until one day the argument was over. Ended.

Eddy would have most certainly designed and constructed Mike Todd as permanent understudy. Mike picked up the myth machine where Eddy had left it. There were differences, of course, but they were both born promoters. Both loved the game. Both were married, but only Eddy had been unfree. Mike moved about unconstricted.

Eddy had been social; Mike was an urchin. He made his own rules, his own language, too. Part underworld, part carny, but much Todd—colorful, quaint, explicit. Gypsy adopted some of it, and added a few variations of her own. The love part was a four-page comic valentine. As usual with such cartoons, the blatant coloring was blurred, just a little askew.

Directly under the surface of the slapstick was the need: Gypsy needed a Barnum, Mike needed a backer. They used one another well, while the item-hungry press used them both, so it was a large and happy family of players.

While I was trying to decide whether or not to leave the security of *Pal Joey* and hurl myself into the Hollywood cauldron, they were enjoying the game. Some of the other players weren't in such high spirits. For a longish time it didn't matter, because they weren't the ones who made hilarious copy.

Mike's wife was a small dark woman whose armor must have been hammered over her hide by Thor. She had been brave to the world all through the lady parades, including this last particular float. A small boy had been left on the reservation with her. He too was dark and slim, with deep-down oriental grace. Mike adored them both, but he also adored his freedom to adore elsewhere—wherever, whenever. Nothing remarkable about that attitude, of course, except, when you are operating on Duffy Square in a giant neon arc or two, you are bound to get more attention than the regular run-of-the mill married wanderer.

Eventually there was an accident with some sort of fruit knife. Somehow, the small dark woman cut a vein; she was gone before the bleeding stopped. Accident, that's what the papers said. So anyway Mike Todd was, for the first time in ever so long, not only footloose but totally fancy-free. Free to marry again if he so desired. That sure as hell opened a good-size can of worms. But that came eventually. Mike wasn't free when Gypsy enjoyed his company.

"I don't think I'd marry him, June—no. Even if he had no one at all." She moved her head from side to side slowly. "I'd have to think hard about marriage with Mike. He's more expensive than he is worth as it is."

I knew Gypsy was facing an unexpected finaletto that wasn't simply romance. She and Mike had become big business.

It was Happy New Year time. Nineteen forty-two looked gorgeous from where I stood. I was thrilled when Mr. A. picked me to escort to a great round table, where all the brain and talent that had created *Pal Joey* were gathered to celebrate. Everyone backstage had helped me put myself together. I couldn't tell you what I wore, but I remember the doom-doom beat of my heart, because Mr. George Abbott, known by all for his ability as ballroom pro, had taken it for granted he was escorting someone who was going to be just the best of all partners for him out there on that floor. Ballroom dancing. Social dancing. Me admit I couldn't follow? Couldn't execute one single civilian dance step? And lose out on that party? Unthinkable.

Around the table sat the people who had made it possible for me to take center stage of a Broadway hit, with wonderful songs, great dances, that brought down the house for all of us.

Why wouldn't they consider me a female Tony DeMarco? How could they know that without the music, text, lyrics, choreography, and that five weeks of rehearsal, I had nothing of my own? Except for the kid-stuff routine I was trying to hide, nothing. I didn't have any party conversation, either—still a stranger to newspapers, books, even the world, except for events that touched me directly.

I didn't even know the extent of my unknowing.

Well, I kept saying I'd like to wait for a waltz—after all, New Year's and all that. Mr. A. danced with Mrs. Dick Rodgers, the exquisite Dorothy. Oh, it was lovely watching them glide and float.

As he seated her he said, "You ought to give lessons, Dorothy." She smiled, natch. I busied myself with something or other, so he danced with Larry Hart's date. They were even better. Afterward, he said, "I liked that cha-cha-cha better than any before."

I trembled, but he chose the lovely lady with John O'Hara. That was the best yet. If a judge had held a five-dollar bill over the couples on that floor, they would have been a runaway for the prize. When he seated her, he actually shook hands with John. Then he turned to me.

Countdown. I was on, no way out. Hands clammy, feet in a cramp of anxiety, I rose as Mr. A. pulled back my chair.

"Here at last is your waltz," he smiled.

Maybe I just shut my eyes and clenched my teeth—I dunno. I just can't remember that dance at all. I guess we got through to the end of it, because there was a silence. The music had ended. Mr. A. was seating me. In the center of that quiet moment, he said quite clearly, "June, you have a very strong back."

Mr. A. was right about that. No one asked how it was easy for me to carry 180-pound Jack Durant offstage while singing harmony at the end of one of the numbers in *Pal Joey*. I could have explained easily—and perhaps even collected a few laughs on the way—if I had told about lugging my partners during those hours on the marathon floor. I didn't because I hadn't reached a time yet where I was sure I needn't be ashamed.

Numerous working actors got their first nod from Mr. A. Brilliant at selectivity, his interest usually stopped with your first success. Getting any further into the lives of his discoveries was not his hobby. How could he know, for instance, that he left me unfinished at the winner's circle? That what I needed desperately after the glory was somebody else's head on my shoulders? Even for just long enough to check the rest of me into the next stop?

Taciturn as ever, Mr. A. watched me make a major blunder. He watched as I left the show. My first hit, in a hit—a once-in-a-lifetime combo.

40 ⅏⅏⅏

Cabin fever is sometimes unrecognizable to the oldest of pros. The dreamed-of long run in a beloved show becomes a nightmare to even the most initiated, unless an understanding of the process of repetition can be found or given, or loaned. Hypochondria of every variety lurks behind every performance. Almost the same as being squirrelly when the hours on a marathon floor begin to climb. The mind plays tricks. "Know thyself" should be written across so many makeup mirrors, mine among them. Where is your own particular weakness? An unpredictable back? Trick knee? Are you just a little bit emotionally unstable? Delicate stomach? These evils rarely attach themselves to stagehands, pit musicians, ushers, or the rugged individuals up in the booth. The insidious germ is somewhere within that bright light center stage. There is a growing concentration which remains on you as every other actor exits into the wings, until finally you are alone out there, absorbing those invisible germs. That's the most dangerous time of all.

You are center. Alone. In the spotlight. Loved. Applauded. Blinded. Deafened. It's the moment that can deform.

Oh, for that extra head now . . .

But I did leave the show and I took us on the Twentieth Century, then the Chief, and it was Hollywood. I was supposed to do the film and return to *Joey* in six weeks. I didn't. I didn't even tell anyone I wasn't coming back. I was convinced that nobody would notice I was gone. The convincing was easy, because for counsel I heeded the worst possible source: myself. At the time, there was no other voice. That situation prevailed for a long time, and you can't help but wonder how in hell that happened.

In the early 1940s, the number-one crack train was the Twentieth Century Limited. High-speed luxury on wheels. Plush seats, deep-pile carpeting, subdued lighting. It was hard to imagine showering at that speed, telephoning while the train's voice called, "Whooo-ooo—" Oh, romance. In the dining car, the tables were shrouded in white damask. There were bowls of fresh flowers and silver galore. The train life of my childhood had never been like this.

During the regulation stopover in Chicago, I wandered in and out of memories. I had headlined the State Lake, the Palace, Kedzie—and, in the very beginning, the beautiful Majestic Theatre had been where "Dainty June" had won that coveted three-year blanket contract on the Keith-Orpheum Circuit. Chicago had also been the setting for that nervous breakdown, during which I had found the determination to let vaudeville die without me. To escape. To engineer and foot the cost of failure or success on my own. I put my hand on the small protrusion under my sweater. Inside the crocheted grouch bag I touched was my total capital, adding up to some two hundred dollars. I didn't expect it to go too far in Hollywood.

I think that was the only time I wondered for a moment what had become of that other capital, representing the fifteen hundred a week "Dainty June" had earned in those years. True, a semi-dry spell followed the glorious period. Vaudeville diminished as the Depression spread. But the act did continue to work. Less money, smaller audiences, longer jumps. Well, wherever that money went, the destiny of this two-hundred-dollar boodle had to be different. There must never be an excuse again for sleeping in a depot, or thumbing a truck ride, or stealing buns, or . . .

I'm not alone anymore, I told myself happily. Make a home, make a life for us, for April and me. Boarding the bulletlike silveriness of the Chief, I opened all my pores to the luxury of that fluttering hopefulness known as anticipation. The future was mine.

Green hills. Mountains. Trestle, bridge, tunnel. That trip took three days. Even though those two trains were the fastest transportation on land. Prairie, more mountains, then desert. There were Indians at the Albuquerque station selling wares . . . then. Motionless people; with as little conversation as humanly possible, you could exchange small silver, even pennies, for a hand-wrought bowl, pipe, whittled doll wearing dyed chicken feathers. It was all very romantic . . . then.

Next came miles and miles of orange groves. You wondered if there were enough people in the world to consume all that fruit.

Arriving in Pasadena amid tracts of blossoms, I found the air overpowering, unreal.

My first encounters with film acting were to be synonymous with a series of blunderings, mistakes, and hysterical misjudgments. Some of this, I discovered later, was due to a facility I unfortunately possessed—a rare talent to hide ignorance with such positive force that truly informed, intelligent people around me were compelled to believe I knew what I was doing.

I didn't know.

Not only was I ignorant, I had no manners. Not the slightest hint of what to wear. The disguise I had assumed as a Gibbs shadow had been left in a corner of the little house, and I was outside in the light without a substitute. Gauche? Oh boy.

Alighting from the Chief in Pasadena, I was a patchwork of remnants. There had been one important mover in my recent life: Mr. George Abbott, who either had given up trying to fathom my machinery, or wasn't that interested outside of what happened onstage at the Ethel Barrymore Theatre. A truly taciturn Nordic, Mr. A. was never overly generous with direction or advice. You had to be trained in how to hear training, and I had missed that whole prologue.

I'd never heard of the Royal Academy of Dramatic Arts (RADA), ANTA, a personal manager, or exercises. I believed you just learned it and did it. Did it with love of the entire doing. Your lights blazed, your heart danced, you were part of an act of love, of unfathomable passion. Lots of very successful people shared that concept of the art of acting, people who will never be forgotten—but I didn't even know that.

And I had a beautiful smoke screen to help me stay stupid. I was disembarking from the train from New York as a Broadway Baby. A hit in a hit. The secret formula. All that hoopla was part of what made it appear to the naked eye that I must indeed know my apples. Well, I did know how to be who that character could be—move her, speak her. My discipline was of platinum. Hadn't I been onstage with the rules all my life? I respected the

233

whole damn business of show business as well as the flame.

But I didn't know where the camera was. The lesson: do I ask someone what to do, thereby exposing myself as I take the chance? Possibly confiding in the wrong person, who will simply dub me stupid forever? Possibly spreading the word . . . Or do I go on pretending I know, which will guarantee never knowing?

Johnny Darling was one of my agents; waiting on the platform, he looked more like a movie star. Batiste shirt open against a cashmere cardigan, white flannels, and oh, the subtle shade of suntan. Gorgeous.

"Your trunks can follow," he said, taking in my measurements at a glance.

"This is it," I answered, pointing to the dilapidated bag at my feet. Darling looked down as though something were spilling from my skirt.

"Oh?" There was a slight lift to his nostril as well as the end of the "h." I fanned my anticipation all the way to the car, which was long, low, and sleek.

"We'll go directly to the office. Everyone wants to see you, of course."

Johnny tried talking on that ride, but if I had been overwhelmed by the orange groves, I must have been numbed by the dazzling Darling. However, the grandest glow was yet to come. Pulling alongside a low stucco building somewhere in Beverly Hills, Johnny cast what could only be termed a worried glance in my general direction. I got to recognize that look, and its effect on my machinery. Somewhere inside, my generator stalled, turning off the fan that was trying to keep alive the glow of anticipation. Inside, I was a real Rube Goldberg contraption in need of repair. I hoped it wouldn't show enough to matter to these strangers.

"This is June Havoc." I was pushing out a smile toward a lady who could have been Joan Crawford, if some other lady hadn't beaten her to it.

"Ruth Matthews. You have to get to know Ruth; she runs this whole office." The Crawford double sat behind a desk lined with papers. Red, black, and green dots stood out on the pages.

"His annual party, you know." She waved toward the pock-marked lists. "He's on the phone, naturally, but you can go in."

The door to Leland Hayward's private office wasn't ornate;

in fact, it was ordinary. The whole interior was simple and work-like. Hayward stood up smiling, waving toward a chair as he continued his phone conversation. He was slender and tall. Grayish but not at all bald. His face had attractive lines which may just have been there from birth. He wore a business suit. Someone cut his hair very, very short. As short as a criminal's. His desk was littered with the same dotted lists I had seen outside. Judging from the number of names on those pages, the annual party promised to be the sort of epic D. W. Griffith would stage.

I cannot remember what Leland Hayward said during that interview because I never knew if he was talking to me or into the phone. I'm sure he was very polite. We shook hands eventually, and I followed Darling to the car.

". . . in makeup tomorrow for testing . . . costumes fitted . . . temporary apartment until you get your sea legs."

Why had the excitement gone? I closed my eyes. Then I realized. Of course, I wasn't going to be able to accomplish the arithmetic problem, and Leland Hayward was going to say, "If you don't learn even the elementaries, you'll be ashamed. People will think of you as inferior." A lesson from Jamie? No, this time the headmaster's name was Hayward.

"Names and numbers . . . all those lists . . ." I puzzled.

"Oh, those." Johnny smiled, looking more like an ad than he could possibly know. "The colored markings behind the names? Well, red is for absolutely, because of price, status, and shall we say acceptability? It's a rating method. Very simple. Effective, too." I was taking in the fine points of the clean-cut profile as he drove.

"Acceptability?" I began.

"No, no. First is the earning. The value. The cost of someone. Next, the current rating—how did the last film gross, and so on, understand?"

I wasn't clear. "For a party?" I mumbled.

"Certainly a party. Anything. Tennis, lunch—he can't afford space around him to be occupied by nonentities, can he?"

I watched the road. "And the . . . the acceptability part?"

Johnny's face was somber now. "Nonentities and . . . well, undesirables can blur anyone's image if they crowd into, let's say, a personal portrait. So the dots are a kind of code, you see. How much are you worth? What's your rating at the box office, and what are your choices, both personal and . . . uh . . . political.

Invitations are easier to decide on, you understand. Any residue from the A party can be invited to the B party, of course, and it's easier when you have a workable chart to avoid the . . . uh, unacceptables."

We pulled up in front of a Spanish-style building. More flowers. More palms and fruit trees. Another list. Names.

"This is your assistant. Your studio calls come from him. Here are all the numbers you'll need, including mine. Here are the keys to the car we rented for you."

I looked at the dangling chain. "Do I need to rent a car?" thinking of the expense.

"How else can you get anywhere?" Johnny was closing the French doors. ". . . hate that whore odor—"

I stopped him. "But, it's lovely," opening them wide onto a small patio ringed with flowering bushes. "What are they?" I asked.

He laughed pictorially. "We call that one 'night-blooming jazzhound'—it's a jasmine of some kind. I tell you, the scents, the never-ceasing sun and blue sky are so monotonous. Boring. Well, the car is at the curb. Drive carefully—you'll be the only one on the road who does." He was gone.

"In makeup," he had said, "early tomorrow." I unpacked my jars and tubes carefully. Six o'clock in the morning would be the earliest I had put on my makeup since I was three years old. Twenty years between pictures. I hadn't known then where the camera was. With a sinking heart I realized I still didn't know.

41 ❧❧❧

Of course I found my way to the studio. I was early. "Six o'clock in makeup." I reported at five-thirty in full makeup. Stage makeup.

It's called an industry. Perfect. No factory could present a more industrious atmosphere. Trucks, handcarts, dozens of bicycles, all on the move from way before dawn until mid-evening. Just don't examine the scene too closely. From enough distance, you'd be unable to decipher what people wore, looked like. What those trucks were moving. A closer view would delight any surrealist. Behind the gates and walls of a film studio, the serious business of make-believe is carried on with a hard-hat discipline any steel mill might envy. All the muses corralled, protected, surrounded with a coven of Magic Makers in every field of technological art. Craft?

The most delicate colors of the overall tent, the quickest to fade, to run, were those worn inside and out by the component standing in the center of the arc, the actor, standing unshaded where the light was most powerful, most likely to cause fading. Sad, and ironic, that the weakest should be so far to front and center. Balance of the total structure was hard to maintain. Too many times, balance became the major task—the most important issue. Too many times those delicate colors faded to no color at all because the light was too strong. Too strong.

Weary of sitting on the curb, waiting for the doors of makeup to open, I wandered around the lot. Things had certainly changed since my last movie job, when I was three years old. Most of the work was done outside then. But these streets were lined with huge, hangar-like buildings—windowless, flat. A series of semi-Spanish structures lined the main entrance. These were offices. Among the business-oriented were the writers. Why they had been imprisoned in adjoining cells with auditors, administrators, and manipulators to and of the press was one of many mysteries.

There was a place to get a shave and haircut, a shoeshine, a massage; and a real restaurant with three separate sections. One for executive class only; one for the middle class, including talent; and one for just anyone hungry, such as crew and workpersons. Prices and menu varied according to rank and station. Social lines never alarm a true pro. The earliest knowledge comes as oft-proven fact. You can't run show business on a democratic level—if it's not a dictatorship, it falls apart, etc.

Forget the variables. Everyone found his place here.

Of all departments on any lot, Special Effects, Costumes, and Props are the ones I love the best. Today, anyone with the money can go wild with Disneyland and the like, but back then all that wonder was locked behind the big gates. Craftspeople only permitted within.

Wandering back, I found the doors open. Hugging the cigar box containing my stage makeup, I climbed the stairs. Familiar dressing-room odors grew with each step upward. The purple smell of spirit gum, pinkish odors of powder and rouge. I hadn't applied rouge for years because it wasn't in style, but the rabbit's foot I had used since I could remember was warm in my pocket as I held it for good luck now.

It wasn't just the climb that made my heart beat so hard. This was the very day—the meeting with all this magic would happen within hours. It wouldn't be like the stage, I knew; I wouldn't be moving into the spotlight toward an audience that had been family for so long. No; no audience at all. Chilled, I pushed at the awful fear. "You lucky bastards, you're going to get to see ME" wouldn't work here. I was passing giant closeups of Ginger Rogers. Oh, perfection. Lucille Ball, more of same. Kay Francis, Joan Crawford—what did they use for ballast? For an anchor to keep from flying into a million pieces?

Clutching the cigar box and my rabbit foot, I took a deep breath and stepped onto the top landing.

It was like being caught in a stampede. In a rush of noise, people moved in all directions. Struggling to keep my balance, I backed out of the traffic and braced myself against the wall. One voice rose above the din.

"Get the son-of-a-bitch on the set, I don't care if you have to dismember him. Just push my rotten luck one more day—let me finish this goddam thing so I can afford a nervous convulsion—please!" Almost in tears, the speaker clattered from a room and down the stairs. "Get the damn door open—open!" There was the identical strain in this voice I'd heard so often, from one partner in any marathon, lugging, struggling, to keep the dead weight of the other from falling. Falling and being disqualified.

The general movement now was from the room of those frenzied voices. They were dragging what appeared to be a large corpse. Pulling, panting, everyone giving directions; the idea was to get that body into the men's room. Someone held the door. Some were removing shoes and other articles of clothing from the inert figure.

"You fools!" one hysterical man screamed. "Don't scrape his head on the floor—God! Oh, God, I have enough trouble painting on that hair!" Indeed, a thinnish crop was all that was growing. Someone turned on a shower, the door closed. Voices were muffled. People dispersed into different rooms. I was alone in the hall. Nothing had been unfamiliar, only unexpected.

Peering into the first room, I saw a row of barber chairs. The walls were lined with shelves. Triple mirrors circled by bright lights faced each chair. Bright light also came from above. A few chairs were occupied by people apparently asleep. The hysterical man arrived with a tray. It was loaded down with coffee mugs and danish.

"Oh, yes," he grinned, "welcome, welcome to you. Everybody's waiting over there. Go right in, go on. . . ." He pushed me gently into the opposite room.

There was only one barber chair here. One big triple mirror with lights. More lights above and all around. Indeed, there were three people waiting.

Reality jars. The big jolt comes when you are dealing with a reality that connects in no way with fact. The gentle shock I experienced at wardrobe for my first fitting is a example. The dressmaker's dummy I confronted had my name on its neck. It wore bits and pieces of muslin here and there, but the thing that had to command thoughtful attention was the note pinned to its chest. My measurements were written in a neat hand, but in very clear print at the bottom of the list was an important statement. It read: "Bust, adequate." That was dealing with fact. Easy.

However, in makeup it's a little more difficult.

Sitting in the barber chair, listening to an unfamiliar language, I watched the reaction in the reflection of my face.

"Widen between the brows."

"Lighten those dark circles under the eyes."

"Leave the forehead."

"Upper lip—make it one line."

No one asked a question of me, but questions dotted the air.

"Is that going to be the hair shade?"

"What can you do about that nose?"

At that, I saw my reflection start. The eyes widened. I thought I heard a swift intake of breath.

The Norwegian beak.

"Profile is awful . . . just about ruinous . . . tsk."

"Put it on the chart—it's not going to be your fault. You can't finish what God didn't begin."

Guilt overcame me. It's my fault, I thought. Anything wrong would go on the chart, and that was on me. The other rehabilitation group were in the hall with the corpse, which, while not exactly ambulatory as yet, was being moved on foot. The noise grew.

The leader of my own contingent leaned against the triple mirror I confronted. His voice trembled with suppressed emotion: "Close the damn door! Close it! If I have to look at that one once more this morning, I'll throw up all over this one!" The door was closed. Sounds of the removal diminished, as the corpse was taken to the next recovery depot.

These walls were also lined with pictures of famous faces. Each bore an affectionate inscription. While my nose was being discussed, I examined the matching proboscises of other actors who must have endured this same scrutiny. Bob Hope smiled out of one frame, Jimmy Durante another, Ray Bolger—Victor McLaglen's nose was huge. I hadn't really looked at noses before. My eyes traveled to other pictures. Ann Shirley. Katharine Hepburn. Bette Davis. Ann Harding. All so perfect—mostly nose-wise.

I found my voice.

"Those noses aren't so perfect," I heard myself say. "Look, Bob Hope, Jimmy Durante—why, they even make jokes about theirs, and . . ."

There was a silence, but not for long. The woman among my repair set spoke.

"On a man, a funny nose is like a trademark—endearing, cute—but only on a man, dear." She smiled. "You have to try to be pretty."

I asked, "Why?" Glances were exchanged. "You see, pretty isn't what I do—I mean, why I'm here—I mean, I was funny, too. On the stage. The show—the one that brought me here, and—"

The lady patted my head. "Lissen, honey, you can be funny here, too; nobody's going to stop you. But you have to try to be as pretty as you can manage while you're at it, okay? And that's our job, so just relax and we'll give it a try."

I relaxed and they tried.

If I had a preconceived image of what I looked like to others, it was buried under many more workable items. Here again was the self-evaluation learned from another planet. How would it be possible for these judges to weigh the sound of laughter that could not be heard on a sound stage? How making a pretty picture had no connection for me to the business of making direct contact with an audience?

I stared back at the stranger in the triple mirror. The first of the following twenty-five or more years of doubt haunted the eyes staring back at me. In time I would be back and forth across the country for over forty films, but I'd never conquer the conviction that I needed to apologize to everyone on any lot, any set of any film on which I worked.

My chart was looking like a tick-tack-toe in Arabic as the door burst open. Flushed and disheveled, it was one of the resuscitation crew who had been working on the corpse.

"Okay," he yelled, "take it from here, Bud. He's on his feet! You got five minutes to rehearsal on stage two!" Panting, the harassed one disappeared.

"Rehearsal, my ass." The man whose name, I gathered, was Bud moved dejectedly toward the door. "Hamlet, from Ashtabula to Kankakee, but has to read it from the idiot boards. Jesus! Even I know the damn thing!" His voice trailed behind as he left, "To be, or not to be . . ."

I found myself moving to the stairs. The corpse was on his feet, all right, but the eyes were puffy, bloodshot, and glazed. Three huskies were shoring him up. As Bud approached, a very small glow of recognition seemed to pass over the bloated face. I think he tried to smile. A trickle of saliva escaped his mouth. I had never seen John Barrymore in person before.

42

I didn't do just the one film at RKO. I did three, all perfectly forgettable, except for the people involved. People who otherwise would never have been such an important part of my life. Also, I wouldn't have been in California for the divorce, so it could have been harder to get.

Somewhere between *Four Jacks and a Jill, Sing Your Worries Away,* and *Powder Town,* I discovered that, no matter what was needed, you could find out who had it, where to find it, or if it was wiser not to try for it at all, by going straight to the Publicity Department. Ever since my earliest encounter with Perry Lieber and the rest of that crew, I had gone to one or the other for everything. They never failed me.

Our friendship had begun with the initial "fact-gathering" coffee meeting. Not unusual with a newcomer to the studio; the only unexpected element of the event was the facts gathered at that particular meeting. Remember the year 1941? It was nice girl or boy time, apple pie, down on the farm, or just like the kid next door. . . .

"Where did you attend school?"

"Well, I didn't, you see, I was, uh—"

"College?"

"Uh, no—"

"Well, your folks. Where from?"

"Actually, I don't know my father, but—"

"What?"

"I mean, I would, maybe, if he hadn't been removed so early, and—"

The facts tumbled out. Around second-cup-of-coffee time, it was decided I needed a whole new backdrop.

"Say, for instance, she's an orphan, see? And—"

"Yeah, and those people who ran the orphanage saw she had something, huh?"

"No, no. Lissen. A hick town buried somewhere unfindable, so—"

Perry Lieber held up his hand. "You forget, friends, she has hit *Life, Time,* you name it, and this—this yarn she tells, well, look here," he spread a sheaf of magazines and papers on the table, "there it all is."

They gazed sadly at the evidence. Finally, a kind-faced lady wearing matching cameo and earrings spoke. It was a lovely voice, soft, with a trace of Eastern elegance.

"Not one of the fan mags will scratch it." This was followed by a thick silence. The thought struck me. Was I an "unacceptable"? Was this what part of being "out" or "in" was made of?

Perry Lieber broke the silence.

"You are legitimate, aren't you?"

"Well, I have been. At least since *Joey.* "

They cast nervous glances about.

"Joey who?"

"My show. *Pal Joey.* That's strictly legit."

Well, the being married that young, the marathons . . . Aside from simply failing to comprehend what their big problem was regarding anything about me, it was a long meeting.

When it was over, I really loved that group. They really tried a million ways to make me "acceptable," according to the rules of that time, and I finally understood what it felt like to be a social leper. It wasn't anyone's fault, really. It just meant that, when one didn't have a usable backdrop, their job was harder because there was a lot of cleaning up to do.

All during those first three films, Perry Lieber and his crew scraped, whittled, and tried to refinish what God hadn't begun. They found a house for me in a nice neighborhood: Beverly Hills. They knew I had no furniture, so asked the prop department to give me what I needed. It wasn't their fault that I fell in love with the twelve-foot-tall stuffed gorilla who served as coat rack in the foyer. The prop department obliged, in fact, were generous in the extreme. I guess Perry's crew didn't realize I needed a decorator—or at least a restraining hand.

I loved the house. There were ten bedrooms. Little by little they were occupied by refugees from *Pal Joey.* First was the beautiful Amarilla, the Texas girl who had made such a hit in the show; then Van Johnson, who was being tested by Warner Brothers; Gracie Albertson, whose husband, Frank, had been sent overseas by the Navy before she knew she was pregnant; and a few other stragglers. I was working but getting nowhere—at least, I felt that way about it.

We had big hopes for Amarilla, though. So big that we all pitched in for a couple of caps to go over her front teeth, which were too far apart. The very first day Amarilla sallied forth to smile into the camera with them she swallowed the damn things and we were out $50.

Then Van failed at Warner's, even though they dyed his hair brown. His eyebrows were tinted, also—poor Van—the dye came off on all his pillow slips and ran down his face when we went swimming.

Whoever came to eat at the huge round table brought their own plate and weapons. I chose the round table because Elsie Mendl had told me it was perfect for table discussion. Good for conversation. She knew her business, all right. At the time, Sir Charles Mendl was one of my most beloved friends. "Listen to

Elsie, but watch me." He sang arias from any opera, in whichever language you asked for. He liked singing best at Malibu, with a gentle surf at his feet. At almost ninety years of age, he used a gnarled walking stick, wore a Jamaican straw hat and long shorts tied at the waist with a gorgeous sash of rainbow-hued silks. No one told stories with the dazzle and charm of Charles.

"You've got to write all these stories, do a book," I told him.

"Oh, my dear child," he smiled, "I can't possibly do a book, all that writing. I'm not budgeted to live that long."

It was at one of the Mendls' gorgeous dinner parties I learned an awful truth about myself. I was watching the beautiful people gliding about from the top step of the stairwell, when the most attractive male creature alive started upward step by step. Tall, dark, and unbelievable, Cary Grant had almost reached my perch when I noticed his mouth was moving. Stricken deaf with thrill, I only knew that he was saying something—saying something to me. I blacked out in delight. When I came to, he of course was gone. Charles and Elsie were annoyed with me.

"The most desirable man in town—or anywhere, for that matter—tries to begin a conversation with you, and you—oh, June, you say something like that to him." Elsie was upset, but Charles was stern. He was a stickler for good manners. He didn't like an uphill battle.

"Honestly," I apologized, "I don't remember what I said, but it never occurred to me that he was actually coming up those stairs to talk to me. I still can't believe it."

Elsie sniffed, "Well, you can, because he was, and you did."

My voice was wet with unshed tears. "What? What did I say to him?"

Charles looked down his aristocratic nose at me. "You directed him to the bathroom."

I held those tears back until I got home.

Around that time, April's tonsils had to be removed. Neither of us had a fondness for ether. I had planned that she would awaken to the sweeter smells of life, so I sat on her hospital bed laden with flowers, reading a *Variety*. A smallish item caught my eye: "Once Great Vaude Star Suicide."

I read on: "Julian Eltinge, headlined for decades as the 'Creole Fashion Plate,' died today of an overdose of sleeping pills. . . ."

Sadness enveloped me. I remembered Julian Eltinge well.

He was over six feet tall, and wore gowns and furs like no other female impersonator in the business. The pathetic ending of such a spectacular life was unnecessarily cruel, I thought—why? And Barrymore, intent on another sort of self-destruction—why? The question burned in my mind. These men were at the very top of their chosen profession. A long time at the top—on reaching the summit, was the view so disillusioning?

"Don't cry, Mummy, I'm alive."

April's voice was a scratch. Her face was pink. Filled with compassion for me. I leaped up to get her the ice cream I'd been told to have nearby.

"I know, oh yes, I know, darling." I was suddenly overcome with relief—joy. True, I thought, we are alive. We won't do that to ourselves. Nothing must ever cloud over the brilliance of just being alive.

"Don't try to talk, I know it must hurt so." I babbled on, "Brave—oh, you were wonderful!"

April sat among the pillows in a bower of scented blossoms, trying hard to swallow the ice cream. I put the dark thoughts at the very back of my mind. Soon we would return to a house filled with others who were intent on the future, not the past. Who laughed, and enjoyed the gift of now. It occurred to me that April was surrounded by an extended family just as I had been at her age. I had to smile, then, remembering stagehands struggling to teach me to read: " 'N' has only two hills to climb, 'M' has more, see?" The method may be different, but when Van Heflin, Van Johnson, Laird Cregar, or Sam Levene tried the multiplication table on April, their faces wore the same loving expression I'll always remember seeing as I struggled with all those hills on "N" and "M."

43 ⚡⚡⚡

Coming in on the last eight bars of a once-popular melody was getting to be routine for me. Childhood ended with vaudeville dying. Girlhood went down the drain with the outlawing of marathons. By the time I got to Hollywood, the studio system was already frayed to a cobweb. No longer were there pools of embryonic talent in every studio nest. No more Baby Wampums, male or female. The seven-year contract was all that was left of the great plans for finding and developing talent. You would begin with a pittance and end, if you lasted the endless contractual journey, with a modest wage and no fringe benefits—even though by that time you might have outdistanced every hope as moneymaker the studio could have dreamed.

Betty Grable was one long-distance runner of that sort. A contract held her personal earnings to a tiny portion of what she brought in as the highest-paid human of one of the lowest postwar years; splashed all over the covers of *Time, Life,* and all the rest. Agents and lawyers fought the last of studio ownership. Stars who commanded a huge audience had the right to a fair percentage of the big money. So many people fought for that gain that today television stars rightfully collect huge profits—along with all the non-talent. Aside from percentages, stars command prices up to $100,000 a segment on a successful television series.

But that windfall was a long way off. In the late thirties and early forties, residuals hadn't as yet been born. There are still no returns for the actor from any films made prior to 1948. Until 1935 there was no Social Security when you were old. No food stamps and welfare checks when you were in the middle, no unemployment insurance when you were young, just beginning. No. You were on the line. If you wanted to be in show business, you went the rounds. Being witness to the various deaths of several entertainment mediums was part of the trip. Still is. After all, buttons were outdistanced by zippers, the horse by the car—why not vaudeville by radio? Radio by talkie? Talkie by TV, and on and on to whatever goes down the drain next.

My pores had always been open enough to feel the cold air rushing through the empty vacuum to signal finis. I was in again at the last eight bars of a glorious melody. At least this time my feet were planted firmly. I knew who I might turn out to be, now. I even knew I had a fairly good chance. That meant I was free of one trainload of self-doubts. But oh that awful vulnerability when confronted by the necessity to sell. Sell yourself. How— without a stage, play—do you sell talent? Without a picture, if an artist? You can't just "tell" the chooser about a voice like Pinza's or a glorious sound such as Horowitz's without a piano. Who will buy the shell, the more than often unlikely package, without a sample of the goods? The answer is, only a chooser who has equal talent in that particular field.

That's what "going the rounds" was all about. Find a chooser who sees inside your shabby, insecure façade. I learned a lot about all that as soon as I knew I had to. I had squeezed through early survival somehow. All those efforts between marathons to secure any temporary work, even a civilian job, had been educational. Waitress? Cashier? Salesgirl? No go. I didn't know how to make change, my writing was printing, my spelling was my own code. I almost did get one job because all you had to do was stay on the phone and yell messages across a room full of boxes and crates, but the boss at the other end said my speech wasn't good enough.

I had been among the small army who had served time on the bench at the Shubert office whenever I hit New York. I figured that someone would finally snap a finger my direction. Perseverance worked—the snap came. Thrilled to a degree of airsickness, I took a deep breath and moved toward one of the casting cubicles. I couldn't believe my luck. Trotting out my best smile, I squeezed into the six-by-eight chamber, where I came face to face with the impossible dream. After what seemed like hours on the rack waiting for the screws to tighten, there was a stir within the monument of scripts I faced. A small head with enormous eyes further enlarged by magnifying spectacles was turned my way. I felt like Dorothy during her audience with what she thought was the honest-to-Pete Wizard of Oz.

"What are you?" he asked.

What was I? A marathon dancer? A freak child star? What?

"I am an actress." The voice was firm and positive. Best of all, it was mine.

A tiny hand emerged to smooth away whatever tension lay under the transparent skin of his forehead. Then a deep sigh ruffled a few pages of the very top script.

"Never, never." That belle tolled for me. "When an actress is in my aura, I feel something—it's in the air all around her. It's a force, an intangible force."

My mouth fell open with the breathless beauty of it all. I sat down in awe.

"Get up," he said shrilly, "how dare you relax when I am talking?" I shot to my feet.

"But I'm not relaxed, I'm not!" My voice cracked. I felt the heat in my head. "I'm up, I'm up. Only part of me sat down—honestly—I swear it! I'm not relaxed at all, I'm not!" There was only the choked sound of my suppressed hysteria as we regarded one another. I knew dark spots were discoloring the underarms of my blouse, because perspiration trickled down my back and ribs.

"Unreal," he said finally, "no, the air is still. There is no movement, nothing. No life. With you I get nothing."

To my shame I didn't plow into the fort of scripts, tear off his clothes, break his glasses, skin away his Jockey shorts and tie his little penis into a pretty bow. Instead, I mumbled something about advice needed, oh pretty please. The voice was small, almost apologetic. Oh, I had a long way to go.

Standing in a sweat of self-loathing, depending on my tightly clasped knees to hold me up, I waited for the death or life directions from this fount of wisdom, who sat immobilized in scripts as though in a cement casket, who read himself blind, who served as the final shredder for the dregs. First the feast of beauties paraded through the more important cubicles. The aspirants sort of tumbled along an examination belt, the more likely being plucked off at previous stations, so that here at the end cubicle were the abject rejects. I didn't realize then why he hated his job, but he knew.

Finally he worked up enough oxygen to speak.

"My advice? Easy. Marry. Grab the first offer you get." He disappeared behind his mountain.

I groped my way to the back stairs, where I let go. Removing coat and shoes to preserve them, I banged myself against the iron railing. Kicked my feet on the stairs, rolled along the rubberized carpeting, howling inside like a berserk banshee. It was all over in a few minutes. I always felt better after punishing myself. It was years and years before I learned any technical titles for the agony of self-hate. Besides, I wouldn't have given credence to the condition even if the truth came from the top. Not then.

"Marriage!" I thought. Why would a perfect stranger want to insult me? My outrage had to do with my own performance in response to the gross suggestion that I was obviously unfit to stage-manage a life of my own. The little man with the wornout eyes could not have suggested anything more degrading.

Well, I'd managed to get past that part to this part—the part about "What are we going to do about the nose?" I had seen the nose on film in *Four Jacks and a Jill*. It wasn't crooked, it was just long, with a droopy tip at the end. Only noticeable in profile. But the camera doesn't look at you front face only, so off with the problem and onward.

Around this time various terminations occurred, in such rapid succession I lost track of how one might have, in some way, related to the others. I had learned of a showbiz lawyer through the publicity department. His name was Martin Gang. He explained the usual divorce proceedings: "The State of California will consider as adequate grounds for divorce proof of loss of health due to harassment, loss of income due to loss of sleep or health, causing inability to function before the camera, etc." Feeling that I understood the situation, I signed up for the necessary appearance in court. So that there would be no waste of time while waiting, and as long as I was between films anyway, I cut a clipping from the paper which had intrigued me. Featured was the sketch of a profile designed to make the Witch of Endor resemble a Rheingold Girl. Next to this atrocity was a nicer sketch of a perfect profile. The caption said, no matter how awful your nose, this ad and three hundred dollars in cash could make you a nose-happy person—just what I needed to be.

I scraped together the three hundred and drafted a few pals to see me through. Other terminations occurred in tandem. The nose itself wasn't all that awful. The job was done with the speed of a well-planned bank heist. There was no bone removal—for which I am forever grateful, because a few others who came up with the three hundred in cash didn't fare as well. There were two actresses and Carmen Miranda who needed bone removal. Those noses disintegrated. Same doctor.

Aside from running with no warning, my new nose was a great comfort. Just lucky.

With the help of the publicity department, I was very busy. Guest appearances on all the big shows were exciting and more than remunerative. I found more friends. Here was I, on the very Yellow Brick Road, gaining friends, learning my business, losing the unphotographable tip of my nose, dissolving the unworkable marriage, and yes, ending my first agent-actor relationship. It's a montage now. Perhaps it was then. Nose, husband, agent—all background for a face-to-face realization of how it feels to be déclassée. That's the word my sister used. Sometimes there is no substitute for French.

Bing Crosby, Bob Hope, Red Skelton, Kate Smith, and so

many others had radio shows. I appeared on them all, enjoying myself immensely in the comedy skits, the songs, dances. It was all blended in with the same cast of characters met on hundreds of camp and hospital shows for the servicemen.

At first, before the camp shows were organized, the studios sent cars filled with familiar faces, voices, just to say hello at a mess hall, an open installation, a hospital or rehabilitation center. Standing on a mess-hall table, dolled up in some glamorous gown originally created for Betty Grable or Rita Hayworth, just saying a coy "hello to the boys" embarrassed me terribly. Wasn't I a vaudevillian? A song and dance actor? Then why wasn't I doing a real act? Justifying the attention of all those men? That audience? My own costumes, my own self. "Why can't I be me?" My agent smiled wearily. "All those guys want is to look at a female," he said.

"I won't believe that. Aren't they the same people who buy tickets?" I was getting mad and my nose began to run.

"Just wear what you are given and do as the studio tells you." His tone was so ominous I stared. "Oh, yes, you have enough problems, you know. They haven't told you about the Kate Smith guest shot yet?" I had been rehearsing for that show, loving it and everyone connected with it. "You're out."

I didn't think I heard the words.

"They don't want you and so you are canceled."

I went cold. I had never had a happier rehearsal time.

"I know they liked me . . . my work. . . ."

He sighed, "The sponsor, June. They don't even know what you're rehearsing, what you do. They just found out that you are Gypsy Rose Lee's sister." I must have looked my bewilderment. "Surely you understand. That show goes into millions of American living rooms."

I didn't understand. And, although we never talked about it, I watched my sister form her own unit to entertain the servicemen at installations where the chaplains had refused to receive her. I know she played saloons all over the world, but was not booked as a star attraction in any elite supper club or swank hotel spot. Or—and this is the most ridiculous . . . at the big-time Las Vegas spots. Gypsy toured one very long, hot summer as owner of her own concession with a carnival. Doing as many as sixteen shows a day.

"Clocked two hundred and seventy-five thousand dollars in just a couple of months," she told me.

If I hadn't understood the importance of all the money talk, fame talk, publicity talk, that incident of the Kate Smith show put the spangles and the feathers right in focus. We just never discussed this area. Phone conversations that many times ran into hours were about anything, everything else. One time the talk went on for six hours, and the only reason continuance was postponed was because my arm fell asleep and I couldn't hold the telephone. Another time was during a nationwide strike. My call to my sister was relayed to the telephone company's monitor.

"Sorry," she said, "only emergency calls for the duration."

"But this is an emergency call!" my sister cried. "My sister needs my advice."

The operator was sympathetic. "Medical?" she asked.

"No, of course not," Gypsy snapped. "She's been offered a film in Hollywood and she wants my advice, see?"

The lady in charge sniffed. "Well," she said evenly, "I don't see what good your advice would do. You didn't do so well out there yourself, you know."

44

Finally on the stand—facing the judge who would decide whether or not I would be an unmarried woman. It came clear to me—I suddenly understood the intricacies of law, so I picked up my cue and leaned into the wind.

JUDGE: And were you at any time publicly humiliated?
ME: Oh, yes, your honor. My husband referred to all my associates in the theatre as "little bennies."
JUDGE: They resented that?
ME: Yes, your honor. And—and I never got any sleep. . . . I . . . I lost weight and my work suffered.
JUDGE: Can you enlarge on that? Just a little, if you please.
ME: Well, I have five lovely dogs. They always sleep with me. They always have, and my husband—well, he resented that.
JUDGE: How did that affect your loss of sleep?

ME: Well, my husband kept me awake all night, whistling, calling. You see, he wanted the dogs to sleep with him. . . .

I got the divorce, and enough unexpected publicity to please even my sister.

Six films later, I enlarged the act developed from entertaining at camp shows and the Hollywood Canteen and hit the personal-appearance road. It was home again. Packed houses. Marvelous audiences, even with five and six shows a day. And, of course, the USO appearances coupled with radio. What a busy time.

When Mike Todd came backstage at the Chicago theatre, he didn't know me as the urchin who ate everyone's leftovers that time at Lüchow's. He had seen the show.

"Got a great role for you in my new musical."

Even the pit band couldn't match that for sweet music. I couldn't wait to phone Gypsy.

"I told him to catch your act, June. You see? Now we can share this house and save the bills on all those phone calls."

She told me more. "Cole Porter, no less. A huge cast, wonderful clothes, and you'll star opposite Bobby Clark. I'll handle all the business, darling." Then she explained about her own play. "I wrote *The Naked Genius* for myself, June, but Mike doesn't think I can play it, so we have Joan Blondell. We go into rehearsal in a week."

I thought I heard the familiar ache inside the voice somewhere, but as always we talked around the sore spot.

Watching Gypsy laugh while Mike did his routine on her: "Best-known no-talent broad in the business . . ."

Listening as she flattened it all into something wearable—useful; witnessing the smoke disappear in her mouth, waiting for it to finish its tour through the delicate tissues, making a return through nose and mouth simultaneously—she loved her smoke. She loved him. I knew if I went back to do Mike's show I'd be there between them again. I'd have to pretend not to see; to con myself into believing everything she did was good for her—that she knew every step of her way. I half believed she did. Wasn't she older, more sophisticated? Weren't my nagging doubts for her safety part of my own insecurity? What had Mother told me once when she found my sister and I had doodled all over a hotel bill?

"Look at that," Mother said to me. "Your doodles don't ever make sense, June. At least your sister's are constructive. They reflect purpose, a sense of direction. Study them, Baby—you might learn."

I did. Diligently. All I learned was how many ways my sister managed to doodle five letters. Always spelling one word: M.O.N.E.Y.

In spite of Mother's early admiration, that was the word that was foremost in their alienation.

I had always been content living with two pegs and the back of a chair. The last three years had been New York and the road, but always returning to Hollywood. During this time I discovered "home" had closets. It was an evil day. Ever since, I have suffered a profound sense of obligation toward filling those closets. Long-distance commuting in this age was new to many actors, but to me the only changes wrought by time were the fashionable luxury trains and my sudden overabundance of personal effects.

A year or so before this particular glory trip East, I remembered myself standing in the blinding early-morning haze of Hollywood. I was prepared for another out-of-town engagement; my then agent had arrived, tickets in hand, to deliver me aboard the Chief. He was dutifully checking out my luggage. The bellboys in charge of this assortment wore pained, stifled expressions. It had been the same with the chambermaids who cleaned my rooms. For the past six weeks, an anonymous fan had been sending me five hundred mystery gardenias a day. The little blossoms arrived wet and thirsty—it was unthinkable not to water them. The hotel's container supply was full by the second day; by midweek I discovered new arrivals could be accommodated in the containers while the wilting flowers were removed to closets, drawers, sprinkled on the bed and in the bath. For they exuded a nostalgic, mystical scent as they faded, quite unlike the heavy romance of their youth. This way thousands of gardenias happily fulfilled their mission. The anonymous sender was obviously an improvident, cowardly showoff. Anyway, among our many pieces of luggage were six huge florist's boxes. The gardenias were neatly packed in layers of watered cotton cloth. Up till the last moment we had tried to give them away, but long ago all takers were surfeited. We had tried eating them, too—but they resisted rubberly.

Among my wartime dependents were a couple of "duration" dog orphans. They sat among the boxes and cases at a respectable distance from my two legal charges. All four wore pinched expressions, and even my then agent's nose twitched as he counted us off for the journey to the train.

In wartime, actors pulled up stakes and departed from loved ones and jobs just like anyone else; they donned the borrowed wardrobe of the GI and went off to fight just like civilians. When actors I knew, or who knew me, were compelled to leave behind a loved dog, cat, or bird friend, I was the logical foster parent. I made every effort to accommodate these "duration orphans" with the basics of existence as well as affection, showing no favoritism to my own fur people.

At the time, the latter were Grumpy Dumbo Ding Dang Dog (he was billed as a standard poodle), and Napoleon, a tiny Yorkshire terrier. The two boarders were Everybody O'Shea, a West Highland lady, whose master insisted I perpetuate the fable that she was a gent. Everybody was sweetly superior—in fact, a snob. The fourth member of this company was a self-satisfied, smug freeloader whose name I refuse to remember. He was a genuine imitation basset, in spite of anything he may claim. He wasn't impressed with any of the rest of us and went out of his way to make this clear. Come to think of it, his personality was the "in depth" ingredient that made his master such a frightening actor. I don't know who imitated whom, but it was a cinch there wasn't any war big enough to keep them apart very long.

On the drive downtown, my agent hardly spoke through the handkerchief he held over his face. What could be seen of Hollywood around the boxes and dog heads sped by as I looked forward to the peace and quiet of the three-day journey to New York. Surely there would be a few suckers on the train who would adore gardenias. Conductors, waiters, and porters on the wonderful Chief knew me well; I felt certain of their cooperation during the obligatory gestures demanded of me in order to recognize accepted ordinances established by some vague railroad authority. Example: having synchronized our watches, my agent and I checked the luggage, then trotted off separately; each of us in charge of two— mark you—two dogs only. As per routine, I walked briskly to my compartment. Once inside, I explained to Grumpy and Napoleon that good troupers sat silent and motionless in the tiny washroom until they heard their cue. This worked with seasoned travelers such as these gents, which is fortunate for the two war bums, because the ordinance permitted two dogs *only* to each compartment. It was lopsided and unfair to humiliate my gallants by hiding them in the washroom, but it was the penalty for talent. The cue my agent took was the final " 'Board!" from the conductor, who then kindly busied himself with a lantern or some other handy prop. With seconds to spare, my agent hurled himself onto the train—sometimes it was even in motion—as he hung on to dogs and balanced, I often thought, quite beautifully. I stood at the heavy open door, ready to whisk the dogs into the compartment without attracting undue attention. Sometimes, as he completed his feat, I could see my agent's face as he fell slowly backward from the movement of the train, or as he turned with the grace of an adagio dancer and sort of toppled forward. He always ended by sprinting swiftly, but gracefully, into the dimness of the long platform.

Although we never said an official farewell, I knew we were both relieved for the other's safety. And I'm sure he realizes that I still consider him an excellent, first-class agent. We parted a few years ago, only because his timing had not improved with experience. These days, what with air travel, I need a much younger, faster agent.

On the Chief, crack train of the Santa Fe, we were good friends. We had a routine worked out. A fast train, but it stopped magically at just the desired intervals to aid and comfort my fur dependents. A warning tap on the door preceded the three-to-five-minute stops, giving us just time enough to form a flying wedge. At the signal, we galloped through the aisle, down the steps, and into the bushes. A porter kept lookout for us, so that a second before " 'Board!" was heard, we were on the gallop once more toward our compartment. It always took me a few moments to recover, but the leaping, bounding joy of the dogs was such a reward that I looked forward to these excursions.

Unpacking, I glanced at my four friends. Grumpy, my poodle, sat in tall elegance, gazing out the window in worldly ennui. Napoleon, in true Yorkshire terrier style, had inspected every last inch of the place, and now curled under the warmth of Grumpy's smoky coat. As expected, the attitude of our guests remained enigmatic. Everybody O'Shea regarded me stoically, but the open disapproval of that basset was almost more than I could bear.

At lunchtime, there were a few unfamiliar waiters in the diner.

Also, many changes had been made in the décor since my last trip. In spite of all the improvements, something made me a little woozy. Unlike my habit, I slept through last call for dinner. I managed to put four dishes of ersatz supper at polite distances on the floor for the dogs. Lethargy had crept over me. Something was wrong. I tried to focus my eyes, but I slowly dimmed to dark on the baleful countenance of the visiting basset.

A gentle tap woke me with a terrible pang of guilt. I opened the door to a familiar voice. "Take your tray, Miss Havoc?"

I blinked. "Are we stopping? It's time for us to get off for a few minutes?"

The waiter looked puzzled. "No, ma'am, no—" He took the tray.

Where were we? I pressed my face against the glass. Great endless stretches of pale, barren terrain lay outside. There was a full moon, expressionless, flat-faced. I turned back toward the dogs. They too had changed. Their faces wore that lifted, eager look. I looked at my watch. We had been traveling at some great rate of speed for over ten hours. Then it hit me! *With no stop!* I leaped to my feet, apologizing profusely to all four dogs. I must have slept through one or even two of our precious stops; poor darlings must be bursting! Oh! I felt selfish to my toes. Suspecting that the gardenias had finally asphyxiated me, I piled the boxes outside my door, attaching a large sign to the heap: "FREE—TAKE SOME FOR MOTHER'S DAY," then rang for the porter.

"When is the next stop?" I inquired.

He beamed. "No stops, Miss Havoc."

I stammer sometimes when I get nervous: "But, but—on all my trips we—we stop and—and the dogs get off, and—"

He expanded with pride. "We were on the old train last year, Miss Havoc. Slow, stopped four times. Sure, but this is the *new* train. Best, fastest yet—the Super Chief. *We* don't stop at all."

I looked over my shoulder at the taut expressions on those woolly faces, hoping they hadn't heard, but of course they had. I shrugged toward them. Grumpy's eyes filled, and his half smile faded. I avoided the smug expression of the basset; even so, he was no camel. He could be a sage just so long.

"Please get me a stack of newspapers." I turned and faced the music. "Now, listen, gang—" I was factual—"we're in trouble—the wrong train—I'll put down papers—don't be embarrassed—use them."

An hour later, after I had put my hair in curlers, undressed, bathed, there were four inches thick of newspapers on the floor, with no takers. I knelt in front of Grumpy, whose muzzle had moistened to a near drip.

"Grumpy, remember when you were a puppy? On the paper?? Good boy on the paper?!" I turned to Napoleon. His teeth had started to chatter ever so slightly. "Nappy, lots of people go on the paper all the time. Yes! It's the thing to do—it's—Nappy? Look at me. . . ."

Basset's skin had folded further over his face than ever. His eyes were very red. "I apologize," I said. I looked at him again and the tears came. We both sat there and bawled.

There was a gentle rap on the door. I dashed to open it.

"These are for you, I guess." The porter was piling the boxes of gardenias on the floor.

"Read the sign," I implored.

"There's no sign, Miss Havoc, but your name's on the boxes." The door closed.

Helpless, I staggered to the bed and drugged oblivion. I sleep in only my curlers so when the slowing up began, I did grab a coat, but I forgot my slippers. I guess I was fearful of interrupting the gradual halt. When the train came to a crawl—well, slow enough for us, anyway—I yelped, "Everybody out, quick!" I yanked open the trap door, and we sprinted for the outside. No one was in sight. The desert was a dead sea in the slanting moonlight. I started after the dogs, but razor-sharp gravel bit at my bare feet. Hugging the warmth of my coat against the goose bumps forming on my body, I felt a chill wind whistling through my curlers.

"Hurry up!" I whispered loudly. "Hurry up! Good boys! Good, good bo—" The word withered on my lips. Intent on the scurrying little figures darting about in the pale light, only a shivery premonition caused me to turn back my glance. Oh, no! There, snakelike, squirming away into the night, almost in total silence, was my train. The Silver Wonder of the Decade. I stood frozen, wearing nothing but curlers and coat. The desert stretched all around. The train was a good city block away when an ear-shattering wail reverberated from the cloudless sky. The banshee blast scared me as much as it did the dogs. It kept on and on. It was me.

I hollered in all keys as I took to the tracks—gravel or no gravel. My feet carried me, or rather hopped me forward. The dogs tried to keep up, but Nappy fell behind. I grabbed him without pause, galloping and screaming frantically. The train kept gaining speed. Now basset fell behind, panting. I tried lifting him, too, before I realized it was hopeless. The train outdistanced us easily. Refusing to accept the situation, I stood still in the empty desert and let go with everything I had. Basset lifted his head and emitted long purple howls. The others joined in. We howled and howled.

Opening my eyes to breathe in another lungful of yelling air, I saw the miracle of red lanterns swinging amid clouds of white steam up ahead. The train had stopped! Had really stopped, this time. Oh, glorious moment! I limped toward the scene. There was wild disorder. Lanterns flashed in and out as people milled about in the steam. We five gazed around only a moment, then our instinct took over, and we faded into our compartment for a warm, grateful, dreamless, gardenia-scented sleep.

Next morning I promised the dogs we would never ride the Super Chief again, then went to the diner for breakfast. My waiter greeted me with the restrained intimacy of old friends involved in a mystery.

"Heard any more about . . . last night?" His lips barely moved. "Nobody'll admit pulling the emergency switch. It costs thousands of dollars to stop a train like this."

I looked down at my plate. "Who would have a reason?" I inquired demurely.

His eyes glowed. "Reason? Why, any—all—everybody on this train who had ears. All that unearthly howling!" Shuddering, he looked over his shoulder. "The really scary part is they never found the body! Nope! Not any kind of body at all!" Our eyes locked in horror. His voice was almost indistinguishable from the soft "pitty-pat-pitty-pat" of the tracks below.

"You want coffee now or later?" he said, then moved away before I could answer.

45 ᵥᴇᵥᴇᵥᴇ

Arriving in New York, I found my sister prostrate, her face red and swollen with weeping, the canopied bed littered with newspapers. It was the morning following the opening night of *The Naked Genius,* written by Gypsy Rose Lee, produced by Michael Todd, and starring Joan Blondell.

"Read these notices, June," she wailed. "It laid a cake, a goddam angelfood cake! That's how many eggs it took. But that's only part of it. . . ." She blew her nose heartily. "We're in Boston, and it's easy to see we're in trouble, and—oh God, June—George Kaufman gives up. Just gives up. And Mike—Mike tells me he is in love with Joan!" Her eyes were almost swollen shut. "All that's before we ever got here! Jesus, if I had written a play about what went on in Boston, the critics would have a right to bellyache." She tried hard for control. "Hell, Kafka couldn't have got near it!"

She pushed a bunch of newspapers toward me. "Read them, go on—no, don't read them!" She sobbed quietly. Pushing away the mess on the bed, I held her. Tears are contagious, I guess, because we both bawled until the fever subsided. When the noisy part was under control, I made us large cups of the gluelike tea we loved.

Finally, Gypsy announced her decision. "The son-of-a-bitch will never get another red cent from me. I hope everything he ever does from here on in hits the fan he's facing. I mean it! In spite of the investment I have in the bastard, too!" She sniffled. "He is a lying, two-faced, double-dealing—" She sat up straight. "Omigod, June! You start rehearsals tomorrow!"

My voice was a squeak. "Yeah, with Mike producing."

Well, *Mexican Hayride* wasn't a family affair. The cast was so huge, the show so massive, so unwieldy, I had no trouble staying lost through the chaos of early rehearsals. It wasn't difficult to see that Mike was happy with the Barnum & Bailey atmosphere he was creating.

It was the heyday for the prestigious supper rooms at swank hotels. Also, the big nightclubs were treasure troves of talent. Mike had scoured the circuits, signed a half-dozen sensational acts that were to dazzle Broadway. At least he planned it that way.

The early stages of rehearsals resembled a D. W. Griffith mob scene if, let's say, someone had plugged the director's megaphone. Spilling from the stage of the Winter Garden Theatre, filling all large rooms of Nola, the rehearsal hall, into the men's, ladies' rooms, everywhere; there was little or no privacy. The Dorothy and Herb Fields book was being directed by John Kennedy in bits and pieces all over the theatre. Cole Porter music and songs, arranged by Robert Russell Bennett, in separate rooms at the Nola. The big dance numbers, choreographed by Paul Haakon at one place, showgirls at another, choreographed by a Haakon assistant. Specialty people were scattered all over town, polishing and honing with an accompanist at a piano.

Equity decided *Mexican Hayride* was a "spectacle." That meant five weeks were permitted for rehearsal. Running from book to dance to song rehearsals while avoiding Mike was tricky, but after a few weeks of the bedlam, Todd's eyes glazed over, his voice hoarsened. That night I went home to report an initial step to my sister.

"I think he is slowing up, Gyp. He's beginning to walk as though someone put rocks in his pants."

While Gypsy recovered somewhat, our Christmas, 1943, didn't promise much joy. Neither of us dared hope I could squeeze through the mass of people, scenery, and sounds, even if Mike had still been unembarrassed at the very sight of me. Of the hundred and four members in that cast, I was the only one he couldn't face. Mike was ashamed of his betrayal of Gypsy, of his destruction of her play, of their partnership. But, by the time *Hayride* took to the rails for Boston, even that emotion was flattened by the stampede. This time, although it was the same theatrical season, Mike was returning to the Ritz in Boston, this time with one major thought left in his head: a smash. He was desperate for *Mexican Hayride* to establish Todd as a name among the greats. The "too much of everything" syndrome was simply panic. Postponements were inevitable. One production number alone used $30,000 worth of costumes—just for the showgirls. Everything came in dribbles. Scenery was arriving in sections. Mike's walk was rockier.

Christmas week in Boston, Mike's opening attracted more press coverage than any show in years. This was when *Life, Look, Esquire, Pic, Click,* and a score of other magazines always appeared at out-of-town dress rehearsals, in order to run their spreads at the same time as the New York opening; then there were avid columnists waiting for tidbits good or bad but hopefully juicy. Hedda, Louella, Winchell, Kilgallen, and a dozen more. Nine newspaper critics in the big city, plus AP, UP, etc. Lots of out-of-town biggies, too.

Backstage at the Shubert Theatre, I sat in my dressing room numbly. Bronchitis, sore throat, laryngitis, runny nose, and bursting heart. The hammering, pounding, shouting, which are music to the ear of any actor, sounded to me, on that occasion, like the preparation of a scaffold with my name on the rope. How unhappy my sister will be to see me sink under the weight of this monster, I thought. Reflected in the dusty mirror over my makeup shelf was the costume I was to wear for my first entrance. The damn thing was hideous. Playing a lady bullfighter in a big musical that was all comedy. Hassard Short, credited with the overall fantasy, had picked me to represent reality. Weird. Right down to long white cotton stockings, knee-length pants, and flat-heeled matador shoes. I looked like Minnie Mouse in that outfit. Besides, I couldn't move. I told anyone who would listen, but to no avail. I hadn't told Gypsy, I couldn't.

Gummy tears coursed down my fevered cheeks as the weary sobs echoed through the bronchitis. I had worked out the comic movements for my first number, but in that costume I was immobilized. Paul Haakon was in overall charge of choreography. In a last-ditch effort, I cornered him in the basement, working on his hazardous sword dance.

"My God, June, the whole cast out there singing, waving, shouting 'Olé' for your first entrance—what a way to come onstage! What more do you want?" He executed a whirlwind pass with the glistening knives.

"I want something to do once I get center!" I shouted. I had moved to a safer spot behind some trunks. "Big entrance, great," I yelled, "then what? I gotta follow up!"

He dropped the knives with a clatter. "C'mon." I followed him to the men's room, which for once was not being used for rehearsal. I explained that I couldn't move in the costume designed for me.

"And Short said it matches the scenery, and that's that, huh?" I was surprised to hear Paul put it so clearly. "After this afternoon's dress of my knife ballet, June, none of us will have to match the scenery. That will be option number two." He returned to his knives and I to my dressing room.

Adjoining same was a small, old-fashioned bathroom. The toilet was the kind which had been long ago outlawed because any murderer could lose a whole body by pushing it down the big round hole and pipe. It ran and sang continually. Through this oriental-type music came Bobby Clark. His kindly features peered at me anxiously. Framed in the doorway, the top tank was just over his left shoulder. He looked worried.

"You don't mind if they put one of my trunks in your room, do you, Junie?"

I shook my head wetly. Two stagehands grunted under the weight of a huge H & M, the special trunk used by vaudevillians. Bobby patted it lovingly. "You don't mind if I put another one in that little bathroom in between us?"

I said, "Uh uh," then watched Bobby direct the sweating men to place those huge trunks just so. They looked like old friends to me. H & M trunks had special compartments for props and wardrobe. Bobby produced an entire carpentry shop, complete with trick saws, presses, drills—even a percolator. We had lots of coffee.

"Now the work begins," said Bobby. "Goodbye, tinny rehearsal piano. Goodbye guessing." He grinned. "You can't get answers anywhere but from an audience, can you?" I grinned, too. It felt good.

"Listen," he said. The orchestra was tuning up. "Wipe your face and come on."

The first time the cast hears the score with a full orchestra can hardly be compared with mortal thrills. It's a slice of delight known only to members of the privileged unions. I leaned against the proscenium, drunk with listening, as the conductor lovingly led the men around a magnificent arrangement of our number-one hit song, "I Love You." The sound went down my back and worked at loosening all the knots I had carefully tied in myself.

Cole Porter insisted on lots of strings, so the musicians filled the pit as well as the first two boxes stage right and left, bass in one, cellos in the other; they were crowded. I was watching the sweep of the bows when I noticed one cello, almost hidden in the folds of the red drapes, waver and tilt. The small dark man who clung to the instrument slid from his chair and disappeared from view. Apparently, no one else had noticed. I hurried out the big fire door at the side of the stage and entered the box just as he fell. As I searched his pockets, hoping to find the medicine heart-trouble people carry, I called, "Help! Help! Someone!"—but the music was everywhere. I loosened his collar. He was dark blue. Mike appeared.

"Hurry! Get an ambulance!" I cried. "I can't find his pulse!" Mike put his head to the small man's chest. I held the limp wrist. "Get a doctor!" Mike looked up at me for a second, then he closed the red velvet drapes. My tears fell onto the little body I held in my arms.

"Don't cry, June." Mike's tone was soft. "I betcha if he had this exit custom-written and specially produced, he would of wanted it just like this—surrounded by everything he loves, and with that wonderful music in his ears. You gotta admit, if he was really meant to go, he did it awfully good. Go back to work, June, I'll make a call." He drew the curtains and the music hardly paused.

The orchestra hardly paused. The next number was Paul Haakon's knife dance. Magazine photographers crawled all over the house: in the upper boxes, and balcony, onstage as you worked, and even in the pit. Everyone was used to coping with cameras during dress rehearsals.

"May I have your attention, please?" The stage manager was blinking in the spotlight. "Mr. Haakon requests you stay at a safe distance during his rehearsal, please." The photographers, of course, moved closer. "Mr. Haakon has not as yet rehearsed in full light and in costume, so—" he paused as the newshounds gathered to the edge of the stage—"it may prove dangerous and we cannot be responsible."

Electricity was not only within the brilliant lighting, it was in the very air. Harry Sosnik, the conductor, lifted his baton, the cameras moved closer, music enveloped us all—and then, in a dazzle of color, Paul made his entrance. The ballet was to suggest the glories of the bullfight, but poetically. He too was costumed in matador trimmings. However, his costume was made of stretch material, a concession because Paul was actually dancing, not just moving. He looked gorgeous. Long legs beautifully muscled, even in the knee-length pants. But then he wasn't victim to the long and low pear-shaped bottom. No. His was safely flat. Eyes flashing, he lifted his arms, holding his banderillas high.

Then all hell broke loose. As Paul leaped and spun, it became too evident why the photographers had gone mad. They were crawling all over the stage, shooting wildly, as Paul, with a mad gleam of determination in his eyes, kept up with the pounding, crashing music.

Sosnik, too intent on the difficult score, didn't see what was of such interest to the newspeople. No one backstage could see, and if I hadn't been watching from an upper box I would have missed the strategy, too. With the first magnificent leap, Paul's skin-tight, supposedly stretch pants had ripped open front to rear. A true artist, Paul had not missed a beat of his music. The rehearsal was not wasted.

My first number was next, but I was spared. I had hardly begun when Mike stopped the music. I had already torn both sleeves at the shoulders, lost my hat and cape completely, and there were signs of ripping underway as I kicked up one leg.

"Why is June falling apart?" Mike asked the world. "Whadda we got here—breakaway costumes? Fix 'em—fix 'em so the actors can work." It was an order.

Spot dress rehearsals staggered along without a full run of the entire show; when faced with a timing of all components once they were put together, the show would have run over four hours.

Lost in the hysteria was the remaking of my matador costume. Paul's was rushed into completion as an obvious emergency measure. Mike had stopped my music too soon.

"I'll kill myself onstage in front of the whole company! You've gotta come, Gyp! I need you terribly," I wailed over the phone until she said, "All right, all right. But I simply cannot be seen by any of those people . . . or . . . or Mike."

I rushed to assure her. "No one will know you are here. Only me. Oh, please come now?" There was only a slight pause.

"I'll get my sewing box together, stay in your hotel tonight, after rehearsal. Three knocks—that's me, okay?"

Gypsy was well aware of the layout of the enemy camp. How many times had she been closeted in the same environment? When a show opened in Boston for a tryout, it was usual for members of the major teams to take over an entire floor at the Ritz-Carlton Hotel. This kind of segregation assured the management it could relegate the all-night rehearsing, songwriting, script changing, and combined mayhem to one area. Doors on the private floor were rarely closed, as traffic was inevitably heavy. A carefully chosen team of waiters manned the special pantry dispensing all-night food and drink.

This was the gauntlet my sister must walk. Could she make it to my room unrecognized?

Late that night, pacing nervously as I waited for the signal rap that would announce the secret arrival of my sister, I tried to evaluate the personal importance of success or failure at this moment of my professional life. If I couldn't repeat the impact I made in *Joey*, would there be no more film offers? No musicals? Would it all be over so soon? The answer sat heavy on my heart. All the miles of marathons, modeling, all the rounds. The specter of being a has-been once again was unbearable.

After all, it's continuity that proves the worthiness of any contender. This show must be one rung up, not down. Then it might leave me hanging in the middle. The middle . . . purgatory. No. All positions except up would be failure.

Everyone's nerves were frazzled with endless rehearsals to install new songs, dances, sketches. Everyone's voice scratchy, eyes red. The tempo had reached wildness; outbursts of fury, tears, heated arguments were the run of the day and night. Dancers were suffering aching muscles, even charley horses as in a marathon. Singers worried about raw vocal cords. The ever-present doctor went from throat to feet to stiffened back.

Startled by a gentle tapping on the door, I called, "Who is it?" The voice could be a disguise—it sort of rumbled, "Room service." Of course, I thought, Gypsy has come up the service elevator dressed as a waiter.

Swinging the door wide, I stage-whispered, "Tricky, tricky you! Nobody could guess you made it up here! Hooray! Hooray!" I closed and locked the door, then turned to face an interested waiter.

"This is . . . your order . . . Miss Havoc?" He looked trapped. I hadn't sent for service, but the table he had rolled in was spread appetizingly with food and drink. So I nodded. He began preparing the table for four people. There was another knock at the door. Was this one three taps? Before I reached it, a hotel maid entered bearing towels and fresh linen. The phone rang. It was Mike calling from the executive suite down the hall.

"That you, June?"

"Yes, Mike."

"Tomorrow you're doing the 'Abracadabra' number."

"What?!"

"You heard me."

"But we open—"

"You're doing the number tomorrow."

"Like hell, Mike. Now you listen to me. I gotta have rehearsal time when you throw a number at me. . . ." The maid had stripped the bed. She tossed the pillows onto a chair. I saw the waiter pause as he eavesdropped.

"Mike." My voice was controlled but trembling. "I'm not going on in anything if I'm not ready. Furthermore—"

He interrupted. "You do the number or I'll take you to Equity!" He was yelling.

"Take me to Alcatraz!" I was yelling, too.

"Hang up! Hang up!" Mike hollered.

"Hang up?" I hollered back. "I'm not through—"

The phone was grabbed from my hand.

"Hang up, I said!" Mike stood in front of me waving my phone in the air wildly.

"But, Mike, that's you on the phone." The maid slammed into the bathroom, but the waiter stood over his table.

"Supper for four, Miss Havoc," he growled menacingly.

Mike sputtered, "Ya got time for a party for four, huh?" He started toward the door. "Have a nice supper, June. I'll see you at rehearsal tomorrow. Here's your music." Banging the sheaf of paper on the bed, he departed. The door slammed shut. Choking on hysteria, I kicked at that door until my foot hurt.

"You'll be great in that number," the waiter's voice was suddenly warm, "and your sister and I will do absolute miracles with that costume, you'll see." He smiled encouragingly. "You ought to let her out of the bathroom now."

My sister's face was grim as she emerged. The maid's uniform hung askew. I was too exhausted to laugh.

"Where's the coffee?" She took a battered sewing box from a pillow slip.

The waiter was already pouring. "Extra strong," he said. "I just happen to be doing this right now—actually, I'm a designer.

Sugar?" Gypsy nodded. She was unpacking her sewing things. He went on, "You're so right, you know. I mean, about those knee pants and those, for God's sake, white cotton stockings with low-heeled shoes!"

My sister was staring at the costume. "Oh, my God," she breathed, "what time is it?"

46 ⚜⚜⚜

Remembering parts of that night convinces me that I was running a better than average fever.

"I just hope you're not contagious," my sister muttered. She was pinning the line she would cut on the matador pants. We had learned the waiter's name. It was Pete. He was clearing the table, putting all eatables on the windowsill just like a real pro.

"After I strike these dishes, you can do your cutting on this surface." He paused, gazing at us in a warm, friendly way. "I have very good vibrations about us tonight," he said.

My sister looked at him a moment. "Stand against the bed," she commanded. "Now put your arms out straight at your sides, and face June's little clock." Pete obeyed. "Now, make a wish." My sister's voice became hypnotic. "You know the wish to make, don't you?" Pete nodded, closed his eyes. He moved his lips silently.

"Okay," Gypsy ordered, "back to work. That's it for a quarter to three. We'll give it another whack at nine-fifteen in the morning."

I knew those were mystical hours for wishes. You had to stand in front of a clock with your arms all the way out, because the clock's arms were in the same position for that one moment, and mysterious gates were open.

Between fittings, I cloistered myself in the bathroom to learn the song Mike had thrown my way. Addressing lyrics to three white porcelain fixtures was one thing—in the profession it is called being bathroom perfect—but confidence along with lyric usually flees at confrontation with an audience. I thought of Bobby in our combined dressing rooms, at his elaborate trunks, soberly creating "sight gags." Disguised as a Mexican woman in one scene, he added a papoose to wear on his back, but unlike a native child, this one wore Bobby Clark's famous painted-on glasses and smoked a replica of Bobby's famous cigar; by the time we opened it could spit ten feet on target. He was famous for his props and his secrecy. So I could never divulge what I watched being prepared. But Bobby's dogged concentration was something I tried to emulate. So, for the benefit of the bathroom fixtures, I set a routine to the new lyrics. Worked out an attitude for the song itself, and emerged frazzled, a little damp, but ready.

At nine-fifteen, both my sister and Pete stood facing the clock. The wish was tacit, of course, otherwise it didn't have a chance, but all three of us knew: the reason I couldn't stand with them was because the wish was for me.

The condemned ate a hearty breakfast; Pete brought in another table laden with pancakes, eggs, toast. When the coffee was gone, he held up the decanter. It was a silver Thermos, elaborately embossed with the Ritz-Carlton insignia.

"This one is perfect," said Pete. "Put it in the trunk and give me the one you packed away. That one has a crack, and you don't want that, do you?"

That night, Pete said he just happened to have a seat in the lower stage-right box and a blond wig. He said he would stand for that performance, and the wig was left over from some forgotten adventure, so never mind if Gypsy wanted to keep it. We got to the theatre early so she could hide. I was to leave her in the box pretending to read a newspaper. Words fitting the occasion had been uttered. Between us, we had accomplished whatever was possible to circumvent the ultimate humiliation.

"One angelfood a season is one too many cakes for this family to tolerate." Gypsy had tried to be coolly realistic. "You'll get other chances, honey—this isn't the end of the world." We were rolled into the drapes of stage box right. The unforgettable scent Gypsy used was competing with the memory-laden odor of stage velvet.

"You shouldn't have worn that perfume tonight, Gyp." I was trying hard for a funny.

She almost giggled. "But this is when we need it." Fishing around in her bag, she drew forth a flacon. "Hold still, baby, I'm going to baptize you." She emptied the contents over my head. "With this token I pronounce you unbeatable, untouchable . . . nobody can get to you, see?" She wrapped me in her arms. "If you cry, June, I'll beat hell out of you."

I pushed down hard. "I'm not going to cry," I said. "I'm going out on that stage and asphyxiate everybody in the whole damn place!"

The audience began to arrive. We unrolled ourselves quietly.

"Remember, June, remember what home is for. It's where you refuel between races. You'll come home with me and we'll have wonderful fun while we plan strategy and attacks. Just do your best for now." I found my way to the fire door and onto the stage.

A few dancers were limbering. I heard the singers warming up their voices somewhere in the top-floor dressing rooms. Musicians were in the basement locker room. They too were preparing. Some of the stage crew puttered with special lights and set pieces.

Walking across the dimly lit stage, I thought, "A house— any house—is lovely to be in—to own . . . but this is home. If you lose a house you find another, but there is no replacement for here." I stopped center. I could hear the audience moving into their seats through the heavy asbestos curtain hanging between us. "Please," I whispered, "don't send me away again . . . please."

Sitting at my makeup mirror, breathing in the splendiferous scent my sister had all but drowned me in, I thought of what she had said. "We'll go home." I pictured the twenty-eight-room mansion on East Sixty-third Street in New York Gypsy called "home." It was California-style, Spanish Mediterranean, deceiving to the street viewer. Two stories high in front, with a formal entrance Gypsy called "The Lobby," a tiny powder room, an enormous kitchen with servants' dining hall in the basement below; while up a small stairwell were many large and small servants' rooms. The sub-basement housed the largest, most ferocious furnace I ever met, a huge wine cellar, and a storage room.

That was only the front part. Two glass corridors, one up, one down, connected the front with a four-story rear house.

Leaving The Lobby, one passed an enormous dining hall, which looked across a lovely atrium kind of garden into the drawing room. The glass corridors were to the left of the garden, so the walk from the front door to the drawing room was almost as long as half a city block.

A tiny elevator took you to the three big rooms above the drawing room. Unless it was indisposed, of course—then you galloped down the stairs, hoping whoever was ringing at the front door hadn't given up in despair.

The three big rooms over the drawing room consisted of a bedroom and bath (April's and mine), then above that another bedroom and bath (Gyp's). On the very top floor was the library. The lovely house was designed at a time when people all had servants—staffs of servants.

In my closet was a plush-covered ladder leading upward into the closet of Gypsy's bedroom above. When Charles Dillingham lived there, he didn't want the servants to know when he visited his wife's room. Or maybe he just liked climbing red plush ladders in closets.

My sister couldn't resist the beautiful old house when she first saw it in 1942; besides, it was a good buy at $12,500, even though there was a flood in the basement.

During an awful heat wave that summer, a heat wave reserved for New York City alone, Gypsy and I were indulging in a skinny dip. We had managed to squeeze into the tiny pool adorning the atrium garden. It was too small for total comfort, but settling into the center, leaving our legs to dangle over the side, we could enjoy the coolness of the water falling from the mouth of a dolphin above our heads; and so, on this humid, scorching day, we relaxed, wearing our shower caps only. Lovely. We lifted our faces to the cool spray, then sipped tall, icy drinks as we exchanged pleasantries.

We were startled when the doorbell rang, but then remembered that we had recently acquired the questionable services of another in a long line of wartime help. One more who loved the pretty uniform, but who didn't clean, cook, wash dishes, or make beds. Being expert ourselves at these chores, we took on people just to have the door answered. This one trotted across the marble floor of The Lobby.

We heard a male voice, then her reply: "I'm sorry, sir. No. No sir." Then, with authority, "You cannot see them. I am sorry, mister, but the girls is in the bird bath."

The door closed. We never learned who the caller was.

There were to be four years of sharing our lives in that house. Even though I had fallen in love with and bought a tiny home in California, even though we would both go far away on tour, for a film, we called that home our base of operations.

My reverie was interrupted by Bobby. Wearing his stage makeup, which was all foolishness, all clown, the serious technician underneath would never be recognized. Pale base, kinky black eyebrows, the mouth outlined in brown pencil, the famous trademark, of course, in black. This was a very large pair of round glasses. The commonplace features were lit from within. A quiet goodness was the essence of the private man. Whatever wild zaniness one recalled onstage, my memory of Bobby Clark extends from his comic genius to his simple kindness, his tender concern for others.

"Tonight's just another dress rehearsal," he announced. "Don't fall down."

I grinned. "Nor you," I said. "See ya out there."

It was reasonable for Bobby to consider opening night in Boston just one more dress rehearsal. He was so well established, so respected and loved, he could open quietly and take the whole time until New York to experiment. Selecting and discarding dozens of gags, props, bits, and pieces. Polishing. By opening night on Broadway, Bobby Clark would be ready.

"We're here to find out, aren't we?" He pointed his finger at my reflection in the mirror. "Those people out front are the only ones who have the answer, right?" I nodded, only half understanding. "All that work was wishful guessing, June. Hard, much needed, but not the final word." He paused, waiting for me to take hold, to use the strength he offered. Uncomprehending, I hung on his words without realizing their potency. For the first time in my life, the people out front were all judges, strangers; in the dreadful fear of failure, I had closed all my pores to hope. There was only one ally out there for me, and the enemy was so powerful that my champion was in hiding under a wig.

"Well," Bobby's face receded, "see you out there." He was gone.

"Fifteen minutes—fifteen minutes to overture!" The voice moved through the dressing rooms until I heard only a murmur. My hands trembled so hard I gave up adding mascara. There, waiting for me, was my opening costume. Gypsy had done the tailoring. It was musical comedy now. Medium heels, and no white cotton hose. The effect would be in keeping with the scene, workable in my first number. If only I could get past that . . .

"Five minutes, five minutes, please." I froze. Never before having experienced the deadliest foe of actors—to this degree— I thought of running. Just running, as far away as I could. Closing my eyes, I tried deep breathing. My dresser arrived.

"Everybody in the business out front, Miss H. Such a—"

"Don't! Please, don't tell me." I shook myself into the costume.

"I'll have your changes all ready in the tent." She was putting my other costumes over her arm. "Good luck," she said easily, as she left.

I tried to pin down my old standby—"You—you lucky sons-a-bitches—you're gonna get to see me!"—but it didn't work. This panic was new. My heart pounded along with the overture.

"Places. Places, please . . . First act—beginners, please!" Then the whole company was out there in the light singing toward me, waiting there in the wings. Waving, shouting, "Olé!" Just as Paul had said, "What an entrance." Well, at least I had the routine he had taught me, the business with the cape. I didn't just go on and then do nothing. . . . It was over . . . the opening scene was behind me. . . . I stood in the first entrance, waiting for the blackout before my first number alone onstage. Blackout . . . my introduction music, I am center . . . the lyrics hang in the air . . . spotlight is blinding but I see the conductor . . . I hear the ripple of laughter . . . more . . . more laughter . . . I am doing my eccentric dance-walk toward the wings. I stop. Do the trick ending . . . it's over. I take a bow. The applause warms me. The awful coldness abates. Another bow . . . another. My dresser grabs me, hauls me off to the change room as she unzips.

"Your shoes," she whispers, "kick 'em off."

The canvas flap on the door is pulled open. Mike's face is a study. "Get the hell out there! Whaddya doing? Listen to that, willya? Here, get your pants on—get out there!"

Bobby was center with a group of actors trying to start the scene following my number. Mike had rushed backstage because the audience didn't stop applauding. I hadn't heard anything. Half-zipped, I got to the wings. Bobby grinned and shrugged before he moved offstage with his actors. Mike all but pushed me into the spot which Bobby had directed toward my entrance. Across the stage he stood, nodding anxiously toward me.

Numb with happiness, pride, sure—drunk with joy all the

way—I nodded back, then tried to remember the lyrics. Nothing came. The conductor's baton was lifted; I got the bell note to begin—the world stopped.

"Please forgive me," I heard myself saying. "Nobody expected this to happen, so . . . Mr. Porter didn't write any more lyrics. I don't have an encore, I'm sorry and . . . thanks." I actually left the stage.

Bobby's laughter could be heard over everyone's—even over the applause, which again didn't stop. Finally, I went out, put my foot across the footlights, as I had seen Bobby do, and then, because no lyric would come, I double-talked through a chorus very confidently, and did my dancing exit, but before I left the light, I gave a big look to the stage-right box. Even though I couldn't really see her in the glare, I knew she was seeing me seeing her.

From that moment on, it was the same audience I had known all my life. The glare was that flickering light from the newsreel.

"You had to go out in the light of the newsreel to take a bow, remember?" Gypsy had reminded me after the opening night of *Pal Joey*. Bobby had been telling me to trust myself and the audience, but I hadn't comprehended. I had allowed the fear of failure to speak and act for me. How many times a life would I be guilty of this? How do you learn to believe in yourself? Who teaches confidence? Is there a guarantee?

The night before, during all the bathroom study and fittings, I had tried to explain to my sister how I felt about Mother's absence.

"How is it possible this is so different?" I asked. "I know why, I guess, but I don't understand why. Isn't this what all my Baby June, my Dainty June—all those years she loved so—were about? If I only knew why . . ."

Gypsy held up a thimbled hand. "Why? Why do you have to know any why? It won't change anything, June."

"Why do I feel guilty when I can't sort out why I should—"

"Stop it." Gypsy sighed, shaking her head. Then she spoke brusquely. "Okay, now hear this. It'll help put a few whys down for a little while, maybe. Remember that brown suitcase you left with Mother all that time ago? The big one you locked and put in the loft of the barn?"

"I lost the key."

"That's right, June. It was full of those cartoon letters—very personal—very."

"Jamie's letters? . . ."

"Uh huh."

"Mother didn't know they were in the loft. She—"

"Those letters were very entertaining at Mother's parties. Hilarious."

"Oh, God."

"So hilarious she thought you ought to buy them back."

I stared.

"It's the only conversation I've had in years with Mother," Gypsy went on. "I told her people called that blackmail, so she said she would sell them to Jamie instead."

"But he's . . . he . . ."

"I told her that, and her reply? She said, in that case there would surely be someone in his family who would want to buy them . . . in his memory. Surely no one would call that blackmail." We didn't say anymore for a while, but during breakfast she asked, "June? How's the guilt department?"

Perhaps if we had known more about all the whys—why people behaved . . . why others responded with behavior that . . . why ignorance and fear are so predominant . . .

Why? . . . why . . . why . . .

If answers to questions I could hardly formulate tortured me now, how could I hope for a respectful coexistence with my future mature self? Would the time out to acquire the education I had missed make up in reward for the starvation time it would take? Even if I didn't have April to care for, there could be no guarantee the future would be better. Gibbs, the oracle in my life of a few years back, had insisted, "Education can't feed everybody's needs. Hell, the whole world crawls with highly educated morons."

The answers had to come from some other source.

Maybe, if you could just keep from falling off the earth . . . maybe if you could convince yourself you had as much right as anyone to be wrong or to be . . . how did that go? Polonius, who turned out to be just an actor to whom Shakespeare had granted the perfect set of words . . . Polonius said, "To thine own self be true." Not one word about how smart that self had to be, or rich . . . or well born . . . tall, short, or good-looking. Well, maybe if you could just keep from falling off the earth long enough, and you could manage to stay true to whatever self you got stuck with . . .

EPILOGUE ⚥⚥⚥

1954

Mother was dying.

We were all together at last. Mother had won this round. A light snow was falling. Gypsy sat at the foot of Mother's bed. I stood at the window. The chill began at the back of my neck. I was afraid to turn around, but I knew I had to. My sister sat frozen. Watching, as Mother slowly and laboriously crawled toward her on the bed. Her breath came chokingly.

"I know about you," she gasped, "greedy, selfish! You want me to die. I'm the only one knows all about you . . . so, die . . ."

One purplish leg dangled toward the floor. Some buttons on her nightgown burst open, revealing the long suède bag she wore strung around her waist. She clutched at it feebly, wrapping the torn flannel gown around the grouch bag.

"You'll fall!" My sister reached for her.

"NO!" Mother's voice cracked. "You can't have anything back! Just because I'm letting go—it's mine! My house, my jewelry . . ." She swayed on the tumbled bed. Gypsy caught her, trying to lower her gently. They writhed in bizarre rhythm until Mother twisted suddenly, forcing her tormentor against the headboard. My sister's ashen face turned toward me. I started toward them.

"No," she said, arresting my compulsive move. "Don't. No." The voice came cool and strong. Arms intertwined, they lay contorted against the headboard of the bed—face to face, eye to eye.

I must have been bewitched, for I could not move. Could not speak. They remained locked in the grisly embrace for what seemed an eternity.

Then, finally, a voice which might have come from the mouth of some matron pouring tea at a PTA meeting. It was Mother's voice.

"You'll never forget how I'm holding you right this minute, Louise, holding you as strongly as I can, wishing with all my heart I could take you all the way with me—all the way down!"

I must have expected my own horror to be reflected on my sister's face, because I was astonished to see nothing. No expression at all. Mother released her grip, falling back on the bed, eyes closed, motionless. Gypsy slowly got to her feet. She stood before me, swaying weakly. Long minutes passed. We did not look at one another. Then Mother's voice curled around us like a vapor.

"This isn't the end. Wherever you go, as long as either of you lives, I'll be right there—and I swear before God you're always going to know it!" The room was cold. "You'll know I'm there, I'll see to that. So go on, Louise, tell all your classy friends how funny I was, how much smarter you were than me. When you get your own private kick in the ass, just remember: it's a present from me to you. A present from your funny, unbright mother."

We stood there like store mannikins until Mother's breathing came evenly. It rasped in and out as we closed the door. We moved slowly, as in deep water. My sister turned to me; our eyes met.

"Everything she promised," she whispered, "all those things she said would happen?"

I took her hands in mine; they were icy. "Shhh," I whispered back. "Never!" Her hands curled around mine.

"Oh yes, June, they'll happen. Just like she promised. She'll never let me go. Not ever." Her voice dropped so low I could hardly hear it.

"Why only you?" I whispered. "Why not me?"

My sister glanced toward the room we had just left.

"Because you failed her. You didn't turn out to be exciting enough to create the kind of reflection she needed to live in. No tabloids, no carnival, no sirens, no arrests. How many times has she enjoyed a ride in a police car with you?"

We stared into each other's faces.

"You mean, I'm not . . . not . . ."

She finished the sentence for me. "You're not enough glamour, June—no notoriety. She didn't bother to curse you because you had your chance and you flunked! Aren't you glad?"

I couldn't find my voice, but I nodded.